# Selling
# Fear

# Selling Fear

## Conspiracy Theories and End-Times Paranoia

## Gregory S. Camp

**Foreword by
Sherman S. Smith**

**Baker Books**
A Division of Baker Book House Co
Grand Rapids, Michigan 49516

© 1997 by Gregory S. Camp

Published by Baker Books
a division of Baker Book House Company
P.O. Box 6287, Grand Rapids, MI 49516-6287

Printed in the United States of America

**Library of Congress Cataloging-in-Publication Data**

Camp, Gregory S., 1957–
  Out of the shadows : conspiracy theories and Christian prophetic belief /
Gregory S. Camp.
      p.      cm.
  Includes bibliographical references and index.
  ISBN 0-8010-5721-3 (pbk.)
  1. End of the world—History of doctrines. 2. Conspiracies—History. 3.
Prophecy—Christianity. 4. History (Theology)—History of doctrines. I. Title.
BT876.C36          1997
277.3'082—dc20                                                      96-18779

For information about academic books, resources for Christian leaders, and all new
releases available from Baker Book House, visit our web site:
                          http://www.bakerbooks.com/

Dedicated to two of God's greatest blessings in my life:
my parents,
Harry and Dolores Camp

# Contents

# Foreword

Too many Christians are possessed with the idea that secret societies control the world. There have been countless theories that propagate this idea that the world economy and its political and social systems are controlled by a few evil and sinister men belonging to secret organizations that seek to rule the earth.

Books have been written by dentists, economists, ministers, and others, but rarely does a publication hit the marketplace written by someone with authority on the subject. Dr. Camp, a reliable historian, hits the nail on the head in this book. His no-nonsense research puts the facts in order and sets the secret theorists straight. He does this with verity, not with illusions or distorted historical data—something you will rarely find in other books dealing with the matter of secret conspiracies.

Conspiracy believers have done the same thing. They have taken a fact from history here, a fact from history there and have constructed distorted theories that secret people control everything that is happening in the world. Many believe and are caught up in the notion, creating an illusion that is very hard to get away from them.

The Illuminati, the Council on Foreign Relations, the Masons, the Trilateral Commission, and the international bankers

are some of those who, in the minds of many, seek the abolition of private property, family structure, organized religion,
national governments, inheritance rights, and capitalism. Scary
thoughts! Worse than the boogeyman I was afraid of as a kid.

The facts demonstrate that Christian people who believe and
embrace these kinds of theories are in the same boat as athe-
ists, agnostics, and evolutionists. They have thrown God out of
the picture as one who has lost control of his world. This book
will show you how biblical happiness is predicated on the truth
of the Bible—the hope of the Christian who has strong faith in
God. That is, God is in control of everything and nothing happens one second before or after he lets it happen.

I have personally spent many hours communicating on the
phone and through the mail with Dr. Camp. I believe his biblical perspective is correct and that is the bottom line to all this
paranoia about how the world is controlled.

There are conspiracies; make no mistake about that. Unfortunately there is a dark side to the world. Throughout history
there have been despots who have tried to seize control of governments and their citizens. I am positive this is the plan of
Satan. However, never has there been one successful ploy over
any great length of time because the heart and mind of a person cannot be controlled forever. The heart and mind of a person belong to God. When someone figures out how to control
them, I will embrace these theories Dr. Camp so successfully
destroys.

Dr. Sherman S. Smith

# Preface

The author wishes to thank the many people who were of great help in the researching and writing of this project. Ranging from employees at bookstores and publishing houses to librarians and research specialists, many people went out of their way to be of service. I greatly appreciate their kindness and patience. Also, for financial support of my research, I thank Dr. Dale Elhardt, dean of Minot State University's College of Arts and Sciences, and Dr. Jonathan Wagner, chair of the Social Science Division. Heartfelt thanks must also be extended to Michael Cooper and Jake Popejoy for being supportive and encouraging, as well as to Dwight and Brenda Vaught for their friendship my wife and I so highly treasure. Likewise, to Tom and Diane McCleary I have owed so much over the years. Thanks and a heartfelt I love you. So, too, to the many people with whom I have crossed paths at Shiloh over the years.

I owe a special debt of gratitude to Tal Brooke of Spiritual Counterfeits Project of Berkeley, California. Tal was always available for my questions and proved to me what I had concluded from his writings: that he is one of Christian America's intellectual and spiritual treasures. His book, *When the World Will Be as One,* is in my opinion one of the best books pertaining to the New Age movement that evangelical Christianity has produced in the past quarter century. I may not agree with the conspiratorial portions of it, but that in no way diminishes its great value. Someday I hope to bring Tal to the Northern Plains and show him what winter is *really* like! Likewise, to William Alnor *(Soothsayers of the Second Coming)* of Philadelphia and Sherman Smith *(Exploding the Doomsday Money Myths)* of Napa, California, a special word of appreciation needs to be extended. To Robyn Miller, our division secretary, I also owe a debt of gratitude for her help in the preparation of this manuscript. On several occasions she helped with preparation and printing on short notice—not to mention tutoring me on a new computer.

Finally, to my family, who had to put up with me while I was researching and writing this book, I offer my heartfelt thanks. My wife, Cindy, was particularly supportive of my efforts. My two sons, Arlo and Aaron, patiently waited for me to finish as well, something I had hoped to do before the major league baseball season started. Ironically, I finished the rough draft of this manuscript just as the major league strike began. Nonetheless, our conversations on our mutual love for the Baltimore Orioles were always welcome—now, if the Orioles could only play up to their talent potential! To my little girl, Abigail, I must also extend gratitude for her understanding and patience while Dad was working on the manuscript. I am sorry I was gone for such extended periods of time.

# Introduction

The question of how the world around us functions and who, if anyone or anything, is in control has been asked for hundreds, even thousands of years. Most of us believe that there is some semblance of order in the world's political, economic, and social systems, and that these systems are under varying degrees of public control. Still, among certain groups in American society—among them conservative Christians—there is a haunting fear that perhaps things in politics, economics, and society in general are not as they appear on the surface. Over the past two hundred years this fear has taken the shape of a belief that an unknown but immensely powerful secret cabal has sought to gain world domination. Belief in a worldwide conspiracy is not confined to any particular political or religious belief, either.

Members of both the political left and right have their own theories concerning a shadowy "Them" who are using their influence and making things happen according to a preordained plan. An irony is that both left- and right-wing groups often point to the same villains. The culprits most often mentioned as responsible for this intrigue include the Illuminati, Freemasonry, Communism, International Bankers, the Vatican, the Council on Foreign Relations, the Trilateral Commission, and history's perennial victims, Jews. For contemporary Christians believing in conspiracy theory, these ideas and end-time pondering are important because they shape their view of the past, present, and future. If perceptions of the past are in error, views of the present will similarly be skewed to a degree. If nothing else, this book is a call for caution to Christians holding conspiratorial views and using them to interpret world events.

The alleged perpetrators of the Oklahoma City federal building bombing are among those holding conspiratorial views of the sort I will detail in this book. Because they try to justify such actions, it is important that those with conservative Christian beliefs concerning prophecies, whether they are evangelical, fundamentalist, Pentecostal, or Charismatic, distance themselves from mixing conspiracy with prophecy to form an end-times scenario. What many of the rank and file holding these beliefs do not realize is that these same ideas have been around for decades, indeed centuries, and have reaped a harvest of racism, mistrust, and intolerance. Sadly, the numbers of those holding these views are growing at an alarming rate. The huge market for prophecy-related publications, some of them drawing on secular conspiracy theories, bears this out.[1]

Conspiracy theory can and often does degenerate into scapegoating on an enormous scale. An ideology of this sort provides the believer in such a theory with easy answers for how and why things happen as they do. Instead of random events and unforeseen happenings, believers in this theory see directors with a very definite script acting as a hidden hand behind the scenes to further an evil agenda. In the following chapters I will look at some of the many individuals and groups that have held these beliefs, including American Christians, and how they have at times been tied to traditional teachings about the second coming of Christ.

I came into contact with the whole world of conspiracy theory as a teenager, when I had the opportunity to hear some recordings about political intrigue that were quite impressive to the first-time listener, especially a young one. Like most people first

# Introduction

exposed to conspiracy theory, I was amazed at the seemingly comprehensive nature of the so-called world conspiracy.

It was December 1971, just a few weeks before Christmas, when the small turboprop plane I was aboard made its turbulent descent into Pueblo, Colorado. Waiting for me was a friend who had invited me to his in-laws' ranch just outside the small southern Colorado community of Penrose. Located not far from Canon City, best known for the nearby Royal Gorge tourist attraction, the terrain around Penrose at that time was a window to the Old West. The land was ruggedly beautiful, with majestic mountains and sweeping plains. Of particular interest to me, even at the young age of fifteen, were the many deep gullies or creek breaks hiding historical and archaeological evidence of Shoshoni-speaking native peoples. What appeared to be grave sites and pottery shards were scattered over several miles in these small canyons, and I was respectfully careful to keep my distance and not disturb anything.

With my parents' blessing, my visit was meant as a time of reflection. I sought advice of a man whom I had come to respect as a Christian and as a friend. John[2] took time to show me much of the beauty of the place, instilling in me a deep love of the wilderness—especially in the Southwest—that is with me to this day. The breathtaking vistas provided a dramatic backdrop to the political information and viewpoints I discovered during my weeklong stay. Little did I know the paths I would eventually tread as a result of hearing a few recordings.

One Saturday morning, when it was simply too cold to do much out of doors, my friend asked me if I would like to listen to a few long-playing records on political issues of great importance. I was somewhat less than interested, but his demeanor was quite serious and, not wanting to be an ungracious guest, I agreed to listen. The message presented contained information and political viewpoints I had not heard before. The records were by the late Myron Fagan, famed Hollywood producer, director, and playwright. Acting as narrator, Fagan laid out a story of conspiracy, treachery, and betrayal against the United States of titanic proportions. Names then unknown to me, such as Adam Weishaupt, Jacob Schiff, the Warburgs, the Rothschilds, the Morgans, and Rockefellers were brought forth as major players in this betrayal, a conspiracy that, according to Fagan, was nigh unto two centuries old. Moreover, institutions with strange names were "exposed," although very few of these made sense to me at the time. The name "Illuminati" in particular was spoken of with fear and loathing, as was what Fagan believed to be its contemporary American embodiment, the Council on Foreign Relations.[3]

What I came away with after hearing the recordings was a sense of overwhelming helplessness and even fear. If the conspiracy was as Myron Fagan described, it was immensely powerful and capable of superhuman political, economic, and military feats. Despite its physical, tangible attributes, the struggle was presented as ultimately a spiritual contest. The spiritual forces involved, Fagan claimed, were of the darkest evil and with the most malevolent intentions—whether its human agents were aware of it or not.[4] It was a story of great sweep and interest, but was it true? At that time I was frankly unable to decipher it all and make any sense of it. As I grew older and eventually made history my profession, I had opportunity to do some investigating.

A few years ago, while researching an unrelated topic, I came on some government memos that seemed to suggest the possibility of an economic collapse in the near future. In the body of the memos, mention was made of the Federal Reserve system, its setting of interest rates, and the growing rate of the yearly deficit and compiled debt, and in general a tone was set that caused me to be somewhat bemused. For a while I began researching the history of the Federal Reserve and the nature of national debt, for it all sounded as though string pulling at high levels was taking place. In the process I was led to a host of books from the conspiracy theory camps that insist that the Fed is nothing more than a front for groups such as the Illuminati and its current embodiment, the Council on Foreign Relations and Trilateral Commission. The arguments, weird as they are, nonetheless contain grains of truth. After digging much deeper into the whole conspiracy theory world (including the Federal Reserve), I became convinced that conspiracy for control on a global or national scale by a small, faceless cabal is little more than fanciful thinking with less-than-compelling logic behind it.

Moreover, once a person becomes convinced of the "truth" of conspiracy theory, it is nearly impossible to reason that person out of his or her point of view. Instead, the True Believer in these theories tags those arguing against them as "uninformed," "lacking in true insight," or worse still, "spiritually deceived," for those from a Christian background. Those who see the "truth" behind conspiracy become a sort of illuminati of their own—the bearers of the true light of historical interpretation. The point here is that if a professional historian can at least be impressed with some of the conspiracy message, how much more so are those without a background in history? It is seductive, but it is also quite false.

When anyone brings up conspiracy in connection with history, one's guard immediately goes up, as well it should. To understand the dynamics of this method of historical interpretation one has to consider two general assumptions conspiracy advocates hold in common. First, they say, there are people of immense wealth who are using their resources to acquire and consolidate power in their hands. After all, as conspiracy theorists are wont to point out, is it difficult to imagine a large oil company's or other corporation's involvement in price fixing? If a company can act in such a manner, is it not also possible that individuals could do the same? Of course, there would be tremendous limitations on their ability to carry out a conspiratorial scenario to fruition. Timing, differences of opinion, politics, nationalism, economic policy, and the logistics in implementation are just a few of the obvious complications. These obstacles do not deter conspiracy believers; indeed they too often fall into the error of assuming the Planners are something akin to omnipresent.

In a second area of common ground among conspiracy believers, many attribute the Plan to supernatural forces under the control and direction of Satan himself. In this scenario, earthly forces in favor of global government are themselves mere pawns in a cosmic game of chess. This view does solve many of the logistical problems given in my first example but obviously necessitates at the very least a belief in the metaphysical or spiritual world. It also ties into many Christian end-time apocalyptic beliefs concerning the end of the age. It is at this point where some of the greatest danger lies. Groups who have an apocalyptic worldview and hold to conspiracy theories can read into any number of events in the world around them some terrible planned evil meant for the harm of the church or the United States. There are other tendencies found among some believers in this view of history, perceptions that have been terribly consistent over the past two thousand years.

The most notable example is the despicable tendency to attribute conspiracy to Jewish people as a whole. This virulent strain of anti-Semitism has reared its ugly head all too often over the past two millennia, always with tragic results. To this day sizable portions of conspiracy believers blame Jews or Jewish influence for the world's evils. Hateful documents such as the long-discredited *Protocols of the Learned Elders of Zion* are resurrected to "prove" a Jewish/Zionist plot. Almost without exception, some anti-Semitic groups try to separate themselves from others by claiming that they are in fact against Zionism, not Jews as such. This ploy is used by groups as diverse as the Palestine Liberation Organization, Institute for Historical Review, and Liberty Lobby. The latter two organizations have gone so far as to actively support the notion that the Holocaust did not happen. Obviously, this thinking is the intellectual equivalent of a flat-earth society. As one might deduce, these same people are vitriolic in their condemnation of the state of Israel. Besides the enormous harm done to the innocent people persecuted as a result of these flights of delusion or willful misguidance, these baseless ideas serve as something of a red herring when looking for possible evidence of real conspiracy. Postulating a Jewish plot for global conquest is as lacking in credibility as suggesting a Lutheran conspiracy or Seventh-Day Adventist conspiracy for world domination.[5]

A major reason I have decided to connect the beliefs of conspiracy advocates with Christian beliefs in the second coming of Jesus is their commonality in a few key areas. Christians and conspiracy advocates, at least in the late twentieth century, hold that a world government is coming that will result in the rise of an all-powerful leader. Christian teachings speak of a coming Antichrist, a person who will be either possessed of Satan or be Satan incarnate. Conspiracy advocates hold that there has long been a move afoot for a world government and that it is just now coming into the final stages of completion. Christians and conspiracy advocates have merged beliefs in some circles, making for the possibility of some dangerous theories about the world around them. Conspiracy theory's anti-Semitism is just one of the more obvious of these dangerous theories. Should that become a staple of conservative Christianity, it could very easily turn ugly for one or more minority groups.

I must clarify that I am not trying to convince anyone that a belief in the soon return of Christ is in error. What we have to be careful of, however, is insisting that we *must* be in the end times. It is therefore all the more important that Christians inform themselves about the world around them and not jump to conclusions. As we near the end of the twentieth century and the beginning of the new millennium, I can guarantee that you will hear increasingly shrill voices insisting that the end is at hand. The same thing happened during the years 999 and 1000. People simply assumed that history was calling it quits because the next thousand-year period was dawning. Christians and non-Christians alike need to take talk about the end of the world or conspiracies with a grain of salt—or in some cases, a livestock salt lick.

A last point needs to be made concerning conspiracy theory. Although I am not an advocate of "The Conspiracy"—capital C—I do believe that people and organizations have engaged in conspiracies—lowercase c—for political power from the time the human race first put a system of government together. There are hundreds of examples in the history of Western civilizations to back the fact that powers have risen and fallen as a result of plotting. Any revolution, after all, is by nature conspiratorial. There is trouble, however, when one tries to tie everything together into a massive cosmic event that has been planned from the very beginning. What I have found in the course of my research is a lot of evidence that individuals or groups have sought control with varying degrees of success. What I have not found is proof of a worldwide conspiracy. But again, common sense alone would dictate this. There is simply no prima facie evidence to support any conspiratorial interpretations. Although political and economic groups with their various agendas have become increasingly adept at presenting their message, it simply stretches credulity to the breaking point to suggest there is a collective of conspirators headed by an elite board of directors running it all.

In the following chapters I discuss a number of individuals and organizations who have been alleged to be part of a worldwide conspiracy. Although there have been and still are individuals and institutions who desire a fundamental change in the way nations deal with each other and are willing to commit time and money to their cause, the question is this: Is there anything new about this? Haven't there been people seeking this or something akin to it for centuries? And if so, does that necessarily mean that these shared ideas constitute an active conscious conspiracy? In my opinion, the answer is no. It is also important to state that the overwhelming majority of conservative Christians in the United States reject these conspiracy theories out of hand as the false teaching they are. The groups I refer to in this study are a small but vocal minority. As is true of all things concerning faith, philosophy, or politics, we must come to our own conclusions.

A final word about my use of sources. The reader will find that throughout this book I have used a host of conspiracy books and articles in cases other than direct quotation. Please do not misconstrue this to mean my support for conspiracy! Unlike some of the examples I provide in this book, I absolutely do not consider them to be authoritative as accurate interpretations of history. I felt it important to familiarize the reader with the arguments, specious as they may be. An appendix identifying conspiracy books can be found at the end of this book. The researcher should also be aware that many, indeed, most, of the books found therein are not written from a Christian point of view.

# The Illuminati

In the area of secular and Christian conspiracy theories, there have been few longer-lasting legends than those concerning a mid-eighteenth-century group that called itself the Illuminati. That it existed there can be little doubt; records from the period clearly prove this. What has remained a source of controversy among conspiracy theorists and historians is the role it has played in political, economic, and even spiritual history. At its worst, some believe that this secret society delved into occult practices and tapped into the greatest conspiracy of all: the desire of a fallen Lucifer to have absolute control of Earth. Other believers in the Illuminati legend contend that the organization has lived on since its founding in the 1770s and grown in power and influence. Still others hold that the society disappeared after a few decades but its ideology was adopted by others and lived on in the nineteenth and even twentieth centuries. In our own time, groups such as the Council on Foreign Relations and the Trilateral Commission seem to be the favorite targets of conspiracy-theory believers who see these institutions as modern-day representatives of the Illuminati Plot.[1] Whatever its present status—or lack thereof—a look at the origins of the Illuminati will provide a good basis for understanding how and why these stories have lasted so long.

## Prophecy Belief and Teaching in the Colonies

In the late 1790s, when rumors of an Illuminati plot for world control became public knowledge in the United States, some Christians were convinced that the end of the age was near. During the seventeenth and eighteenth centuries, a good many American Christians held the view that theirs was truly the last generation. The vicissitudes of earlier colonial economics, the colonial wars, and the troubled times during and after the American Revolution led many to conclude that Christ's return was imminent. For instance, seventeenth- and early-eighteenth-century Puritan leaders Increase and Cotton Mather frequently incorporated prophetic messages into their sermons. Both men, and thousands of other Christians of the time, were of the firm opinion that current events pointed to the soon return of Jesus. Providing examples from the news in a manner much like that of contemporary prophecy teachers Jack Van Impe or Doug Clark, their style and reputation (particularly Cotton Mather's) had a significant impact on the listeners. Their influence did not lose any steam as the eighteenth century rolled on; by the time of the American Revolution, many Christians still pointed to current events as fulfillment of both Scripture and Mather predictions. Conveniently forgotten was Cotton's penchant for setting dates for Christ's return: 1697 (while King William's War and the War of the League of Augsburg raged in New England and Europe respectively) and later 1736. Despite these errors, his reputation was such that any mistakes on his part were quickly forgiven.[2]

Jonathan Edwards, perhaps the most imposing intellectual and spiritual leader of colonial America, was himself taken with prophecy and the perceived nearness of Christ's second coming. In his 1742 publication, *Some Thoughts Concerning the Present Revival of Religion in New England*, Edwards postulated that the Great Awakening was a sure sign of the nearness of the millennium. As Paul Boyer points out in his brilliant *When Time Shall Be No More*, the tendency of Christian leaders in colonial America to tie current events to prophetic predictions would have a long-term influence; this would last at least until the

Revolution, and in my opinion continues to the present.[3] If someone of Edwards's monumental intellectual capability can fall into this trap, it shouldn't surprise anyone that others much less brilliant would later make the same mistake. It is into this frame of reference—the anticipation and uncertainty about the future of the young republic—that talk of an occult group known as the Illuminati arose.

## Birth of a Conspiracy and Occult Legend

The leader of the Bavarian Illuminati so vilified in the United States and Europe was one Adam Weishaupt. He has been cast as something akin to a demon for his work with the secret organization. Indeed a published booklet in the 1930s referred to Mr. Weishaupt as a "human devil" for his part in shaping the secret society. It has been suggested that Weishaupt was born of a Jewish family; in truth there is little proof of this. An extremely bright individual, Weishaupt attracted the attention of the Jesuits, Catholicism's "shock troops" and apologists for the papacy. Ever vigilant against heresy, Jesuits were considered the best and brightest Catholicism had to offer. The young Weishaupt trained under these impressive intellectual leaders, eventually obtaining a professorship in canon law at the University of Ingolstadt in 1772.[4]

Weishaupt's studies exposed him to many philosophies other than Christianity. During this age of Enlightenment, it became apparent that the young man had a deep love and respect for the philosophies that exalted reason and the value of the individual at the expense of church dogma. In the Holy Roman Empire itself, Weishaupt was keenly aware that a number of princes were embracing Enlightenment philosophies. Frederick the Great, King of Prussia, ranks as probably the best example. Because Weishaupt was a Jesuit, his support for Europe's secular intellectual Renaissance was a dangerous position to voice. It is for that reason that when Weishaupt did form a society of like-minded individuals in Bavaria, it was kept secret.[5]

On May 1, 1776, Adam Weishaupt founded the Order of the Illuminati, a term that means "bearers of the light." This organization borrowed a great many of its ideas and views of world order from other groups, some established many years before Weishaupt came along. The Ingolstadt professor's sources include a number of organizations that had as their object the overthrow of the established social order and replacing it with elitist rule. Apparently Weishaupt did not object to borrowing organizational ideas from the Society of Jesus (Jesuits) either; his secrecy, however, far outstripped the Catholic institution he had apparently come to despise. The Illuminati system also included a hodgepodge of Rosicrucianism, Cabalistic mysticism, Gnosticism, and teachings of Masonry. Of course, the latter is said to be philosophically built on a number of Near Eastern ideas as well, ranging from Egyptian mysteries to Babylonian cosmology.[6]

Weishaupt apparently put a good deal of thought into the secretive nature of his new society, as it was set up in concentric circles: the outer circles were the initiates; the inner circle was composed of those deep into the teachings of Illuminism. According to its charter, the Illuminati intended nothing but the highest good for humankind. In Weishaupt's own words, "Our secret Association works in a way that nothing can withstand, and man shall soon be free and happy."[7] The Illuminist Charter also states:

> This is the great object held out by this Association: and the means of attaining it is Illumination, enlightening the understanding by the sun of reason, which will dispel the clouds of superstition and of prejudice. The proficients in this order are therefore justly named the Illuminated. And all Illumination which human reason can give, none is comparable to the discovery of what we are, our nature, our obligations, what happiness we are capable of, and what are the means of attaining it. In comparison with this, the most brilliant sciences are but amusements for the idle and luxurious. To fit man by Illumination for active virtue, to engage him to it by the strongest motives, to render the attainment of it and certain, by finding employment for every talent, and by placing every talent in its proper

sphere of action, so that all, without feeling any extraordinary effort, and in conjunction with and completion of ordinary business, shall urge forward, with united powers, the general task. . . . And what is this general object? THE HAPPINESS OF THE HUMAN RACE.[8]

Weishaupt's Illuminati defined happiness as making men good; this in turn was achieved by "enlightening" the individual to the truths of Illuminism. Enlightening also carried with it the rejection of what Weishaupt called "the dominion of superstition and prejudice." Critics contended that this enlightening meant nothing less than the abolition of Christianity and the placing of Illuminist agents in high places in kingdoms and nations around the world: in essence, a world system dominated by a new, yet at the same time ancient, mode of thought. Critical revelations of this secret society showed it to be dominated by the megalomania of a few men in its innermost circle. Such an organization would stop at nothing to achieve its aims. Truly, Weishaupt's philosophy was one of the ends justifying the means. In this case, both the means and the end are most repugnant to those cherishing individual freedom and liberty.[9]

One of the disputed portions of Illuminati history has to do with whether or not Weishaupt was a member of a Masonic lodge when he formulated his society. What is known is that sometime around 1771 a man named Kolmer introduced Weishaupt to a form of Egyptian mysticism. Between that time and the official founding of the Illuminati in 1776, Weishaupt based his own secret society on Kolmer's occultism and melded it with Masonic teachings. Joining the Munich lodge in 1777, the fledgling organization quickly spread to other German lodges, effectively becoming a secret society within a secret society. Adam Weishaupt reflected this in his private opinions of both Masonry and the Enlightenment movement. In his correspondence he sarcastically lambasted the followers of the Enlightenment for worshiping all things Greek and Roman while at the same time being impotent to produce anything themselves. Some researchers go so far as to suggest that although Masonry provided the organizational structure of the revolutionary movements of the late 1780s and 1790s, it was the Illuminati that gave the movements their blueprint. Weishaupt, it would appear, considered himself among the truly enlightened; in his arrogance he came to believe he knew better than the rest of humanity what was best for it.[10]

In time, lodges embracing Weishaupt's philosophy became known as Illuminized Masonry. Membership in the Illuminati was certainly not open to all, nor were the Illuminists entirely forthright in their proselytizing practices. Prospective members were asked a series of questions that would ascertain their "worthiness" to join. It must be pointed out that Adam Weishaupt's identity as the head of the Illuminati was a closely guarded secret. He even took on the name of "Spartacus" and used it when corresponding with his lieutenants.[11] Other high-level members of the Illuminati followed suit and adopted false names. The requirements for joining the organization were most unusual, too, and had occult overtones within them. Consider the following description of a required initiation ceremony.

> Marks were made with blood on the prostrate nude body of the candidate. His testicles were bound by a pink and poppy-colored cordon; and he renounced all other human allegiances before five white-hooded phantoms with bloody banners after a "colossal figure" appeared through a fire. Finally, the bands and marks were removed and he was accepted into the higher order by drinking blood before seven black candles.[12]

A requirement for joining the Illuminati was to make an oath promising hatred for the monarchy and all its symbols. Refusal to do so would almost surely disqualify a prospective initiate.

The organization of the Illuminati was based on a pyramid model. At the top, of course, was Weishaupt. Below the head of the organization were highly trusted lieutenants who in turn had two "commanders" below them, and so on. In this way commands could be quickly spread through the dozen or so levels of Illuminism without the lower initiates knowing who was in charge.[13] The first lodge, in Bavaria, moved to Frankfurt when it became clear that word of their society was leaking out. On setting up the organization in Frankfurt, the fortunes of the Illuminati improved when infusions of capital made it possible to spread the message to other German lodges. By the 1780s Masonic lodges across western Europe had accepted, by varying degrees, Illuminism. By that time, governments began to take notice and eventually took action.[14]

Freemasonry on the European continent during the 1770s was in something of a state of disarray. This was especially true of France and the Germanic states. The Illuminati sought to obtain converts to their version of Masonry by taking advantage of the general confusion and seeming lack of leadership. Baron Adolph Knigge was a leading Mason from Hanover. When he joined Weishaupt's inner circle in 1780, he helped to increase interest among other influential members of Knigge's Masonic level, the Strict Observance. A known occultist, Knigge fit right in with the dark ceremonies performed under Weishaupt's direction. An additional change in Illuminism took place at this time as well: The Illuminati became increasingly political. This is important because it made the group attractive to potential members who might have been put off by what they had heard about the arcane mysticism, rituals, and tightly guarded secrecy.[15]

In 1782 representatives of a number of lodges met at the Masonic Congress of Wilhelmsbad. Some conspiracy theorists have alleged that it was here that Weishaupt and his Illuminati brethren unveiled their true plans for restructuring Western societies along the lines of their occult and mystical beliefs. In a true stroke of political genius that would have done Alcibiades or Richelieu proud, the Illuminists in attendance set themselves up as the "true" Masons. Their contentions were mainly that portions of European Masonry had been either infiltrated by Jesuits or simply lost the society's true vision. As bearers of the light, they cast themselves in the image of saviors of the ancient order. To Weishaupt, Masonry was to be used as little more than a training ground for deeper mysteries and then discarded. The twelve levels of Illuminism were to lead the believer to a point of spiritual and political egalitarianism, a sort of self-deification or godhood for those who had made their way into the deepest mysteries of Illuminism.[16] Many Masons in attendance were shocked by what they heard. The Comte de Virieu, a member of the Martiniste lodge at Lyon, returned from the meeting obviously troubled. When asked to elucidate his concerns, de Virieu stated only "that all this is very more serious than you think. The conspiracy which is being woven is so well thought out that it will be, so to speak, impossible for the Monarch and the Church to escape from it."[17]

Rumors of the Illuminati's intentions to overthrow the existing political and social order eventually reached the ears of officials in Bavaria. Understandably, the government was concerned enough to look into the matter and ascertain the veracity of the stories. Investigators received a break in 1785 when lightning struck and killed an Illuminati courier. The papers he was carrying, apparently meant for Illuminati lodges in France, told of plans that were by all accounts subversive. Weishaupt's house was searched, as were the homes and businesses of other exposed Illuminati leaders. In the end, the Bavarian officials were convinced that a plot did indeed exist that had as its goal the overthrow of governments with a view of replacing them with "enlightened" (Illuminati) leadership.[18]

Despite the unwanted exposure, Illuminist ideas and even organizations continued to meet and put forward their agenda. France in particular, as well as some Germanic states, saw continued Weishaupt influence of his particular brand of Masonry. Illuminati sympathizer Count Mirabeau revealed in his book, *The Prussian Monarchy under Frederick the Great (1788)* (coauthored by former Illuminist Jakob Mauvillion), that "the great aim [of the Illuminati] was the improvement of the present system of governments and legislations." This book perhaps more than any other helped to popularize the Illuminati with the reading public of the day. Mirabeau helped to influence a number of younger intellectuals and provided some Illuminati history and inner workings for anyone interested.[19]

In France, Nicholas Bonneville also played an important role in pushing Illuminism. "The [integral] man is God" perhaps best sums up his position on the subject. In yet another work,

*The Jesuits Driven from Freemasonry,* this Illuminati writer makes the case that Illuminist thinking was essentially the salvation of Masonry—the "true flame." Illuminists in France just prior to the Revolution were adding touches of their own to the Weishaupt model. Men such as Christian Bode, who in fact had converted Bonneville to Illuminism in 1787, and the Saxon physician of Philip of Orlean helped to add to the growing number of influential members of the sect. The leader in France, however, was probably Sylvain Marechal. It was in all likelihood his ideas that made their way into print through men such as Bonneville. After all, the strict code of silence and secrecy would forbid the revealing of inner-circle members. It was Marechal who nonetheless became somewhat noteworthy for his use of the title l'HSD *(l'homme sans dieu),* or "man without God." I could not think of a more appropriate short description of Illuminati ideology. By 1789, when the French Revolution broke out, Illuministic ideas were known and discussed among the intelligentsia of that kingdom and across Europe. Many found the ideals of Adam Weishaupt to be something of a culmination of the Enlightenment movement, the "final result" or action Weishaupt had scorned them for failing to take. It is at this point, the French Revolution, that the influence of the Illuminati is most debated.[20]

## The Illuminati and the French Revolution

Could the Illuminati have pulled off the French Revolution? By itself, no. The seething cauldron of French political and social unrest was such in the 1780s and 1790s that any Illuminati ideas would have provided more of a backdrop than a driving force. To suggest that secret societies alone were responsible for the collapse of the French monarchy defies historical fact. It does provide an easy, quick answer but it fails to take into account the magnitude of events beyond anyone's ability to plan. There were simply too many grievances among the lower classes to explain away the uprising as mere opportunism. The earlier excesses of the Sun King, Louis XIV

(1643–1715), followed by Louis XV (1715–74) and the resultant losses to Britain in the great Wars for Empire are but a few of the myriad factors contributing to the collapse of the French monarchy during Louis XVI's reign. Corruption and unrest in the three French social divisions called estates were also quite pronounced. Among the First (clergy) and Second (nobility) Estates, corruption was so bad that the Third Estate (peasants) was simply given no choice but to finally toss off the yoke holding them in abject political and social destitution. The Third Estate, which made up about 90 percent of the population, simply had no say in government, and when the national debt crushed the French treasury, they were the ones to feel the brunt of the burden. Moreover, Louis Philippe, Duke of Orléans, often pointed to as a primary Illuminati conspirator during the French Revolution, was, according to Henry Cabot Lodge's multivolume *History of Nations,* intellectually incapable of conspiratorial planning. Although he loaned his name to a number of conspiratorial and even popular movements, it would be a gross overstatement to attribute one of the greatest revolutionary movements in history to his efforts. At most, I believe the secret organization exercised its influence through finance, advice, and at times terror.[21]

It is my contention that at least the Illuminati Enlightenment ideas lived on and most certainly had an influence on some of the revolutionaries of the 1780s and 1790s—not to mention future secret societies and revolutionary movements. It has been popular in works by Richard Berkhofer, David Davis, and others to suggest that the Illuminati survived in legend alone. Though it is true that not enough concrete evidence exists to support the contention that the Illuminati survived the nineteenth century, it is virtually indisputable that its ideology and philosophy did. Weishaupt's ideas continued to influence, inspire, even thrive in some quarters. But even this does not mean active conspiracy. Its impact was nonetheless felt across the Atlantic Ocean in the young United States, a nation that watched with alarm as the French Revolution went from popular uprising to Reign of Terror. More disturbing still, it was rumored that the Jacobin/Illuminati movement had spread its influence to the new republic.

## America's First Illuminati Scare

The United States in the mid to late 1790s was anything but a quiet nation enjoying the independence won from Britain just a few years earlier. After the contest over dumping the Articles of Confederation in favor of the Constitution a decade before, America's political system was sharply divided. Political parties, something we consider normal in today's republic, were thought anathema; yet they had formed in what historians call the First Party System. Those, such as Alexander Hamilton, in favor of a strong central government and those against it, under Thomas Jefferson's leadership, were at each other's throats for control of the nation's future. George Washington bemoaned the fact that these two members of his own government were so bent on political rivalry. Things did not go very well with the change of administration, either; the United States found that some problems simply did not disappear with the changing of leadership.

When Federalist John Adams was elected second president of the United States, he had to deal with some serious domestic and foreign issues. On the foreign front, what became known as the XYZ affair made news in the United States when it was revealed that French Foreign Minister Talleyrand had sought a bribe in exchange for cooperation in ending the undeclared war against American merchant shipping. In the domestic arena, John Adams had something of his own scandal when he and the Federalist Party endorsed the Alien and Sedition Acts. Briefly put, these laws sought to limit immigration, stiffen residency requirements, and most controversial, make it illegal to criticize the government verbally or in print. The Anti-Federalist Party challenged these laws immediately. The leading Anti-Federalist, or Democratic-Republican, was Thomas Jefferson. He encouraged the passage of what became known as the Kentucky and Virginia Resolutions—bills that if they became law would allow individual states to nullify laws they considered unconstitutional. It is into this partisan argument that the Illuminati controversy arose.[22]

In 1798 a most electrifying book was published in the United States. First put in print a year earlier in Europe, *Proofs of a Conspiracy* shocked the American public and political establishment. Written by John Robison, a professor of natural philosophy at the University of Edinburgh, it laid out a hidden conspiracy within European Masonry for the overthrow of governments, religion, and society. A recognized intellectual of the first order, Robison's charges drew immediate attention. This Edinburgh professor stated that continental Freemasonry had been infiltrated and largely overtaken by a sect known as the Illuminati. Adam Weishaupt himself had earlier approached Robison (also a Mason) to bring his considerable intellectual abilities to work for the Cause. Robison refused the invitation. In fact, he was deeply disturbed by what he uncovered about Weishaupt and his underground movement. When Robison's book hit American shores, it was immediately thrown into the fray of domestic politics.[23]

In May 1798, Boston Congregational minister Jedediah Morse delivered two sermons to his flock on the dangers of Freemasonry and in particular "Illuminized Freemasonry," which, he believed, had made its way to the United States. Using a prepublication copy of Robison's book, Morse shocked his congregation when he stated that "the world was in the grip of a secret revolutionary conspiracy, engineered by the Order of the Illuminati . . . and that the Republicans [Jefferson's Democratic-Republicans] in America . . . were dupes and accomplices of this same pernicious organization."[24]

The implications were clear: A number of American Masonic lodges had been infiltrated and "illuminized" and sought the ultimate destruction of the new American republic. The political dupes on our shores, according to Reverend Morse, were led by Thomas Jefferson. Jefferson, it should be recalled, was a big supporter of the French Revolution and of the infamous Citizen Genet (French Ambassador to the United States) until both—the Revolution and Genet—became unpopular due to their excesses. The timing of the announcement, at least in New England, helped to shore up support for the Alien and Sedition Acts as necessary actions to halt the influence of the Illuminati.[25]

Reverend Morse was not alone in his warnings against illuminized Freemasonry. No less a public official than Yale President Timothy Dwight blasted the Bavarian movement during a Fourth of July speech. Dwight went so far as to suggest that Jefferson was himself a willing accomplice to the plot, "the real Jacobin," to use his words. To an American nation in the midst of economic and foreign policy problems, it sounded like a very plausible explanation for their troubles. Even ex-President George Washington chimed in that he believed that the Illuminati had influence in some American lodges (Washington was himself a Mason) but did not elaborate on which ones were involved. In time, the Illuminati controversy died when it became apparent that neither Morse nor Dwight could provide any concrete evidence that American lodges harbored advocates of Illuminism.[26]

## Thomas Jefferson an Illuminati Agent?

While many supporters of the Federalist Party railed against the perceived involvement of Thomas Jefferson in The Conspiracy, there were likewise Anti-Federalists making accusations of conspiracy of their own. The most noteworthy of these is probably Abraham Bishop's *Proofs of a Conspiracy against Christianity, and the Government of the United States* (1802), in which the author accused the Federalist Party of selling out the American Revolution in the interests of money. The chief villain in this scenario was, of course, Alexander Hamilton. Hamilton had been a fiscally minded individual bound and determined to get the United States on a firm financial footing through tough-minded policy that included rapid payment of debt and the chartering of the First Bank of the United States. Hamilton's close ties with Britain did not earn him very many friends; Britain was to the United States in the early 1800s what the Soviet Union would be to the United States in the 1950s.

Bishop ripped into Hamilton and other Federalists for what he believed to be the fanciful writings of a "royalist," John Robison. In sum, he didn't think the Illuminati was a real and present danger to the United States. Instead, he perceived the real conspirators to be the Federalists right here in the United States. The conspiracy craze of the 1790s and early 1800s had thus come full circle.[27]

When Thomas Jefferson was elected as our nation's third president, there were many who feared that it would mean the end of the republic. Jefferson's deistic beliefs, his intellectual abilities, even his "Jeffersonian Bible" all were looked on as proof that the country could not possibly be in worse hands. In the minds of Jefferson's foes, the Virginian was sworn to dismantle the entire government structure since the adoption of the Constitution. What was also galling to Federalists was what they considered Jefferson's rank hypocrisy. Here was a man, an aristocratic slaveholder no less, claiming to be on the side of the "little guy." Today he would be called a mink-coat liberal, I suppose. There were other fears about the administration of Jefferson: Religion, it was said, would be assailed; war with Britain likely; close relations with France solidified; and most dreadful, a Jeffersonian-run American "Reign of Terror" instituted.[28]

Despite the criticism, Jefferson performed his duties well; and, though not remembered in his own day as a particularly good president, he has since come to be regarded as one of our best. None of the terrible things the Federalists feared came about, and Jefferson's own revolutionary zeal for France waned. Democratic-Republicans instead saw their rise to power as something of a mellow revolution in its own right, a correction of the ship of state. As is often the case, especially in American politics, rhetoric and reality are usually spaced far apart. Like the Federalists before him, Jefferson had to face the problems of constant war between Britain and France and the lack of respect the United States received at the hands of both. He acted, frankly, as probably any other Federalist would have done in similar circumstances. The fears that he was a Jacobin, an "Illuminist," were unfounded.[29]

The United States was doubtless hampered internationally during the first fifteen years of the nineteenth century. Undeclared war with France and Britain over the issue of freedom of the seas was a genuine test for the American government. Desiring conflict with neither France nor Britain, the three presidents during this period found it increasingly difficult to continue international trade without becoming involved in the political affairs of Europe. When various tariffs and veiled threats failed to bring about the desired outcome with the perpetually fighting Britain and France, an ultimatum was delivered to both, threatening war if the illegal stopping of American ships did not cease. France responded favorably first, so America declared war on Britain—even though Britain was about to rescind her policy of impressment and seizure of U.S. vessels. Objecting Federalists of New England called the result "Mr. Madison's War," what we today call the War of 1812. Ending in late 1814, this conflict helped to provide a sense of unity for the United States that it had not known since the Revolution. This sense of purpose continued for a few years after the war in what became known as the Era of Good Feelings.

By the end of Jefferson's second term in office and the subsequent administrations of Madison and Monroe, believers in conspiracy theories faced a problem those of like mind have had to contend with ever since: proving the existence of conspiracy and exciting the public to action. The ability to awaken a slumbering public to danger is based on the ability to prove one's position. The result of this problem is one that has been repeated time and again over the past two hundred years: Without proof—the "smoking gun"—the public remains largely uninterested or unconvinced.

## Why Conspiracy When Common Sense Will Suffice?

This writer must admit that it is extremely difficult to believe that an organization as young as the Illuminati was in the 1780s could have had the influence necessary to cause the French Revolution or exercise sway over Federalist-era America. Many conspiracy theorists, however, hold to a belief that the Illuminati continues to exist and has grown into a nearly all-powerful clique that can do essentially what it wants when it wants to in the political and economic world. How, it must be asked, can a conspiracy last for more than two hundred years? How does one pass on the revolutionary vision needed? In any revolution, secret or otherwise, a major problem is ensuring the continuation of fervor and zeal for change. There has yet to be a revolution that has not lost its steam over the years. This is true of political movements (Communism in Russia, China, or Cuba) and religious movements (Puritanism in New England). These declines happened over a few decades; but a successful, not to mention secret, movement carried on for generations?

It is my belief, then, that the Illuminati ceased to exist as a real political threat early in the nineteenth century, if not during the French Revolution itself. Later political and occult groups borrowed from its organizational structure, but this is nothing akin to an ongoing conspiracy. Between 1875 and 1900, when occult groups such as Madame Blavatsky's Theosophy Society and the Ordo Templi Orientis (O.T.O.) arose, Illuminism was resurrected, albeit in quite a different form. For instance, the O.T.O.'s most famous member, Aleister Crowley, delved heavily into many occult ideas similar to those once taught by Adam Weishaupt and, along with the Enochian Magick of Dr. John Dee, came up with his own creed. These are set forth in the *Equinox*, Crowley's journal epitomizing early-twentieth-century European and American occultism. These extensions of Illuminism, however, are a far cry from any sort of global conspiracy.[30]

## Conclusion

The greatest enemies of conspiracy theory are not those who do not believe; rather, they are the extremist True Believers whose rantings the public takes as seriously as a late-night-television used-car sales pitch. Outrageous claims of worldwide conspiracy and drug dealing by the Queen of England, for instance, as Lyndon LaRouche supporters suggest, are but one example. During times of social and political stress, some in the public sector turn to fanatical conspiracy theorists to explain contemporary problems. During the nineteenth century in the United States, there was still suspicion of conspiracy just under the surface. This suspicion was to be found in government, religion, and business, and it produced some predictable paranoia.

# Nineteenth-Century Conspiracy Theories

Conspiracy theories did not disappear between the Illuminati scare of the 1790s and early 1800s and the end of the Civil War. While Manifest Destiny, sectionalism, and the slavery issue caught nearly everyone's attention, interest in conspiracy on an international scale was for a time left behind. There were issues of related interest, such as the chartering of the Bank of the United States, the rise of the Anti-Mason party, the Jackson-Bank controversy, and the fallout surrounding the economic collapse known as the panic of 1837. Taken together, these issues did not constitute a large public awareness of unseen movers, or much of a concern about it. Nonetheless, the Robison-Barruel Illuminati stories were kept simmering through this period.

## Early American Masonic Conspiracy Theories

A chief target of conspiracy theorists over the last two centuries has been the Masonic Lodge. The Lodge was attacked at various times throughout its history for allegedly harboring subversive, anti-Christian, or other perfidious ideas. In the United States some of the young nation's most prominent leaders, including George Washington, Thomas Jefferson, and Ben-

jamin Franklin, were Freemasons. During the ceremonial lay-
ing of the Capitol building's cornerstone, Washington was
attired in his Masonic regalia in honor of the event. Despite
this, there was from the beginning a widely held public suspicion that Freemasonry contained something not entirely whole-
some. This suspicion led to charges and countercharges of conspiracy at the end of the 1790s and into the early 1800s. As
pointed out in the last chapter, some Americans were convinced
that an Illuminati plot was wrapped in Masonic clothing.

Although the fear of Freemasonry waned during the Jefferson administration, it never entirely disappeared. By the time
our sixth president, John Quincy Adams, came to office in 1824,
a new round of anti-Mason feeling had arisen. So strong did
the sentiment become that by the time of the 1828 election it
had coalesced into a political party, aptly named the Anti-
Masons. The Anti-Mason Party arose from a number of deep-
seated fears, but it erupted in popularity over the death of a former Mason, Capt. William Morgan.[1]

Morgan was a member of a Batavia, New York, lodge. After
having several disagreements with members of his lodge, some
of them near-violent altercations, Morgan decided to get even
with his fraternal mates by publishing a book revealing the
secret rites of Freemasonry's first three degrees. Published in
collaboration with the local town paper, *The Advocate,* Morgan
and the newspaper's editor quickly cranked out copies of *Illustrations of Masonry* or *Exposition of Freemasonry* in 1827. Out-
raged at this behavior, Morgan's former fellow Masons became
intent on silencing him. First, the newspaper's page proofs of
Morgan's book were confiscated, and then the offices of *The
Advocate* burned to the ground. Still not successful in deterring
the ex-Mason, the Masons had Morgan arrested on trumped-
up theft and nonpayment of debt charges. He was released for
insufficient evidence after both cases went to trial.[2]

What began as harassment quickly jumped to threats of violence and later kidnapping and murder. Morgan was taken from
a waiting carriage and smuggled to Fort Niagara, where he was
held in jail for a few days before he was drowned in the Niagara River. This led to a general outrage over the activity of

some overzealous Masons, and soon anti-Mason organizations grew up, later solidifying into a political party. In the 1828 election, many noted that Andrew Jackson was a high-ranking Mason whereas John Quincy Adams was not. This caused many among the Anti-Masons to oppose Jackson, if not support President Adams. The irony was that in general, opposition to Masons was based on the notion that they represented the rich and powerful. Adams, the non-Mason, came from a wealthy New England family; Jackson, the frontiersman from much humbler origins, was actively involved in the secret society. This was very difficult for politicos of the time to explain.[3]

## International Banking Conspiracy Theories

The Bank of the United States, as it was chartered in 1816, came about as a result of the upheaval of the period before, during, and after the War of 1812. The horrendous economic conditions of those times caused even some of central banking's chief opponents to finally acquiesce in favor of the order such an institution was supposed to bring. The Democratic-Republican party of Jefferson was against it from the beginning; in the wake of the war, however, they decided that such drastic measures were needed. After fighting the renewal of the Bank when its charter expired in 1811, Anti-Federalists opted to back it in view of the economic uncertainty following the War of 1812. The result was that in 1816 the Second Bank of the United States was created. Its charter was good for another twenty years; little did anyone know that efforts in the rechartering of that bank would result in a huge political fight with international implications.[4]

The initial idea behind the Bank of the United States was one of monetary stability. This premise was based on the theory that by buying up state bank notes and demanding repayment in hard money—gold and silver—state commercial banks would be forced to be conservative in issuing paper money. By doing so, supporters of the Bank suggested, the monetary supply would not overexpand, resulting in deflation. Many people,

Andrew Jackson included, believed that instead of offering stability, the Bank was the cause of instability. Opponents of the Bank were insistent that the financial institution was of more use to the wealthy and other bankers at home and abroad than to the average American. By the time Andrew Jackson became president in 1828, he brought his undeniable anti-Bank sentiments with him and ultimately destroyed the institution by refusing its recharter. Although the government owned approximately one-fifth of the Bank of the United States stock, Jackson and his Democratic allies believed that the other 80 percent was controlled beyond our own shores. Fearing economic colonialism under Europe, Jackson was convinced that Bank president Nicholas Biddle was little more than a figurehead for his masters in Europe, particularly the banking House of Rothschild and other London interests. The Democrats were ultimately successful in destroying the institution, and the Bank became merely one of Pennsylvania's state banks and ended its regulation of other financial lending agencies.[5]

In the wake of the Bank's demise, the United States's economy experienced a sizable economic collapse. Indeed, what was known as the panic of 1837 was the deepest depression the nation had known up to that time. Many blamed the economic downturn on the failure of the government to renew the Bank of the United States's charter; still others blamed European bankers for a planned act of revenge. One sure cause of the collapse was Jackson's, then Martin van Buren's, enforcement of accepting gold and silver alone in payment for loans from what were then called "wildcat banks." These state banks were unregulated and would make loans on the least imaginable security. To stop inflation, the famous "Specie Circular" was sent to banks throughout the states demanding payment in a medium of recognized value. The ripple effect was quite intense, causing the United States to undergo financial upheaval. So severe was the downturn that bankers and even the U.S. government were forced to seek loans overseas to help tide them over until times improved. In 1842, one such effort for help came in the form of meetings between Duff Green, a U.S. Treasury Department official, and James Rothschild, head of the Rothschild family interests in Paris. The meetings produced only an enraged reply from the European banker: "You may tell your government that you have seen the man who is at the head of the finances of Europe, and he has told you that they cannot borrow a dollar, not a dollar!"[6] Although America did survive the economic problems of the time, they added to a growing sense among some Christian believers that the end of the world system and the return of Christ were at hand.

## The Second Great Awakening

Between 1800 and 1840, a religious movement afterward known as the Second Great Awakening swept the nation. Basically a rebound in religious interest after a very difficult time for Americans in the wake of the Revolutionary War, the Second Great Awakening ranks as one of the most important social and religious movements in our nation's history. Religious leaders such as Charles Finney and Lyman Beecher were just a few of the leading voices calling a nation back to God. Emphasizing personal salvation through receiving Christ as Savior, this movement differed from most earlier revivals in that it also advocated an experience described in the Book of Acts as the "Baptism in the Holy Spirit." The revivals swept out of places such as western New York State, the "Burned-over District," to all corners of America. Camp meetings like the massive affairs at Cane Ridge, Kentucky, became symbolic of the movement. It didn't take long for the movement to influence society.[7]

A number of reform organizations grew up as a result of the revival of religious interest advocating change in social institutions, such as hospitals, prisons, and schools, as well as the abolition of slavery, better treatment for Indians, and women's rights. Also involved were temperance supporters and prohibitionists. Few mass public movements have equaled the long-term effects these reformers had on the nation. Still, because there was and is a strong sense of anticipation for the second coming of Jesus within Christianity, there were groups who saw in the massive spiritual movement and the nation's financial problems the signs of the end.

## End-Time Date-Setting in the 1840s

William Miller was one person who became convinced that Jesus was about to fulfill his promise to return to Earth very soon. Miller wrote that in 1818 he began a study of the Books of Daniel and Revelation. As a result of his lengthy study, he worked out a system whereby he decided that the times and days spoken of in Daniel referred to years and could, therefore, provide a system to closely guess the time of Christ's return. He shared his findings with just a few friends at first, and it wasn't until the 1830s that his position became known and popular.[8]

Miller believed that Jesus was going to return sometime between March 21, 1843, and March 21, 1844. Checking and double-checking his figures, Miller became increasingly bold in his pronouncements that an important epoch was at hand. As the day approached, there was undeniable excitement among the rapidly growing faithful. The appointed day came and went, and the final deadline approached. When March 21, 1844, passed, Miller fine-tuned his calculations and came up with a date of October 22, 1844. As this day approached, there was again a great deal of anticipation among adherents; among nonbelievers there was growing criticism. The October deadline also came and went, leading to what Millerites called the "Great Disappointment." The movement fell apart thereafter, with the notable exception of a small group that became known as the Seventh-Day Adventists. Miller's miscalculations were not the first, nor would they be the last, to predict the return of Jesus of Nazareth. What is worth noting is that the combination of religious fervor and a severe economic downturn led many to conclude that Jesus was about to return. There is a lesson here for us to learn.[9]

## Post-Miller American Eschatology and British-Israelism

Both during and after the Millerite episode, other Christian "experts" postulated that the end of the world was at hand.

Samuel Baldwin, a Methodist minister, published a book titled *Armageddon,* with the extended title given as follows: *The Overthrow of Romanism and Monarchy; the Existence of the United States as Foretold in the Bible, Its Future Greatness, Invasion by Allied Powers; Annihilation of the Monarch; Expansion into the Millennial Republic, and Its Dominion over the Whole World.* Published in 1854, Baldwin's book contended that the Millerites had misunderstood the dates and "signs of the times" in Revelation and Daniel. Offered as a correction of Millerism, Baldwin did not fall into the error of stating specific dates for the end but nonetheless became convinced that the United States was the Israel spoken of in Scripture. This "United States as Israel" or "Church as Israel" idea first became popular in the form of British-Israelism and continues in our own day through the teachings of the late Herbert Armstrong and some Dominion theologians. One of Baldwin's stranger interpretations of Scripture had the United States the subject of a Russian-led invasion. Like modern-day prophecy writers, Baldwin believed the Gog and Magog of Ezekiel 38 and 39 to be Russia; combined with his Christian Israel ideas, he saw it as natural that the predicted invasion would be of the United States, not Palestine. Baldwin, like the Millerite movement he criticized, was wrong in his interpretations.[10]

Fountain Pitts of Tennessee was a preacher whom Baldwin had influenced. Preaching in the wake of the Millerite "Great Disappointment," Pitts blasted William Miller as being everything from a poor theologian to a madman. Like Baldwin, Pitts believed that America and Christianity (sometimes indistinguishable in the minds of Christians, then and now) had taken over for Israel in the covenant relationship with God. Like Miller, Pitts used the days and weeks mentioned in the prophetic books of the Bible to try to predict when Christ would return. He too believed that the United States would be invaded in the near future by Russian and allied forces. Perhaps to an even greater degree than Baldwin, Pitts expected America to be the New Israel. This is something of a departure from other Anglo-Israelites; here an influential preacher with a national reputation went so far as to relegate to the United States—not just

Christians—the role of the "Chosen People." Although not quite as dramatically, Pitts's teachings were also relegated to the ash heap of history.[11]

The lesson these Christian prophecy teachers present is that even very sincere believers in Christ are capable of egregious error. And just as we have prophetic teachings today insisting that the end of the world must be at hand, we need to be very cautious when assigning these promoters prophetic status. It is also easy to say that the church today could not be duped into believing such false statements. Consider the acceptance of nonprophetic but equally false teachings: "name it and claim it," the prosperity gospel, and personal godhood teachings among faith teaching groups.

Nineteenth-century prophecy speculation did not end with Miller, Baldwin, and Pitts. Indeed, one of the most important trends in prophetic interpretation would come to the attention of the faithful with the teachings of John N. Darby (1800–82). A member of a small sect known as the Brethren, Darby was a firm believer that politics and ties to "worldly organizations" were to be rejected. This obvious break from the prophecy pronouncements of both Baldwin and Pitts ultimately attracted a great many more adherents among the faithful. In a word, Darby introduced the American Christian community to the theology of dispensationalism. Though not a new idea, dispensationalism was at its core a belief that in terms of salvation God dealt with the human race differently at different times in history. Darby's teachings were heavily laden with prophetic expectations, especially the deeply held belief that God was about to end the dispensational period known as the "Church Age" with an event known as the rapture. Although the word *rapture* does not appear in Scripture, it had been a staple of Christian end-time belief from the beginning. Darby, perhaps borrowing from some in the Millerite movement, held that the Church Age would end with the removal of Christians from Earth at the beginning of what was called the tribulation, a seven-year period of horrible plagues, war, and famine. The notion that the tribulation would occur before the second coming of Christ was a bit different than what had been traditionally taught, but it was warmly embraced among nineteenth-century American Christians. By the time of the Civil War, prophecy enthusiasts, like other believers before them, were expecting Jesus to come at any time.[12]

## The Rise of Corporate Conspiracies

The United States did eventually emerge from the economic difficulties the panic caused, mostly as a result of westward expansion and the discovery of gold during the 1840s. By that time, and especially during the turbulent 1850s, sectionalism would emerge as the main concern of politicians and citizens alike. The eventual war between North and South, America's greatest tragedy, produced as many ills as it cured. During the war, industries grew on an immense scale and new words entered the American political lexicon. "Monopoly" and "trust" soon came to describe business practices that were not, in the eyes of most, conducive to the welfare of the average American. As a result of the rise of large companies, conspiracy-based theories of history made an impressive comeback.

The years after the Civil War were not stellar examples of political honesty and competence. With the election of Ulysses S. Grant, a new low in scandal, dishonesty, and outright political stupidity was reached. It is difficult to compare Grant's two terms in office with any other administration before or since. Though a competent and daring Union general during the Civil War, Grant simply had no understanding of government and how to deal with very powerful interest groups. Still, it would be unfair to characterize Grant alone as lacking in ability or honesty during the Reconstruction period; the nation's business community for the most part reflected these shortcomings.[13]

The Reconstruction period in American history rarely finds historians with a lack of opinion about the era. For our purposes here, I will try to zero in on the general business atmosphere and how it had changed since the war. Risking overstatement, I think it can be said that the nation's political and big business leaders had a healthy lust for riches and power and were willing to walk over anyone or any institution to obtain their desired ends. Cynical businessmen constructed monopolies and crushed competition through a variety of unprecedented or illegal means. Politicians were willing to be bought and sold for their favors to whatever business or industry could help fatten their bank accounts. In the midst of this President Grant found himself being wined and dined by the wealthy and powerful, businessmen whom he naively came to consider his friends. For the president, his associations provided the appearance of his being an insider and willing accomplice: that, or a witless dupe. Being guilty of either corruption or gross stupidity is hardly desirable for a political leader.[14] Scandals during the Grant administration seemed to sprout like mushrooms overnight. Just a few of the more publicity-grabbing episodes included the "Black Friday" gold conspiracy masterminded by Jay Gould and Jim Fisk, the infamous "Boss Tweed" ring in New York City, the Credit Mobilier Scandal involving kickbacks for railroad officials and their friends, and the "Salary Grab Act," which involved the 1873 Congress's attempt to increase members' salary by 50 percent, retroactive to two years earlier. The business climate, too, grew in size and complexity, and unfortunately, so did corruption in business during this period.[15]

Along with the tremendous expansion of American business during the war, industries also benefited from a massive influx of immigrants and the cheap labor they provided. Taking advantage of their poverty and immediate needs to provide for their families, factories of all types hired the newcomers for pennies a day and in some cases demanded sixteen-hour workdays in sweatshop conditions. The result of this heinous labor crime was growing resentment against the corporations and government; it also resulted in the rise of labor unions. Groups such as the Knights of Labor and the American Federation of Labor proved highly popular to growing numbers of working-class people tired of living in squalor and working under dangerous conditions. Among the largest and most influential industries to grow up in this atmosphere of corruption and protectionism were steel (Andrew Carnegie), petroleum (John D. Rockefeller), grain milling (Washburn and Pillsbury), meat packing (Armour and Swift), and railroad companies.[16] Taken with a general distrust of the established political system, the corruption encouraged many to seek to create their own political party.

## Christian Politics and Conspiracy Theory in the 1890s

The rise of third parties during the late 1880s and 1890s was an expression of the indignation among rank-and-file America against what was rightly perceived as political and business interests gone amok. It was radical in the sense that, aside from specific reforms, it demanded government action on behalf of the common citizenry. A common theme among third parties was one that has been repeated in conspiracy movements before and since: There was something in the past—the "good ol' days"—when there was something akin to a utopia. For many it was a combination of a time and a myth: Jeffersonian democracy and the agrarian myth combined to provide a powerful image. It seemed to many as though something had happened along the way to sidetrack or derail the ideal; an unknown someone or faceless group had stolen what was rightly theirs.[17]

By the late 1880s the seriousness of the economic problems on the northern Great Plains and in the South became acute. Despite what they might have said about who was responsible, the farmers' problems were real. Farmers' alliances sprang up to meet the needs of the people, at first as social organizations, such as the Grange, and then into full-blown political action groups. On the northern Great Plains there was the National Farmers' Alliance; the South had its Farmers' Alliance and Industrial Union. The latter was the largest of the two, with well over a million members by the early 1890s. When a number of politically active groups including the Grange organized into the People's, or Populist, Party in 1891, the causes of discontent among farmers (and working classes elsewhere), were more clearly stated. Among those problems: falling farm prices tied to deflation, high interest rates and massive loans, unprotected crop prices, and lack of any kind of insurance protection against crop losses.[18]

So quickly did the political nature of these groups grow that the People's Party ran a candidate in the 1892 presidential election, James Weaver. Other leaders of the People's Party included Ignatius Donnelly, William Jennings Bryan (later a Democrat), "Sockless" Jerry Simpson, Mary Lease, and "Pitchfork" Ben Tillman. Populist leaders and a good many of their followers tended to distrust government and business in the extreme, so much so that explanations for national problems were often put in conspiratorial terms. Indeed, the platform of the party that election year addressed a good many issues it considered to be eating away at the integrity of rural life. Attracting particular attention were the nation's currency laws. In short, the Populists sought to increase the number of greenbacks in circulation and to vastly increase the gold and silver available to the public.[19]

Conspiracy became a readily identifiable part of Populism as early as the 1892 election. Leaders of such eloquence as Ignatius Donnelly went so far as to author a conspiracy fantasy entitled *Caesar's Column*. Published under a pseudonym, this book became one of the best-sellers of the 1890s. Within its pages, Donnelly described his vision of what an American utopian society might be like—even though the book is set in Africa. Behind the struggle between the powerful and the producers was another broader theme that would become a staple of Populism, namely a secret society and/or the international banker conspiracy. Of course, as seems to be distressingly common in conspiracy theory, the idea was put forth that those behind-the-scenes planners were all or nearly all Jews.[20]

### Mary E. Lease

The fear of foreigners and the loss of land—particularly the once vast public domain—caused other Populist writers of the conspiratorial bent to seek out yet more hidden reasons why things were amiss in America's heartland. One such writer was truly a Populist original: Mary E. Lease of Kansas. At times called a "demagogue in hoopskirts," Lease was a firebrand author who lived up to that sobriquet. In her book, *The Problem of Civilization Solved,* Lease set forth what she considered to be the final solution to the world's problems of anarchy or despotism. Her solution was to have a massive migration from overcrowded areas, resulting in a gigantic resettling of the world's peoples in such a manner that peace would be an "automatic" result. Beyond that, she also advocated a racist policy that would place the tropical areas of the world under the control of white peoples while members of the Oriental and Black races would serve as little better than farmhands. That Lease considered the Caucasian race superior is beyond dispute; she deemed such a dominance to merely be the result of the natural order of things, and claimed that if the white civilization would merely take its rightful place of leadership in the world, the other "lesser" races would celebrate the change.[21]

Conspiracy as tied to international money power was anything but rare among Populists. It was a common assumption among farmers and wage laborers that a wealthy clique of unknowns was taking advantage of them. As Richard Hofstadter points out in *Age of Reform,* ". . . it remains true that Populist thought showed an unusually strong tendency to account for relatively impersonal events in highly personal terms."[22] People who have been subjected to injustices or economic deprivation can find it easy to blame a nameless, faceless "other" who is the cause of their problems. The farmer or factory worker thus becomes the victim, indeed the target, of great evils hatched in distant boardrooms.[23]

A good, although tragic, contemporary example of this mindset can be found on the northern Great Plains, particularly in North Dakota. A conspiratorial group known as the Posse Comitatus grew in influence during the 1970s when interest rates and farm foreclosures plagued farmers across the Grain Belt. The Posse had simple, quick answers: It was the Jewish bankers who were after not only their farms, but their freedoms as well. Nothing less than a takeover by a one-world system was behind their misfortunes. In North Dakota, known for its low crime rate and friendly citizens, ideology of this sort resulted in the shocking deaths of two U.S. marshals near the small community of Me-

dina. Gordon Kahl, his son, and another gunman were responsible for the shootings but claimed they acted in defense of their
lives and property against the "conspiracy." Kahl was later killed
in Arkansas in a shootout with the FBI. The surviving participating members of the Kahl family are in prison and still apparently believe their actions were in self-defense.[24]

### Ignatius Donnelly

Ignatius Donnelly and the Populists of his mind-set held
something of the same views, albeit ninety years before Gordon Kahl. Donnelly claimed that "a vast conspiracy against
mankind has been organized on two continents, and is rapidly
taking possession of the world."[25] Moreover, it was said among
the Populists that the conspirators were busy keeping the population at large in the dark about their plans, befuddling the
common man in such a fashion that he would not recognize
the Plan even if he saw it. Known as the "Anglo-American Gold
Trust," the conspirators of the 1890s bear a remarkable resem-
blance to the same group described prior to and during World
War I, the New Deal, Communism, and virtually every conspiracy theory since.[26]

Another aspect of the 1890s Populist conspiracy theories that
bear striking similarities to contemporary "secret plans"
involves monetary issues. While today many believers in conspiracy theories hold that the dollar will lose its value because
of federal fiscal mismanagement over the last half-century,
many also contend that Federal Reserve notes will be replaced
with some sort of worldwide currency. During the Populists'
day, the general perception was that the coinage of silver at a
16:1 ratio with gold would eliminate or at least greatly lessen
the farmers' monetary crisis.[27]

### William Jennings Bryan

William Jennings Bryan, a powerful voice in the Populist
uprising and a fundamentalist Christian, also held very certain
views concerning the currency issue. Although a Democrat,
Bryan's political views and geographic point of origin made

him popular among Populists. He stated as early as 1890 the desire for "free coinage of silver" in place of paper or "fiat" money of the day. His considerable oratorical gifts made his ability to state his position quite impressive, even if it was apparent he was not entirely well versed in economics or monetary policy. Bryan even went so far as to admit ignorance of the difference in monetary policy between silver and paper money but continued nonetheless to support the silver side of the debate. By 1893 he was a favorite speaker of political groups backing such a policy. One such group was the American Bimetallic League, an organization formed in 1889 and comprised mostly of western silver mine owners. In time, this organization took to a young lawyer and publicist to present their case to the public. His name was William H. Harvey.[28]

### William "Coin" Harvey

Money, being so important to everyone in modern-day society, is understandably at or near the center of any conspiracy theory. "He who has the gold makes the rules" the saying goes, and it seems to be believed by many fearful of some sort of planning on an international scale. During the Populism heyday of the 1890s, one person in particular pushed the silver (and gold) issue to the forefront, even more so than did William Jennings Bryan. This "silverite" was known as "Coin" Harvey, and his main contribution was a book called *Coin's Financial School*.[29]

William H. Harvey was born in 1851 in Virginia, the fifth of six children. His schooling seems to have been limited to a few years spent at a small academy in Buffalo, Virginia, and later at Marshall College, also in Virginia. Studying law on his own, he was admitted to the bar at the age of nineteen. Harvey moved on after 1870 to West Virginia, and by 1875 to Ohio. There he met and married Anna Halliday in 1876; their marriage produced four children. Still employed as an attorney, Harvey worked for a number of wholesale houses before moving to Colorado, where he apparently first had contact with the metal that was to play such a prominent part in his life: silver. Harvey's desire to move about separated him from the mine business for a time, as evidenced by his legal practice and recently added real estate business interests in Utah and Oregon. By 1893 Harvey had moved back to Chicago, where he established a publishing firm dedicated to the coinage of free silver. Being in the right place at the right time was to serve Harvey well during the Populist era.[30]

Richard Hofstadter referred to "Coin" Harvey as a money crank. This is an appropriate description of both the man and his publications. Uneducated in economics other than his own personal experiences, he became convinced that hard currency—gold, but especially silver—was the only true currency and that paper money was at best a counterfeit method of exchange. He believed that the monetary system as it existed in his day was highly subject to manipulation and that virtually every panic (such as the one in 1893) was the result of long planning by the money barons. Silver, that magic monetary elixir, was the tonic that would save America.[31]

By 1896 the silver issue was at its peak when it became an important part of the national Populist political platform. Ironically it was that same year that silver began a precipitous decline in its value as a result of the discovery of new gold deposits. Harvey did not give up entirely on the precious metal but he did lose a considerable amount of his former zeal. The next phase in Harvey's career took him even further into the conspiracy complex, as witnessed in the publication of his 1899 book, *Coin on Money, Trusts, and Imperialism.*[32]

Harvey's next venture was every bit as unusual as his previous interests. His chief concern appears to have been imperialism and how it would affect the United States. It also becomes apparent that the former silver advocate had an increasingly despondent view of what the twentieth century would hold for the nation and world. Falling deeper into a sort of messianic complex, the aging Coin had, by the end of World War I, constructed a "Great Pyramid" of his own. Purchased over a quarter of a century earlier, Harvey's 325-acre resort at Monte Ne near Rogers, Arkansas, was the site of the pyramid, a monument to the failure of the twentieth century and, not incidentally, to himself. For the most part, his obsession with the Ozark retreat took him out of any further publishing or business enterprises, although he did run for president of the United States in 1932. In 1936, at the age of eighty-four, Coin Harvey died.[33] Harvey's proclamations join the many doom-laden scenarios that have come forth out of conspiratorial thinking. But, as is the case in all conspiracy views, there was an element of truth in them.

## Prophecy Expectation in the Age of Populism

During the last half of the nineteenth century, Christian groups recovered from their shock over the Civil War and once again engaged in prophetic speculation. Some of the more prominent prophetic writers of this era included William Blackstone, whose book *Maranatha: or, the Lord Cometh* (1870) remained a popular prophecy tome for decades after its publication; Dwight Moody, after whom the Moody Bible Institute is named; and Isaac Haldeman, whose *Signs of the Times* (1910) typified conservative Christian attacks against "runaway capitalism" during the Progressive Era. Nonetheless, there were few Christian leaders of the nineteenth or twentieth century to equal the influence of Cyrus Scofield (1843–1921).[34] Most all were dispensational in the Darbian sense of the word, but it was Scofield and his Bible commentary that would prove the standard by which all other prophecy writers were measured. Scofield's writings provided Christians with a blueprint for the progression of the ages and offered those believing him some degree of certainty as to what would lie ahead. Scofield's Bible commentary proved so convincing that to many in the first half of the twentieth century it took on the authority of holy writ. Scofield's teachings would continue to shape prophecy doctrine decades after his death.[35]

This embracing of prophetic teachings was not limited to Christians of that era, either. Many today cling to the teachings of contemporary prophecy pundits as if their musings were equal to Scripture itself. Despite frequent proof that the prophecies were based on erroneous information or downright ignorance, hundreds of thousands of conservative Christians continue to financially support the ministries that proclaim them.

Although interest in prophecy waned during the first decade of the twentieth century, it picked up again with the outbreak of World War I. The quasi-Christian group the Watchtower Society (now called Jehovah's Witnesses) expressed interest in the topic. The group had already been propagating the idea that Jesus had made an invisible return in 1874 and taught that the year 1914 had special significance.

By 1918 interest in conspiracy theory was static; no one seemed particularly interested in the world of politics and international affairs. Despite this lack of interest or understanding, there was in truth much going on in the United States that would later play into the combination of prophecy belief and conspiracy theory. Although ignored in church circles at the time, the creation of the Federal Reserve system in 1913 would in time attract attention, much of it grossly undue.

3

# Money Trusts and the Federal Reserve

If the Illuminati is the favorite target of conspiracy theorists for the last quarter of the eighteenth century, the Federal Reserve system carries that distinction for the first quarter of the twentieth century. Much legend, myth, and distortion surround this organization, an institution set up to serve as the central bank of the United States. Ostensibly created to stabilize currency fluctuations, the Fed, as it has since become known, instead became the fiscal czar of the nation, essentially dictating economic policy for whichever political party happened to be in power. It became, perhaps, something quite beyond what many of those voting in favor of it intended. The background, principal players, and rationale behind its creation are the subject of this chapter. So, too, are the contentions some, including Christians, have that the Fed will be the centerpiece for bringing the United States into a one-world economic system.

## Fiscal Disorder and the Push for a Central Bank

To understand the national fiscal dynamics surrounding the establishment of the Federal Reserve system, one must look to the decade of the 1890s and before for some precipitating influences leading to its creation. The panic of 1893 and the economic upheaval it produced frightened many in both the business and labor sectors. The panic was in no small way responsible for the rapid increase in silver and gold advocates. Unsuccessful reformist plans were introduced to steady the currency of the nation. Popularly called the Baltimore Plan of 1893 and the Indianapolis Plan of 1897, these offerings, as well as many others under Congressman Charles Fowler's sponsorship, failed to attract enough support to become law. As pointed out in the previous chapter, those in favor of such "hard currency" policies failed to make any real headway in the nation's fiscal and banking practices. It would take nearly a decade and a half and another currency crisis to finally incite much more serious attempts at reform. The proposed reforms were a good deal different than many in the Populist movement had suggested, however, and were, according to some interpretations, unconstitutional at worst and extraconstitutional at best.[1]

Much as the 1890s bore witness to wholesale distrust of government, monopoly, and big business, the first decade of the twentieth century saw a growing distrust of the monetary system in general. To be sure, Populists of the 1890s had demanded great changes in the nation's monetary policies to the benefit of producers and users; what was happening during Theodore Roosevelt's administration was more than that. Both inside and outside the halls of Congress, there was growing criticism of what opponents were calling the American Money Trust. Much as there were trusts in big business, it was feared that control of the money supply of the nation and perhaps Europe was in the hands of a very few, often faceless individuals.

## Opposition to the Central Bank

One of the chief enemies of the Money Trust was Charles Lindbergh Sr., U.S. congressman from Minnesota. Perhaps best remembered as the father of Charles Jr., the first pilot to traverse the Atlantic Ocean in flight, Lindbergh was highly suspicious of the super-rich. "The governments have delegated to the rich the privilege of making Money," Lindbergh wrote, "and

charging the rest of us for its use."[2] The Minnesota representative went so far as to outline what he saw as a three-step plan
the super-rich would take in order to gain their ultimate goal:
control of the banking system of the United States. The steps
were, according to Lindbergh, as follows:

Act No. 1 was the manufacture, between 1896 and 1907,
through stock gambling, speculation and other devious methods and devices, of tens of billions of watered stocks, bonds,
and securities.

Act No. 2 was the Panic of 1907, by which those not favorable
to the Money Trust could be squeezed out of business and the
people frightened into demanding changes in the banking and
currency laws which the Money Trust would frame.

Act No. 3 was the passage of the Aldrich-Vreeland Emergency
Bill, by which the Money trust interests should have the privilege of securing from the Government currency on their watered
bonds and securities. . . . The main thing, however, that the
Money Trust accomplished as a result of the passing of this act
was the appointment of the National Monetary Commission,
the membership of which was chiefly made up of bankers, their
agents and attorneys, who have generally been educated in favor
of, and have a community interest with, the Money Trust.

The fourth act, however, is in the process of incubation only,
and it is hoped that by this time we realize the danger that all
of us are in, for it is the final proposed legislation which, if it
succeeds, will place us in the complete control of the moneyed
[sic] interests.[3]

Whether or not Representative Lindbergh overstated or exag-
gerated his position is a matter for debate, but what is certain is
that in the wake of the panic of 1907 some definite changes in
the banking system were needed. The financial upheaval of 1907
resulted when one of New York's venerable banking institutions,
the Knickerbocker Trust Company, collapsed, sending shock
waves through the nation's markets and banks. Prior to the creation of the Federal Reserve, it was principally the large New
York banks that acted as stabilizers for the nation's financial institutions, propping them up in the event of imminent failure. With

the New York banks themselves now threatened, it seemed prudent to supporters of centralized banking to put together an agency to act as a bulwark against financial collapse. For some, however, this all appeared unusual and even suspicious.[4]

It is at this point, earlier according to some, that much bolder attempts to gain a centralized banking system would begin. What the late Georgetown University Professor Carroll Quigley called "monopoly capitalism" surely did exist by this time, differing from finance capitalism of the Adam Smith variety. What is at work here is what some have described as capitalism gone mad, individual bankers on at least two continents gaining tremendous wealth and tightly controlling the availability of credit. It seems clear that most Wall Street bankers and their interests had abandoned the Democratic Party decades before, instead obtaining what they wanted through Republican administrations from the time of Ulysses S. Grant.[5]

## J. P. Morgan: Super-Banker

Without a doubt the leading monopoly capitalist banker at this time was J. P. Morgan. The name to this day is synonymous with power, wealth, financial monopoly, and outright greed. In his own day he was a favorite target of editorials and political cartoonists. He was a giant in the field of finance, a power with which an industrialist had to reckon. His friendships were few, but he stood in the company of fiscal Olympians. Among his friends and adversaries in high finance both here and in Europe were the Rockefellers; Kuhn, Loeb, and Company; Dillon, Read, and Company; the Mellon Group; and Brown Brothers and Harriman.[6] Between them, their control and influence spread across the nation and even around the world.

Bankers such as J. P. Morgan ran their businesses with a ruthlessness equal to or exceeding anything we might see today in the corporate world. Whenever a loan was given, it was under the tightest of conditions to first and foremost benefit Morgan and his interests. First of all, he would insist on ensuring that the business in question would make enough money to pay the bare minimum needed to keep the loan current. He accomplished this, not by checking the books, but by putting his own agents in the company to see to it that solvency was maintained. Second, the House of Morgan would try to create what he called a "community of interest"—a monopoly to anyone else—to limit competition for the company receiving the loan. Finally, Morgan would insist on having his people on the board of the company and essentially take it over in all but name. Failure to acquiesce to these demands meant no money; to give in meant loss of independence. If, after giving in to the House of Morgan a person sought to break free, it would not be unusual for the business to suddenly become loaded down with excessive debt in the form of watered stock. The result was usually bankruptcy and total banker control. By 1907 financial giants such as Morgan, Rockefeller, Baker, Stillman, Schiff, and Warburg controlled much of America's industrial might.[7]

In what is a startling yet plausible interpretation, Professor Quigley states that Morgan, either in concert with Rockefeller or by himself, could have wrecked the economic system of the nation by merely tossing securities on the stock market. In so doing, prices would fall and then stocks could be purchased for pennies on the dollar.[8] It was something Morgan in fact did do in 1907. The result was known as the panic of 1907 and set the stage for legislation that would eventually result in the birth of the Federal Reserve system. The belief that Morgan was behind the panic was stated over and over in newspaper editorials across the nation. He quickly became something of a dark celebrity. Proponents of a central bank for the United States used the panic to suggest that regulation was needed to prevent the Morgans of the world from having too much control of the nation's money supply. This was an extremely popular position to take. Because Morgan was so universally unpopular, legislation could be crafted with public support to change all of that. Ironically, the institution that was supposed to end Morgan's reign as finance mogul was itself sometimes given to dictatorial and arbitrary practices. Before we get to that, however, we must first take a most unusual train ride to an exclusive club in Georgia with the cryptic name of Jekyll Island.

## The Formation of the American Central Bank

In the wake of the panic of 1907, some of the chief supporters of the creation of a United States central bank met secretly
in an effort to hammer out a plan for its implementation. One
of those present was Rhode Island Senator Nelson Aldrich, one-
time head of Teddy Roosevelt's National Monetary Committee.
The committee had made a number of studies concerning finance
and national economics, even traveling to Europe for nearly two
years on what was supposed to be a fact-finding tour. With still
no final report with suggestions for reform, Aldrich and a number of other central bank advocates retreated to Georgia at a prearranged site to begin work. Some of those accompanying
Aldrich were A. Piatt Andrew, assistant secretary of the Treasury;
Frank Vanderslip, president of the National City Bank of New
York; Charles Norton, president of First National Bank of New
York; and Henry Davidson, senior partner of J. P. Morgan and
Company. Joining this already impressive crowd were other officials from Morgan concerns as well as European banking house
representatives: Benjamin Strong, one of Morgan's right-hand
men, and Paul Warburg of Kuhn, Loeb, and Company.[9]

The meeting of such influential people did not go unnoticed.
A few among the press noticed the gathering and sought some
answers as to why the dignitaries were present. No response
was given, leaving the reporters to speculate. Although the
retreat was originally purchased as a hunting club, it was clear
that the delegation that arrived in November 1910 was not there
to bag ducks. Instead, their plan was to write up the framework
for a central bank of the United States. In essence, those in
attendance were composing the report that the Monetary Commission was supposed to write. The Commission's "findings"
instead became the ideas and ideals of men representing Morgan and Kuhn-Loeb. Taking up residence at the club for nine
days, the group ironed out differences of opinion to produce
what eventually became known as the Aldrich Bill.[10]

The Aldrich Bill provided for the incorporation of what was
essentially a central bank for the nation to be run through a
national board and its strategically located branch banks.

National banks were eligible for membership, as were state banks and trusts willing to conform to the standards as set forth in the bill. Membership was entirely optional. Those institutions choosing to become part of this system would serve as clearing houses for the national board. The rules dealt with cash and reserve requirements, discount and rediscount to banks in their respective districts, transfer policy, issuance and redemption of National Reserve Association notes, and domestic exchanges between member banks. The corporate body was singular, so to speak, and was to be embodied in the National Reserve Association. The final say in banking policy as stated in the Aldrich Bill was to reside in the hands of the Association.[11] As will be demonstrated, when the Aldrich Bill was finally brought out into the light of day it immediately attracted opposition from those who perceived in it the potential for abuse and manipulation. Despite what those supporting the Association said about government checks and balances, the truth was that this framework for a central bank would put the institution and its stockholders virtually above the law.

It must be here admitted that critics of Federal Reserve opponents have stated that the story of Jekyll Island was little more than a fanciful yarn. For several years after the meeting in 1910, reports of the secret gathering were merely brushed aside as the blathering of conspiracy-minded quacks. And, as author and conspiracy-believer Eustace Mullins points out, no one ever mentioned Jekyll Island in connection with either the Aldrich Bill or the Federal Reserve Act—at least not initially. In Paul Warburg's mammoth history of the Federal Reserve, he speaks of meetings but does not mention the Georgia retreat. Later, in a biography of Nelson Aldrich, Warburg was quoted as saying, "The matter of a uniform discount rate was discussed and settled at Jekyll Island."[12] Other participants later revealed something of the nature of the meetings as well. Frank Vanderslip let it out that he felt something of a conspirator as the group moved surreptitiously to Georgia and then took oaths of secrecy. One of his most telling statements was as follows: "I do not feel it is any exaggeration to speak of our secret expedition to Jekyll Island as the occasion of the actual conception

of what eventually became the Federal Reserve System."[13] On
the conclusion of the meetings, the participants and their allies
set into motion the public relations machinery needed to support the soon to be introduced legislation. No less a participant
than Paul Warburg later admitted that secret discussions in
1910 became the framework for the Aldrich Bill.[14]

Although considerable effort was made to help pass the
Aldrich Bill when it was introduced, the ultimate result was the
failure of the American people and Congress to accept a central
bank for the United States. Arguments that European nations
had long since been under centralized banking made little headway with opponents of the bill, who were quick to point out that
the finances of Europe were, for the most part, in the hands of
a few powerful international bankers. Possessing such enormous financial power could render nations servants to bankers
in the area of foreign policy. Andrew Carnegie himself admitted as much in his book *Triumphant Democracy* when he stated
that a handful of individuals in Britain could plunge that nation
into war or commit it to alliances without Parliament's consent.[15] Many feared that the Aldrich Bill's National Monetary
Association would grow into the very same thing. The result was
the defeat of the bill but not of the efforts of those wanting an
American central bank. The proponents came back very quickly
with another proposal that was, by virtually all accounts, merely
the Aldrich Bill with different wrapping.

With the defeat of the Aldrich Bill through the efforts of men
such as Representative Lindbergh of Minnesota and Wisconsin Senator Robert LaFollette, many thought that the danger
of a money trust bank had been averted. In truth, it had merely
been forestalled, and not for very long at that. After the considerable publicity the Aldrich affair caused, combined with
the somewhat sensational Pujo hearings of 1912 over money
trusts, those fearful of big money—international money—
hoped that a solution was in sight. After all, many people still
considered the panic of 1907 a contrived event of J. P. Morgan;
those who would benefit from the panic would be bankers of

international stature who wanted the control a central bank necessarily provides.[16]

## Public Hearings on Central Banking

The Pujo hearings, named for Congressman Arsene Pujo who held them in 1912, saw some of the biggest names in money and finance appear before the committee to answer questions pertaining to "money trusts" and international banking. J. P. Morgan and Jacob Schiff, among others, sat before the inquisitors to answer questions pertaining to their roles in the issues at hand. It was less than a year before Morgan's death, and at the hearings he appeared clearly tired of the mistrust and accusations and of the very term *money trust*. It was at this meeting that Morgan made his famous "character alone" statement concerning his criteria for making loans. Jacob Schiff, representative of Kuhn, Loeb, and Company, was not held to any tough line of questioning throughout the meetings. Interestingly, the interlocking and labyrinthine nature of international banking and business ties was scarcely addressed. When the meeting ended, little had been resolved, and the bankers were satisfied with the outcome.[17] This is especially unusual when one considers the fact that the issue of banking—creating a central bank, that is—became an important part of the 1912 presidential election. Indeed, the Republican Party endorsed the Aldrich Bill, while the Democrats made the Owen-Glass Bill part of their platform. Ironically the bills were virtually identical, despite the declarations of both sides that each had the best banking bill. It was but one of many strange events surrounding the Federal Reserve issue and the election that year.

The presidential election in 1912 was affected by a split Republican Party. William Howard Taft, who had taken up the mantle of leader of the progressive end of the party from Teddy Roosevelt, had increasingly disappointed the political leadership and electorate. He was, fairly or not, becoming tagged with the "ineffectual" stamp as his administration drew to a close. A number of Republicans feared the loss of the White House and closed ranks around Teddy Roosevelt when he announced his candidacy as an alternative to both Taft and Democratic candidate Woodrow Wilson of New Jersey. The Roosevelt name just did not have the same magic it had had in the previous decade, and the result was a split Republican vote and the election of Wilson as president of the United States. Always casting himself as the consummate progressive, Roosevelt's running for office was unusual. Perhaps wanting a last political hurrah, his Bull Moose Party was ill defined and its stands on issues sometimes vague. With the election of Woodrow Wilson, it was almost guaranteed that the Owen-Glass Bill would pass and thus establish the Federal Reserve system.[18]

## The Foundation of the American Federal Reserve

Among those seeing the Owen-Glass Bill as a highly supportable piece of legislation meant to create a central bank for the United States was Paul Warburg, the powerful representative for both Kuhn, Loeb, and Company and the Rothschilds. When asked his opinion about the new bill before the House Banking and Currency Committee in 1913, Warburg replied:

> In the Panic of 1907, the first suggestion I made was "Let us get a national clearing house." The Aldrich bill contains some things which are simply fundamental rules of banking. Your aim in this plan [Owen-Glass bill] must be the same—centralizing of reserves, mobilizing of commercial credit, and getting an elastic note issue.[19]

Warburg continued to push behind the scenes for the passage of what would become the Federal Reserve system. Many who had opposed the Aldrich Bill were shocked to see how quickly the forces in favor of central banking came back with yet another bill. Given the power and finances of the big bankers, and what they had to gain from the creation of a central bank, no one should have been surprised. Lindbergh summed up the new proposal as simply a slight variation on the Aldrich Bill.[20] It should have been a foregone conclusion that what we know today as the Federal Reserve system was destined to become law. Woodrow Wilson, the new president of the United States, was committed to it. His chief advisor—essentially his alter ego—Col. Edward Mandell House, saw passage of the bill as being of the utmost importance. Backing him, in fact acting as intermediary between Wilson and interested European bankers, were powerful men like Jacob Schiff.

### *Colonel House and* Phillip Dru

Colonel House—who did not earn his title in the military—used his influence with Wilson to gain support for the bill in an effort to help fund American involvement in World War I and place the nation in a similar position with other sovereign powers with central banks. In a novel House was said to have written in 1912 titled *Phillip Dru: Administrator,* the author made it quite clear that a central bank was of vital importance for the betterment of society and that the system in place up to that point had been a miserable failure. Incidentally, it was not merely banking that was a failure in House's eyes: It was the American system of government. Nothing less than an overthrow and starting over would cleanse the nation of the mistakes of the past. Of course, men like Phillip Dru (House) would be the leaders of such a "noble" experiment. During this age of Progressive politics, utopian ideas of this variety were not unusual.

Many in the conspiracy-theory camp point to *Phillip Dru* as House's (and Wilson's) manifesto, a blueprint for changes they would like to see come about in the United States. In truth, it was a less-than-compelling novel hardly worth the attention conspiracy advocates give it.[21]

### *Bank Support at the Highest Levels*

As far as Woodrow Wilson was concerned, he exhibited something of a Jekyll and Hyde personality when writing or speaking of the money trust and the power of business monopolies. Given his considerable intellectual and political capabilities, it is difficult to believe that he was unaware of the banking control many corporations were under. Wilson gave a blistering speech before a joint session of Congress on June 23, 1913, in which he attacked forces against the Owen-Glass Bill. At the time, the Aldrich-Vreeland Law was in effect. This was a law many in favor of centralized banking believed was far too weak. Wilson lambasted monied interests in his speech but at the same time supported a bill that would essentially turn control of the nation's banking system over to those same people. Again, if Wilson was merely stupid or naive, he may possibly be excused; but being in possession of a first-rate mind, I do not believe he could plead thickheadedness or ignorance. There are many who suggest that he was put in a position where he could do nothing but support Owen-Glass; that, or he was in favor of central banking all along.[22] This raises the question of just how much influence monied interests had over Wilson from the time he was nominated as Democratic candidate for president. Having Colonel House, with his ties to big money, as his chief advisor certainly added to this speculation.

## The Federal Reserve

On December 18, 1913, the House version of the Federal Reserve Act (Glass Bill) passed the House of Representatives by a vote of 287 to 85. The Senate passed its version the next day by a vote of 54 to 34 with 12 senators absent. Although there were considerable problems over policy and procedure, they were resolved in an amazingly short period of time. While in committee the bill was altered to a degree, resulting in a final vote on December 22, 1913, of 282 to 60 in the House and 43 to 23 in the Senate. Many of the absent representatives and senators complained bitterly that they had been told that the final vote would be held after the Christmas break. It was too late, no matter the uproar over when the vote was held. The United States now had a central bank.[23]

One of the strangest aspects of the creation of the Federal Reserve system has to do with public perception, particularly in our own day. I doubt that there are more than one in one hundred who understand that the Federal Reserve system is in fact the central bank of the United States. Nonetheless, it is privately owned, and as such is beyond the power of the U.S. government to do much in the way of regulation. It has great powers to cause economic fluctuations, some of them considerable, by merely suggesting a possible raising or lowering of the prime rate. Throughout the 1990s the Federal Reserve has been a source of controversy among both Republicans and Democrats. Some politicians, including Senator Byron Dorgan of North Dakota, have gone so far as to demand greater public control of the Fed to limit its power.

What of Federal Reserve control? The board and its chair, though politically appointed, are virtually independent of any interference from the president on down. Twelve regional banks were created and are owned by the bank stockholders themselves (in effect, "banker's banks") and subject to their own central agency. Final authority was to reside in the Federal Reserve Board, a provision proponents argued would guarantee public control because the board members were appointed by Congress. The regional banks created private corporations that had a degree of control over the nation's money supply. In addition, as the Federal Reserve Act allowed the issuance of elastic "notes" to be used as currency, the regional (and thus national) Federal Reserve system has control of the nation's money supply (M–1)—the currency in circulation; and as pointed out earlier, the Fed itself is a private institution subject to neither state or national control. Conspiracy theorists have screamed that this meant an end to American economic independence. Still, one has to ask some basic economic questions: Do we really want a currency based on the gold standard? If so, an ounce of gold would have to be revalued to perhaps upwards of a hundred times its current value to balance the supply with the needs of the nation. Presumably silver would undergo a similar revaluation. As the world's economies become increasingly intertwined, a nineteenth-century concept like gold and silver as the foundation of our currency is less likely to be accepted on the international scene. It simply is no longer the sole vehicle by which modern economies operate. We may question whether or not those setting up the Fed had pure motives, but certainly eventually precious metals would have to be phased out of the nation's money system.

### An Incorporated Independent Central Bank

The names of the chief stockholders of the Federal Reserve, though they were supposed to remain secret, leaked out soon after shares were put up for sale. The New York branch of the Federal Reserve was, of course, the lead bank and essentially dictated policy to the other regional banks. Thus, the institutions or people owning stock in the New York Federal Reserve bank could in theory control the fiscal policy of much of the nation. Those shares were quickly swallowed up by Kuhn, Loeb, and Company, First National Bank, and Chase National Bank, among others. Economic conspiracy theorists are quick to point out that these member banks in turn had sizable portions of their stock owned by the Rothschilds, Lazard Feres, Lehman Brothers, Goldman Sachs, and the Rockefellers. In effect, they argue, the money trust so publicly trounced during Teddy Roosevelt's day and springboard for currency reform turned out to be the largest beneficiary of those changes. Indeed, now under the Federal Reserve Act they could exercise power and influence as never before.[24]

Before we scream conspiracy, as many such theorists have done, an obvious overlooked point has to be made: Who would know how to set up and run something as mammoth as an American central bank better than those with experience in international finance—those with central banking experience themselves or with experience dealing with people in central banking? For conspiracy theorists, the Fed was immediately seen as tied into a plan for global economic control, a tool of the Rothschilds. Unfortunately such a view has tainted any subsequent investigation into the organization. Here is a great example of jumping to a conclusion based on some interesting but not case-closing evidence. To be sure, there were behind-the-scenes workings to establish a central bank in the United States; still, this does not prove a cosmic conspiracy, a view so popular among some of the more extreme conspiratorial groups.

In 1913 there were important pieces of legislation that made their way into law. Besides the Federal Reserve Act, Congress authorized and the nation approved passage of the Sixteenth Amendment. Now affecting every taxpayer, this amendment allowed the government to tax personal income, albeit only the highest earners. What is important to remember is that the true significance of the income tax amendment is that it established a precedent. It would not be long before taxable income included middle-class wage earners; it is simply the nature of taxes and those who collect them to expand their reach. Government assurances that this new tax would affect only those in the upper 2 percent notwithstanding, it would not be very long before collection of income tax would be something we all would experience. Together, the Federal Reserve Act and the Sixteenth Amendment marked a turning point in American domestic policy.

## "Legal Tender for All Debts Public and Private"

When the dust had settled concerning monetary policy, the United States had gone from the issuance of Treasury notes to Federal Reserve notes redeemable in gold and silver. This changed to only silver a few decades later, followed by an interesting change on the Federal Reserve note itself: "This note is legal tender for all debts, public and private." Never again would Americans use money or think of taxes in quite the same way. For some conspiracy theory believers and Christians, the rise of the Fed was a sign that the end was at hand. Many Christians of this period simply did not fathom the significance of the new fiscal policy, while later generations questioned whether the United States needed a central bank. By the late twentieth century, Christian leaders such as Pat Robertson restated warnings that the Fed is in fact an important part of financial control of the nation's monetary system (at least M–1) and a beneficiary of a debt-ridden society. Other leaders of faith have done likewise, making for some dangerous interpretations in the area of prophecy. Of course, international banking and the U.S. Federal Reserve were also then necessarily tied to an international conspiracy.[25]

# The Council
# on Foreign Relations

Most Americans have never heard of the Council on Foreign Relations. Located in the Harold Pratt House at 58 East 68th Street, across the street from the former Soviet Embassy in New York City, the stately structure houses one of the most talked about institutions among conspiracy theorists. The Council on Foreign Relations, or CFR for short, has been accused of being a twentieth-century version of the Illuminati—a virtual shadow government of the United States. For decades conspiracy theorists have looked with suspicion on this agency and its members, seeing it as little more than a front for international government and banking. Its impact has doubtless been significant in helping to formulate American foreign policy, especially in the last half of the twentieth century. Whether it has done more than offer a forum for its members to debate policy and issues is the topic of this chapter. Although I do not believe it is a secret government, it will be shown that its impact and influence this century has been considerable, so much so that its relative anonymity to the public at large is rather puzzling. Indeed, for the level of influence it has exerted during the twentieth century, very few mainstream publishers have bothered to release articles or books on this important topic. For a look at its foundation and early years, we must first go to Britain and its numerous Round Table organizations founded during the Victorian era.

## Early Round Table Societies

The Council on Foreign Relations is not uniquely an American invention, nor is it the only organization of its type in the Western world. Toward the end of the period marking the end of British predominance in world affairs, roughly from 1880 to 1905, powerful and wealthy members of Britain's social, economic, and political circles sought to maintain the gains their impressive empire had made over the previous 250 years. Support from men such as John Ruskin and his Oxford student Cecil Rhodes went far in the creation of what eventually became known as Round Tables where issues of the day were discussed and possible solutions set forth. Ruskin had a number of other followers at Oxford in those days, including Arnold Toynbee, Lord Alfred Milner, Arthur Glazebrook, Sir George Parkin, Phillip Lyttleton Gell, and Sir Henry Birchenough. Discussion groups of this sort sprang up at Cambridge and other English colleges as well. Still, none were as influential as the Oxford group.[1]

The basic premise for this group was the preservation of what they termed the "extension of the English-speaking idea." In 1891 Cecil Rhodes created a secret society that would act as the prototype of the Round Table organizations: a behind-the-scenes think tank that treasured its anonymity above all. It sought to become the hidden advisors, providing the British government with advice and personnel to carry through their agenda. One of the first members of Rhodes's organization was Lord Alfred Milner; it was Milner who was the nuts-and-bolts organizer of the discussion groups and ultimately came up with the Round Table name.[2]

By 1910 Milner's Round Table had branches in other parts of the English-speaking world. They were sometimes known as the Cliveden Set, named for a country estate where they sometimes congregated. Consistent with the goals of Ruskin and Rhodes a generation earlier, the Cliveden Set sought to further the interests of the English-speaking world, while ostensibly aiding in the development of what would later be known as the Third World. Within the Commonwealth these groups were generally called Institutes of International Affairs, and in the United States they were the Council on Foreign Relations. Both groups became part of a post–World War I movement in which twelve nations housing similar Round Table groups networked with each other in an effort to foster international understanding. Some of these early nations included South Africa, India, Canada, Australia, and New Zealand.[3]

This is not to suggest that all members of these Round Table groups were always in agreement. Indeed, there were times when they were split along any number of lines, ranging from nationalism to the purpose of the League of Nations. In the case of the latter, some members of the English group thought it best that the League be relegated to mere cooperative efforts of mutual interest, such as controlling the drug trade. This was in part due to the fact that with the absence of the United States from the League, there was precious little the rest of the membership could do in the way of international police actions. Later, in the 1930s, there were even more disputes between Commonwealth Round Table members over the course of action to be taken regarding Nazism.[4]

In the United States the Council on Foreign Relations was officially incorporated in New York on July 29, 1921. As noted above, the CFR was to be part of an international effort, particularly between the United States and Great Britain, that would result in Round Table discussions on subjects of mutual interest. Although they were independent of each other, the two bodies (as well as affiliated groups in other nations) maintained close ties. The CFR may sound like a rather bland, even boring group, the chief purpose of which was to sit around and talk about world affairs. From the very beginning, however, money was being made available to the organization, money that would allow the Council to become very selective in whom it chose as members. J. P. Morgan and Company would be among the major contributors to this organization, causing some to call it merely a front for the banking interests of that firm. Other major contributors included the Rockefeller family, as well as certain Lazard Brothers associates. Arthur Schlesinger Jr., one of America's most respected historians, states as much in *A Thousand Days* when he calls the Council little more than a front to house the American establishment and its interests.[5] Schlesinger's view is not merely opinion; it was clear from the beginning that some of the best minds in finance, government, and politics were supporting either the Council or members in it. It is therefore understandable how some conspiracy theorists have come to believe that with the wedding of big bank money and advocation of world government, the Council on Foreign Relations is a tool of those monied interests—all at the ultimate cost of American sovereignty.

## House and Quigley

Col. Edward Mandell House, Woodrow Wilson's chief advisor, was one of the founding members of the Council on Foreign Relations. And, as a staunch supporter of the newly formed League of Nations (brainchild of Wilson and House), the colonel made sure the CFR was also pro-League. One has only to look at the early editions of the organization's publication, *Foreign Affairs,* to prove this.[6] Another position strongly supported in *Foreign Affairs* is that global government is the final solution to the world's troubles. Of course, not everyone in the Council, then or now, backs the notion of a one-world government; nor has every article in the journal gone to lengths in open advocacy of such a position. Still, it is not an overstatement to suggest that the CFR does, on the whole, back political globalism as a means of ending seemingly unresolvable world problems.

The Council was from its inception dominated by financial interests of an international nature. Dr. Carroll Quigley, Georgetown University professor of international relations, Bill Clinton mentor, and a favorite author of many conspiracy theorists, says this:

[T]here grew up in the twentieth century a power structure between London and New York which penetrated deeply into university life, the press, and the practice of foreign policy. In England the center was the Round Table Group, while in the United States it was J. P. Morgan and Company or its local branches in Boston, Philadelphia, and Cleveland.[7]

Quigley also claimed that much of the major press of that day was dominated by the forces that helped to create the Council on Foreign Relations. Quoting Dr. Quigley again,

The American branch of this "English Establishment" exerted much of its influence through five American newspapers *(The New York Times, New York Herald Tribune, Christian Science Monitor, Washington Post,* and the lamented *Boston Evening Transcript).* In fact, the editor of the *Christian Science Monitor* was the chief American correspondent (anonymously) of The Round Table . . .[8]

Dr. Quigley, who authored the most comprehensive and detailed history of the influence of powerful groups such as Round Tables or the Council on Foreign Relations, was in fact sympathetic to the causes and objectives of these groups. He clearly set forth that the semisecret organizations, of which the CFR was but one of many, sought what he saw as laudable goals: the maintenance of peace and furthering the aims of the English-speaking world. To a certain extent, this included what has become known as the "White Man's Burden," the perceived duty of white, European civilization to "share" the benefits of its culture with the rest of the world.[9]

Another truism that emerges from a study of groups like the Council on Foreign Relations is that they have an agenda completely their own, apart from either right- or left-wing ideologies. If their programs happen to agree with one side or another, fine; but in the end it is the furthering of their own goals that is most important. Again, it would seem that a superficially democratic global government is the objective. Whatever it takes to get to that point is acceptable. This gives rise, as you might expect, to cries of conspiracy among theorists of that mind-set. When discussing the Round Table groups, there is at least the appearance of conspiracy. I cite Dr. Quigley a last time:

> There does exist, and has existed for a generation, an international Anglophile network which operates, to some extent, in the way the radical Right believes the Communists act. In fact, this network, which we may identify as the Round Table Groups, has no aversion to cooperating with the Communists, or any other groups, and frequently does so. I know of the operations of this network because I have studied it for twenty years and was permitted for two years, in the early 1960's, to examine its papers and secret records. I have no aversion to it or to most of its aims and have, for much of my life, been close to it and to many of its instruments. I have objected, both in the past and recently, to a few of its policies . . . but in general my chief difference of opinion is that it wishes to remain unknown, and I believe its role in history is significant enough to be known.[10]

One has to wonder why such an organization would want to remain unknown unless it feared the reaction of public exposure. It could well be that these many groups, the CFR in particular, are reticent about public coverage out of concern that their aims will be misunderstood. That or, in their arrogance, they truly deem themselves the most fit to offer opinions on a host of issues, both foreign and domestic. Conspiracy theorists, of course, hold to the latter view as the accurate one. They believe that given the money behind the CFR and other Round Table groups, the hidden hand cares not whether a Democrat or a Republican sits in the White House; the CFR would have, in a meaningful way, the last say.

## Prophecy during World War I

In this same period, some Christian prophecy writers and preachers became convinced that the last days had arrived. World War I provided fertile soil for prophecy writers of the time. Some had postulated that Kaiser Wilhelm II was the Antichrist; others suggested that the outcome of the war was merely the precursor of a ten-nation confederacy that would ultimately produce the true Beast. When the Balfour Declaration was made in 1917, there arose what historian Paul Boyer described as a "still higher pitch of expectancy" of the end times. The Balfour Declaration, of course, simply stated the British government's favorable attitude to the creation of a Jewish state in Palestine. After World War I, Britain had been given the mandate for governing much of the Middle East, making the declaration all the more important. For conspiracy theorists, the fact that Zionists such as Chaim Weizmann (eventually Israel's first president) and Lord James Rothschild were involved suggested evil intent. For most Christian believers in prophecy at the time, the events of the day suggested just the opposite.[11] Another sure sign of either conspiracy or prophecy fulfillment or both in the minds of many was the fall of Russia to Communism in 1917. To further our story, we must now turn to how and why the Round Table groups were interested in helping the Bolshevik revolution in Russia.

## Bolshevik Revolution and Conspiracy

Conspiracy theorists have long maintained that it would have been well-nigh impossible for the Bolshevik revolution in Russia to have succeeded without the help of Western nations— that is, the international banks in those nations. These same theorists have said that the survival of Communist regimes between 1917 and 1989 was made possible as a result of constant infusions of money to prop up the moribund economies socialism seems to inevitably produce. To these and many other questions, there are no clear answers. There is suggestive evidence that the United States through later CFR supporters did indeed help the Russian Revolution to come to fruition.[12]

In the twentieth century it often seems to be a truism that unless there is big money backing revolutionary movements, those radical groups tend to fail in their objective. The irony in this is that the Bolshevik revolution in Russia, supposedly based on the hatred of and dedication to the destruction of capitalism, had as some of its chief supporters the very class of people it hated most. One has to admit that this seems to be a glaring contradiction: Why would monopolistic capitalism seek to support a socialistic or communistic government? Are not the two diametrically opposed to each other? On a simplistic level, yes; and it is for that reason that many dismiss any talk of communist-capitalist cooperation between 1917 and 1989. What would the capitalists possibly have to gain from it?[13]

Some in conspiracy circles have suggested the following scenario to explain this cooperation: Under a capitalistic system, individuals and corporations can amass tremendous amounts of wealth at the expense of those beneath them. Moreover, the super-wealthy can then shelter their enormous fortunes in foundations, rendering their wealth for the most part tax-free. In a socialistic system, such individuals and corporations are not allowed, or at least it is so contended. Such a system could potentially be a brilliant financial shelter. By putting funds into a closed economic collective where the people have little or no economic power, where all decision making regarding finance is in the hands of a small group of people, the invested monies would benefit from a fiscal monopoly—a money trust. Would it not make sense for those with hundreds of millions or billions of dollars to sink money into those governments in exchange for certain concessions? After all, with a tightly centralized government, the fiscal policies can be made very quickly and without the red tape more common in governments in the West. Underneath it all, short of a nuclear war, bankers in the United States and Europe would in fact have a great deal to gain from such investments; no matter which side won a cold war, their investments would come out on top. Given the control they could exercise in those closed societies, when these same nations no longer served their purpose, they could quickly be dropped and allowed to sink into economic oblivion. Again, conspiracy theorists state, it matters very little to people on the highest levels of finance who comes out on top in the ideological conflict; with their wealth and influence in nations around the world, they are the final winners.[14]

Carrying this further, planned-history advocates contend that the financial power brokers saw in Vladimir Lenin just the instrument they needed to make the resource-rich Russian nation a source of income. The German government was also involved in the transporting of the revolutionary from Switzerland to Russia at a crucial time during World War I. Germany apparently thought that by sending the radical Lenin and his band of Bolsheviks to Russia, it would be tantamount to introducing a deadly virus into the body politic of the Czarist regime. By all accounts, in the minds of financial backers and revolutionaries alike, the incompetent and cruel Czar Nicholas II was ripe for the picking. Sent to Russia aboard a sealed train with some $5 million in gold from German financier Max Warburg, Lenin returned to his homeland after signing a statement promising to stay away from Germany. World War I had gone badly for the Russians, and the additional problems Lenin was causing at home made the possibility of a collapse more likely. The czar had since abdicated, only to be met with a hail of bullets effectively ending the Romanov dynasty. It was into this fray that yet another Bolshevik revolutionary, one living in the United States at the time, was sent to Russia with a very similar purpose. Leon Trotsky, however, had the backing of some very big-name, albeit secretive, bankers in his venture back to Mother Russia.[15]

At the time that Czar Nicholas II abdicated and Russia was thrown into the turmoil of domestic uncertainty and ongoing war with Germany, Leon Trotsky was residing in New York City. Living on the Lower East Side of Manhattan, Trotsky was an unusual character who apparently lived on the money he made writing articles for various New York newspapers on events in Russia; that and funding from some other source, which allowed him to live in relative comfort. Around the time Lenin returned to Russia, Trotsky also began preparations for a homegoing. Provided a passport with the aid of American officials, Trotsky was also provided a ship to take him and some three hundred of his comrades to Europe. With them, in the hold of the ship, was $20 million in gold bullion to help finance the revolution. The source of this generous gift was none other than Jacob

Schiff: capitalist, financier, and later supporter of the Council on Foreign Relations. Schiff's support, and those of the bankers he represented, was earnest money of their investment in what would become the Union of Soviet Socialist Republics—one of history's most repressive and despotic governments.[16]

Many of the individuals in the United States who backed the Russian Revolution, either financially or morally, were to become founding members of the Council on Foreign Relations. It may be that many of these founders of the CFR had seen in Lenin's Communist state the acorn of that final political oak tree. Whatever they thought of the repressive regime in the USSR, it is plain that the Council, insofar as is reflected in *Foreign Affairs,* was at least supportive of a global government.[17]

## Economic Collapse

During the 1920s the Council on Foreign Relations had a minimal impact on American foreign policy. This is easily understood when one considers the public temperament of that decade. Isolationism and self-indulgence were part and parcel of the Roaring Twenties, a time when Americans seemed to collectively forget foreign affairs and simply enjoy the increasingly prosperous good life here in the United States. Calls for internationalism fell on deaf ears both in and outside government, aside from treaties established to regulate or reduce the size of naval forces. Prosperity seemed without limit during this interesting decade, although it was soon learned that the prosperity was essentially on borrowed time and on loan. By early 1930, after the reality of the stock market crash of 1929 had sunk in, this lesson had been learned—at least by that generation. It is ironic how in our own time Americans still seem to think yearly deficits adding to national debts can go on without end; like the good people of the 1920s, we too will find that the fiscal piper demands payment. It would be efficacious at this point to take a look at the Great Depression and its impact on the United States and the world, as well as what the CFR had to say about it.[18]

The crash of the American stock market in 1929 marked the beginning of the Great Depression in the United States. At the tail end of a decade of considerable prosperity and growth, the crash was akin to a harsh alarm clock going off for the nation; the decade that followed would require getting out of bed and shoveling the economic errors of the 1920s out of the nation's driveway. The crash, in retrospect, should not have come as any great shock to the economists or the government. Over-speculation in a variety of commodities markets, notably gold, the rapid profit-taking in the market during the late summer and autumn, and a drop in the money supply all signaled trouble. Choosing to either ignore or disbelieve the mounting evidence, the United States was thrown into a headlong crash that, when combined with the collapse of international markets, plunged the nation and world into depression.[19]

There was something of a rebound, popularly known as a "sucker's rally" during the first few months of 1930, but the die had already been cast. Business and industry such as it had existed prior to the crash and Great Depression were things of the past. What the nation was about to enter into was the modern American economy. No longer a free market in the traditional sense of the word, the U.S. economy would, from the 1930s on, find itself increasingly fettered and controlled until, by the late twentieth century, the economy scarcely resembled a system that would encourage small, private enterprise.

Boom and busts have, of course, been part of American economic history from the very beginning; indeed, around 1920–22, there was an economic downturn (a recession in today's terminology) of short duration. It would not serve as a warning of the impending collapse of the market by the end of the decade but instead convinced many Americans that any slowdown was but a bump on prosperity road.

By 1926–27 the nation's economy went into yet another slowdown. This one lasted much longer and should have been seen as a signal that perhaps a long-term slide was beginning. Factory orders only trickled in, workers were laid off, and a general sense of foreboding seized those with the eyes to see what was just ahead. By 1928–29 the stock market prices surged to the point where average stock values were inflated to more than 40 percent of their value, in part due to capital gains taxes recently levied against businesses. The result was obviously simple: Realizing that the market was overinflated and overpriced, many heavy hitters got out while they could and purchased commodities, real estate, and other properties overseas. The rest of the investors lost their shirts when the collapse came; some committed suicide rather than face creditors who demanded payment on loans used to purchase overpriced stock.

In what became known as Black Tuesday, the ripple effect swept across the nation. People frantically sought to withdraw their money from bank accounts, causing banks to close. Businesses closed, workers were laid off, and the general sense of the unending nature of American prosperity was finally laid to rest. The Great Depression had slammed into America and was being felt around the world. Specifics concerning why the market fell are legion. The following are but a few of them.

1. *Overvaluation of Common Stocks.* Commodity prices dropped to the point where many stocks were devalued as much as 40 percent.
2. *Tax on Capital Gains.* Taxing of business profits made it more likely that the market would see more stock purchased as companies would be unwilling to pay the "revenue enhancement." This opened the market to bear runs at the hint of panic.
3. *Business Recession.* Combined with capital gains taxes, simple overextension in terms of borrowing and expansion helped to raise prices, further causing a sense of concern among investors and the buying public.
4. *Gold Withdrawals.* As the public, but mostly the "big players" in the stock market, smelled a possible recession or even depression, they withdrew funds from the market and purchased gold and silver bullion. When the collapse did come, the precious metal commodities did quite well until the Franklin Roosevelt administration.

5. *Federal Reserve Policy.* Finally, the Federal Reserve's policy of contracting money supplies in the year prior to the crash certainly had an impact.[20]

It is interesting to note that some of these indicators, along with money supply, are rearing their heads in the mid-1990s. Although we are in a different time and under different circumstances, this is an interesting comparison, especially with a president who is fond of taxation and not at all serious about debt reduction, regardless of his rhetoric.

Whatever the reasons, the fact remained that in the 1930s the United States was now in the midst of the worst economic crisis in its history, dwarfing any before it. It demanded bold action—government action, of course—which would ultimately mean a much more intrusive role for Washington to play in the lives of everyday Americans. During the Depression it would by and large be welcomed; when the economic emergency passed, the government's involvement did not end.

The prosperity of the 1920s, then, came to a close quite literally with a crash. The American public, as is often the case, will blame an individual for a disaster that was not of his or her making. It may be said that Hoover lost the 1932 election not so much as a result of blame being placed at his doorstep as it was the perception that he was doing little or nothing to solve the problem. An old-line Republican economist, Hoover was of the opinion that the market would correct itself and ultimately return to normalcy. For a desperate American people, this was not enough. It was for that reason that they turned to a one-time Democratic vice presidential candidate named Franklin Delano Roosevelt.

## Prewar Relations between FDR and the CFR

Franklin Roosevelt campaigned on nothing less than an economic and social revolution. Under normal circumstances, the American people might have rejected his ideas as too radical: Roosevelt sought to introduce government into the lives of

Americans, making it a partner in bringing Americans individually and as a nation out of the despair of the Great Depression. A one-time governor of New York, Roosevelt and his family had long ties to what was becoming known as the "Eastern Establishment."[21] In 1929 Roosevelt went so far as to publish an article in *Foreign Affairs* advocating active American involvement in the League of Nations: this at a time when the Council on Foreign Relations was located immediately next door to his residence while governor of New York. Some conspiracy theorists will contend that Roosevelt was in fact being groomed for the presidency by the CFR and that with proper financial backing and the right political opportunity (perhaps the Great Depression), he could catapult into the White House. Whether a dupe or merely one who shared the Council's political views, Roosevelt was clearly their man, and eventually he obtained the Democratic nomination.[22]

If the 1920s were a period where the CFR had limited influence in the area of American foreign policy, the 1930s saw the organization exert considerable influence during the terms of Franklin Roosevelt. Probably the most obvious of these views, one which Roosevelt held himself, was the recognition of the Soviet Union. Other changes were afoot, some clearly necessary, which saw the United States come out of its isolationist shell. Roosevelt, as well as most members of the Council on Foreign Relations, was an advocate of a stronger American presence on the world scene. That is one of the reasons why, even with a grave economic depression, America began to exert some influence with League of Nations members.

In the Pacific, Japan was encouraged—unsuccessfully, as it turned out—to take a less militaristic role in that part of the world. With war in China already a reality in 1932, there was little the United States could do but cut back its trade and tighten the economic screws on the island nation. In Europe an increasingly aggressive Germany gave Roosevelt and the Allies pause to consider what actions to take. In clear violation of the armament portions of the Versailles Treaty, Germany continued to build up the Wehrmacht and Luftwaffe—their army and air force—despite protestations against it. By the late

1930s Roosevelt had taken the nation from cautious, even paranoid notions of foreign involvement to openly supporting a number of initiatives openly meant to strengthen American interests. For instance, in the Western Hemisphere the Good Neighbor policy helped improve American influence and image south of the Rio Grande; in Europe and Asia, despite a number of neutrality laws put into effect, the nation nonetheless was on a preparatory footing. On the home front, however, there were conservative Christians who saw in the world around them signs of planned collapse and dictatorship. Among the leaders, few were as influential as Father Charles Coughlin.

## Pre-War Conspiracy Advocates

### Father Coughlin: Radio Demagogue

Father Coughlin's weekly radio broadcasts were staple listening for tens of millions of Americans during the dark days of the Great Depression. From his electronic pulpit, the Michigan-based priest spoke to multitudes who shared his view that America was heading down the road to socialism and political ruin. Familiar targets in the conspiracy story were once again put up to public ridicule. International bankers, Jews, and Communists were all said to be part of an international conspiracy to bring the United States to her knees. Although a Roman Catholic priest, Coughlin had many supporters among Protestant conservatives. His claims that Adam Weishaupt was in fact the true founder of Communism found popular support in certain quarters; so too did his blatant anti-Semitism. Few dared to challenge a man who was clearly a demagogue, perhaps out of fear of popular or political repercussion. Because he was a man of the cloth, others thought to counter his statements ill advised for other reasons. This happens even in our own day when a popular religious leader makes statements on politics or matters of faith that don't quite ring true. "Touch not the Lord's anointed" seems to be the attitude among large segments of contemporary Christianity. With the notable exceptions of some ministries specializing in apologetics, few inside the faith raise a voice against some of our modern-day Father Coughlins. The outspoken priest was a good example of the power of fear mixed with faith to produce a potentially dangerous public sentiment. So radical had the priest become that he was even mentioned in Nazi newspapers in Germany as an example of "right thinking" taking root in America. A lesson from the troubled times of the 1930s would serve Christian America well in the 1990s.[23]

### Gerald Winrod: Anti-Semite

Gerald B. Winrod was a Baptist evangelist in the 1930s and 1940s who combined anti-Semitism, conspiracy theory, and prophecy teachings as few before him had. Not until the late twentieth century can we find examples in conservative Christianity of such shameless pandering to nativistic and hate-filled twisting of Scripture and orthodox Christian belief. Organizing a group in the 1930s known as the Defenders of the Christian Faith, Winrod took on everything from evolution to what he called "Roosevelt's Jewish New Deal." He also put out a number of publications to support his loathsome ideas and, unfortunately, had many believing his brand of ideological and theological poison as gospel. It was Winrod who in the 1930s visited Germany and returned with glowing reports of Hitler's government and its dealing with Jews, Masons, and anyone outside Winrod's circle of acceptability.

Winrod's publications, such as *Adam Weishaupt: A Human Devil* and *The Jewish Assault on Christianity,* played up the Jewish threat component of his view of conspiracy and end-time fulfillment of prophecy. That the Antichrist would be Jewish, Winrod had no doubt; any persecution Jews received therefore was acceptable because of their dealings with Satan and rejection of Christ. The Kansas minister also bought wholesale into the ugly writings known as the *Protocols of the Elders of Zion,* a vulgar, anti-Semitic publication forged in the latter part of the nineteenth century in Russia. In Winrod's bigoted mind, all things evil and all things Jewish were synonymous. The coming of war, in Winrod's estimation, was simply the fulfillment of prophecy in the sense that God was using Jewish people despite their evil and disobedience.[24]

### Other Prophecy Ideas in the 1930s and 1940s

Among the many conservative prophetic spokespersons for Christian groups during this period, the following certainly bear mentioning: Wilber Smith of the Moody Bible Institute; Harry Ironside of Chicago's Plymouth Brethren Memorial Church; Donald Barnhouse of Philadelphia—who had a nation-wide radio program on prophecy and published a journal dealing with the topic—and Louis Bauman of Los Angeles—who once claimed to see the "666" symbol in the NRA (National Recovery Act) eagle emblem. In general, conservative Christians were inclined to view the government's New Deal program as a harbinger of one-world government. Another noteworthy belief among prophecy proponents of the 1930s and 1940s was the view that either Hitler or Mussolini, particularly the latter, was the Antichrist. The Italian dictator was seen as the prophesied Beast of Revelation because of his rule from the "City of Seven Hills" (Rome) and his open desire to rebuild the Roman Empire.[25]

## FDR, the New Deal, and Lend-Lease

When war broke out in 1939 with the German and Soviet invasion of Poland, Americans were clearly alarmed about the prospect of yet another conflict that might suck them into its vortex. Roosevelt cautiously yet quite brilliantly engineered aid to Britain through various Lend-Lease provisions, as well as making America what FDR called the "arsenal of democracy." America was indeed becoming that arsenal; it was also quite obviously preparing for war. All during these slow and deliberate steps, the still young Council on Foreign Relations was supplying Roosevelt with as much advice as he needed—perhaps more. It was becoming apparent that the Council had become, during FDR's terms in office, a de facto state department. What also becomes apparent is that by the time of the Pearl Harbor attack, Franklin Roosevelt's positions on foreign policy and the position statements of the CFR were almost identical.[26]

On the domestic side, the depression had opened the minds of the American people to economic solutions they would have rejected just a decade before. The initial purpose of what can best be described as a form of American socialism, euphemistically coined the New Deal, was to bring aid to the millions thrown into unemployment and on the verge of starvation. In what amounted to a veritable alphabet soup of social programs, organizations as diverse as the Civilian Conservation Corps (CCC) and Rural Electric Cooperative (REA) came into existence. The most famous of all, of course, was Social Security. This program was criticized as socialism but defended for providing elderly Americans with at least something of a safety net in their retirement years. The New Deal was truly nothing less than a domestic revolution that forever changed the manner in which American citizens perceived the role of government in their lives.[27] When attention was diverted from domestic to foreign affairs with the outbreak of World War II, it was obvious to all but the most obtuse American citizen that it was only a matter of time before the United States became involved.

## FDR, the CFR, and World War II

Franklin Roosevelt was quite aware that unless the United States was provoked into a conflict, public opinion was behind leaving European or Asian affairs to the parties concerned. Still, if the United States was to have its role as world leader as envisioned by the Council on Foreign Relations, ultimately leading to the consolidation of power in a world body, something had to change. That change came about on December 7, 1941, when the Imperial Japanese naval forces attacked the American fleet anchored at Pearl Harbor, Hawaii. Although the United States had been aware that the Japanese were planning an attack of substantial proportions somewhere in the Pacific, they were not sure where. Some high-ranking officers had warned about the fleet's vulnerability at Pearl Harbor, but the warnings were disregarded. The attack, meant to deliver a knockout punch to the Americans, at best delivered a stunning blow from which the United States could and did recover. The aroused Americans entered World War II with a sense of righteous indignation and purpose. Days later the Germans and Italians also declared war on the United States. War, a sometimes unifying factor between powers with a common enemy, had come.[28]

For the Council on Foreign Relations the outbreak of World War II, for all of its tragedy and human suffering, offered an opportunity to push for the creation of a government structure to avoid wars in the future. In truth, it was little more than rehashed ideas that had been passed about at the end of World War I concerning the League of Nations. Now, the Council believed, World War II was prima facie evidence that such an organization was necessary. Of course monumental problems were still to be overcome before all of this was possible. It should be pointed out that there are a number of conspiracy theorists who contend that World War II was indeed a planned event for the sole purpose of ultimately creating interest—even demand—for a world political body. What was needed was an enemy so evil and grotesque that the world would cry out for relief. A player with a leading role in this drama was a social malcontent from Austria named Adolf Hitler.

Adolf Hitler was born in April 1889 in Austria and grew up idolizing German culture. The offspring of a minor civil servant and his much younger wife, Hitler grew up in a household where his father bullied and his mother spoiled him. Young Adolf, as early as grade school, came to think of himself as a natural leader and deep thinker. He did have a certain aptitude for drawing, especially landscapes and buildings, but when he later tried to enter art school in Vienna he was told that his work was simply not of sufficient quality. His difficulty in drawing the human figure was one of the main reasons for his rejection from a Vienna art academy. Hitler, however, blamed his rejection and lot in life on the wealthy bourgeoisie, Communists, and Jews who, he believed, controlled virtually all facets of life in Vienna and indeed, in Europe.[29] His life was anything but pleasant. He lived in one flophouse after another, managing to make a small amount of money from the sale of postcards.

When World War I broke out, Hitler served as a corporal in the Austrian army. Despite the horror of the conflict, he found a perverse sense of satisfaction in being part of a cause and an organization that warfare provided. While his fellow soldiers longed to go home, Hitler reveled in the stench, death, and wounds around him. Serving with distinction, Hitler won the Iron Cross for bravery. When a mustard gas attack incapacitated him, it allowed him time to think his ideas through and come to conclusions about how the world was run. During his recovery in an army hospital, he received word that the Axis powers had surrendered and the kaiser had fled to Holland. For Hitler it seemed that his world was at an end.[30]

Of course Hitler's world did not end with the collapse of Germany and the establishment of the Weimar Republic. He simply went on his way spouting hatred for the new order and insisting that the betrayal of Jews and Communists was responsible for Germany's loss. It was just a matter of time before Hitler became a leading agitator in Munich and would eventually serve prison time for the failed 1923 putsch. By then, Hitler had become something of a folk hero to thousands who saw in him a spokesman voicing their outrage against the republic. It would be a short ten years after the putsch that Hitler would find himself chancellor of Germany. The Weimar Republic's days were clearly numbered.

In the meantime, Franklin Roosevelt's foreign policy was taking on increasingly internationalistic overtones. One of his chief aides, Harry Hopkins, went so far as to ensure American involvement in the war when consulting with British Prime Minister Winston Churchill.[31] Remember, this was before America had declared war. Though some see conspiracy in this action, I think it is closer to the mark to say that it was mere common sense and enlightened self-interest for the United States to side with Great Britain. Isolationism was fast evaporating, and preparation for inevitable war arose.

## War and the End of Isolationism

By early 1942 the United States was officially at war with Japan, Italy, and Germany, and the age of isolationism had ended. Even Roosevelt's Republican opponent in the 1940 presidential election, Wendell Wilkie, joined the administration in its efforts to unify the nation for war. It was clear that the United States and the world were about to enter a new era, one whose end could not be predicted with any degree of accuracy. What was certain was that the "sleeping giant" was now wide awake and ready to take on the leading role in world affairs. This would not change with the end of World War II, nor with the changing of presidents. Whether future presidents were Democrat or Republican, a basic shift in mind-set had taken place for them. The effect on both international and domestic policies would be considerable.

The introduction of American troops in the Pacific, North African, and later European theaters of operation provided the economic and eventually military clout needed to defeat the Axis powers. Virtually every world leader involved, from Stalin to Churchill, knew that with American manpower and titanic productive capabilities, both the Germans and Japanese would ultimately be overwhelmed. In the Pacific, island-hopping after the Battle of Midway set the stage for direct air strikes on the Japanese main islands. Of course when the atomic bomb was finally created, the island runways provided an easy way to deliver the nuclear payload.[32]

Europe provided different challenges, requiring that first the Russians be reinforced to prevent their collapse, followed by the opening of a second front against the Third Reich. Beginning first in North Africa, the Americans and British landed on the northern and western coasts of what was then Vichy-French territory. The Vichy government had, of course, cooperated with the Nazis after the invasion of France in 1940. By late spring 1943, the last remnants of the once-vaunted Afrika Korps surrendered to British General Bernard Montgomery. From there, the invasion went to Sicily, and then to the Italian mainland itself. The major invasion, of course, was across the English

Channel at Normandy. With the creation of a second and even third front, the Germans were eventually forced to retreat back to their homeland, where a horrible orgy of destruction awaited them at the hands of a vengeful Red Army.[33]

The Allied invasion of Germany also brought to the public's attention what had been up to that point mostly rumor: the concentration and death camps at places like Treblinka, Auschwitz, Dachau, and Bergen-Belsen. The systematic murder of Jews during the 1930s and 1940s totaled some six million and drove home to a stunned world the barbarity that was Nazi Germany. It was for this reason that in 1948 the old Balfour Declaration was revived in the form of a vote allowing the creation of a Jewish and Arab state in Palestine; although the Jewish state—now called Israel—agreed to a partition, the Arabs refused, and the Israeli War of Independence ensued.[34]

Franklin Roosevelt did not live to see the victory in World War II, although he doubtless was certain of the outcome by the time he passed away. Unfortunately, the sickly president trusted Joseph Stalin of the USSR, every bit the monster Adolf Hitler was, with the "administration" of Eastern Europe. Of course this would simply set the stage for the next phase of international problems: creation of a United Nations and the advent of the cold war. It was a certainty that the Council on Foreign Relations would provide its advice and candidates for future administrations.

5

# The Cold War:
# 1945–1963

With the end of World War II, the world entered a new and threatening period. The advent of the atomic age and the ideological struggle between the Communist and free worlds were fodder for powerful arguments among both conspiracy theorists and Christian prophecy believers about the dangerous nature of the world around them. In the minds of millions of Americans and Europeans, the specter of Stalinist Russia was a very real threat needing the full attention of the non-Communist world. The period between 1945 and 1963 was a time fraught with dangers and incredible tensions that very nearly resulted in war between the nuclear superpowers. Fear of war, conspiracy suspicion, and hope in the fulfillment of prophecy made for a powerful mix in those very emotionally charged days. It was a time of high political drama and, if we are to believe conspiracy theorists, planned objectives that have taken us to where we are today.

## The Early Years of the Cold War

Even before World War II had ended it was becoming increasingly apparent that the United States and the Soviet Union had different views of how the postwar world should look.

Despite American concessions to the Soviets involving control of Eastern Europe, the Communist leadership simply felt it could not trust the West and its stated objectives of cooperation in maintaining the peace. This was especially true once the United States had developed the atomic bomb. In Joseph Stalin's mind, the next logical step was for the Americans to use this new and terrifying weapon against the USSR. Between 1945 and 1949, before the Soviets obtained their own atomic capability, Stalin lived in fear of an American attack. Indeed, it could be argued that this paranoia was one of the reasons the Iron Curtain dropped across Eastern Europe. Whatever went on in the tortured mind of the Soviet leader, he at least slept easier once he also possessed the ultimate weapon. Unfortunately for Eastern Europe, their promised freedom and self-determination did not materialize when Russia began building its own nuclear arsenal.[1]

It has been suggested, with good reason, that perhaps both the ailing Roosevelt and his successor, Harry Truman, were simply naive about the intentions of Joseph Stalin. Winston Churchill certainly felt that way about Truman. One does have to wonder about the sagacity of American foreign policy during this period, especially when one considers that Alger Hiss—who was later convicted of perjury and was suspected of being a Soviet agent or fellow traveler, was part of the Truman administration.[2] The willingness to trust a dictator on a par with Adolf Hitler, who along with the Nazi leader invaded Poland in 1939, at least says something about either the blind trust or outright stupidity of the State Department and White House. When it became clear that Stalin never intended to relinquish control of Eastern Europe, it should not have surprised anyone. Still, apologists in the West have made conciliation for the Stalinist regime by claiming it was American imperialism that caused him to behave as he did. Incredibly, some in the United States are still willing to buy the line that Stalin was anything but an international thug and genocidal psychopath.

## Birth of the United Nations

By the end of World War II, calls for globalistic cooperation, and to a lesser extent, a global government, were being heralded both at home and abroad. In many regards, the old dream of the League of Nations had never died, and many who supported that institution saw in the new United Nations the rebirth of their hopes. The truth of the matter was that plans for the United Nations had begun before the war was even over. A significant number among the Council on Foreign Relations, among them Secretary of State Cordell Hull, had encouraged Roosevelt to introduce the idea at the proper time and then back it with the full power and prestige of the most powerful nation on earth.[3]

The first full-scale meeting of the United Nations took place in San Francisco in 1945. Alger Hiss is said to have composed the charter, taken in part from the Soviet constitution. Hiss was a member of the Council on Foreign Relations (something conspiracy theorists are quick to point out), and was only one of more than forty representatives from that organization in attendance. Woodrow Wilson had been rebuffed when he sought to bring the United States into the League of Nations; President Truman, in contrast, oversaw the passage of the bill that authorized the creation of the United Nations. In a show of solidarity with the new organization, John D. Rockefeller Jr. donated some $8.5 million worth of prime New York real estate on the East River.[4] The purpose of the land grant was for the construction of a headquarters for the new organization in the world's leading center of trade, commerce, and diversity.

Aside from the publicity given to the new organization and the hopes being raised, the most obvious question was seldom asked: Who would benefit most from the United Nations? The idealists contended that a war-weary world had the most to gain. It is not my place to dispute what for many were heartfelt sentiments in this regard. After all, it is hard to argue with the fact that the human race had had its fill of violence and carnage over the previous fifty years.

There is no question that the United Nations was at the zenith of globalistic desires for a family of nations. What was clearly necessary from 1945 on was a public relations campaign to sell the institution as humanity's last best hope for peace. As anyone knows who lived through the period, the sale of the organization to the American public did not go well, and most Americans since those early postwar years (at least until the Gulf War) have seen the United Nations as a hapless giant surviving on American largesse. It seemed that in the decades subsequent to its founding, that the United Nations and the laughably "nonaligned" nations used the General Assembly for little more than an arena where the United States and Israel were the chief targets. Faith in that institution was at a nadir during the Carter administration, when the United Nations proved utterly incapable of doing anything about the Iranian hostage crisis or the Soviet invasion of Afghanistan. The United Nations had not had a great track record of speaking out against leftist aggression, and with these crises it finally reached the point where the average American began to seriously wonder just what we were doing in such an inept, corrupt, and politically one-sided institution. Still, there were a few limited successes in the United Nations to report in the first decades of its existence; most of these were in the area of convincing some that a quasi-globalistic approach to the world's problems was best.

Before the United Nations could possibly fulfill its purpose as some sort of world parliament, even the most avid globalistic supporters recognized that a great deal of selling would have to be made to a skeptical American public. Adding to this skepticism was the fact that between 1948 and 1989 the American titan bore the overwhelming majority of the financing of the U.N. mission. Memories of the failure of the League of Nations and American absence therein were still fresh in the minds of many diplomats. Those supporting the new "League" wanted to make sure of United States membership this time.

Despite American generosity in establishing the United Nations, the United States received less than friendly treatment within the walls of the institution. No one expected the United Nations to be a rubber stamp for American policy, but the vitriolic tone of the criticism, the outright hypocrisy of nations under the Soviet heel, made it increasingly clear that the new international forum was anything but fair and impartial. Those who still supported the United Nations were willing to put up with these unpleasantries in hopes that this organization would eventually house some sort of world collective, perhaps even world government. In the atomic age cooperation was needed: Saber rattling in the post–Hiroshima/Nagasaki days could easily find nations forced to decide whether to use their nuclear weapons. American commitment to the United Nations was firm at the highest levels, although it doubtless taxed the patience of any number of presidents. And if the task of supporting the U.N. weren't enough, the United States also had to shoulder the burden of reconstructing Europe and Japan in the wake of World War II.

### The Marshall Plan

When the Marshall Plan to help rebuild Europe was introduced to the American public, it set off shock waves of opinion. It was not a matter of whether or not we should help a fallen Europe; what stunned Americans was the sheer cost of the operation: $5 billion to begin with, upwards of $20 billion before the plan was completed. The rationale behind this policy was the theory that Communism bred most readily in areas of economic and political distress. To prevent this, Secretary of State George Marshall, for whom the plan was named, suggested that immense sums be spent in Europe to rebuild the infrastructure of Europe and Japan before Communist doctrines had time to grow. Ever since the Iron Curtain had fallen across Europe, only the most obtuse observer could not conclude that the Soviets meant to spread Communism farther. The Marshall Plan addressed the economic and political threats of Communism. In answer to the military threat of Communist nations, the United States and her Western allies founded the North Atlantic Treaty Organization (NATO) in 1949. These moves on the part of the United States and her allies were indicative of the highly charged atmosphere of international relations.[5]

### The Berlin Airlift and the Fall of China

The world encountered many surprises and challenges during the early years of the cold war. Among the more noteworthy were the Berlin Airlift, the fall of China to Communism in 1949, and the 1949 Soviet detonation of an atomic bomb. Suddenly the United States was no longer the sole possessor of the world's most frightful weapon; it made confrontations doubly dangerous, as miscalculations could have truly global consequences.

The fall of China to the Communists was also a stunning blow to America. A nation of some seven hundred million people had fallen under a ruthless dictatorship that would, by the end of the Cultural Revolution, be responsible for the deaths of tens of millions of Chinese peasants, intellectuals, and middle-class people.

To the average American the once seemingly unassailable might of the United States was being challenged from every side, both foreign and domestic. Many cried conspiracy and treason as part of the answer for why things had gone wrong so fast. The chief villains, it seemed, were some of our own government officials, spies (such as Ethel and Julius Rosenberg), or alleged Communist sympathizers (such as Alger Hiss). It was a time of frightening change for the United States and the world. For some, it was simply a difficult transition to new geopolitical realities; for others, it smacked of behind-the-scenes manipulation and perhaps the fulfillment of prophecy.

### Mushroom Clouds and Prophecy

There were few prophecy writers and lecturers during the early cold war period to equal Wilbur Smith. During the late 1940s and early 1950s, Smith held forth that the atomic bomb was in fact merely the fulfillment of Scripture. In 2 Peter 3:10, the apostle writes, "But the day of the Lord will come as a thief in the night, in which the heavens will pass away with a great noise, and the elements will melt with fervent heat; both the earth and the works that are in it will be burned up." Smith interpreted all of this as a first-century description of a nuclear holocaust: He contended that it was not possible until the advent of the atomic age for this prophecy to be fulfilled; therefore, he concluded that these must be the last days.[6]

Other prophecy writers joined Smith in similar pronouncements of impending doom and/or the soon return of Christ. Donald G. Barnhouse and Charles Taylor warned the faithful that time was short. The recent creation of the state of Israel (1948) was pointed to with great excitement and held out as a hallmark of God's timetable. According to Matthew 24, they contended, a generation would not pass between the reestablishment of the Jewish state and the coming of Christ. In the early postwar years many believed that the end could come anytime before 1988 because that would mark the end of a generation (forty years) since the establishment of Israel. In addition, Taylor and others made much of the fact that the now Communist Russia fit the description of Gog and Magog referred to in Ezekiel 38–39. According to the prophet, there would be a coming invasion of Israel "from the uttermost parts of the north" by a powerful foe of God and the Jewish state. Through miraculous intervention (or atomic weaponry, depending on whom you believed) the invasion would be thwarted. What was being created was an anticipation of the soon-to-come Armageddon; among Christians and non-Christians alike, this added to the tense atmosphere of the 1950s. It should be noted, however, that identification of Gog as Russia was never universally accepted.[7] Centuries ago, it was assumed that Gog referred to the Muslim kingdom of what became Turkey. Indeed, Paul Boyer, professor emeritus at the University of Wisconsin–Madison, makes an excellent point when he states the following:

> Countless writers casually substituted "Russia" for "Gog" in discussing Ezekiel 38. Such pious linguistic tinkering further convinced readers that Bible prophecy is, indeed, strikingly timely. The historian, reading hundreds of prophecy books published over a two-hundred-year period, can readily see this process of

inserting current events into an archaic belief system. The average believer, encountering the genre for the first time, may be stunned by the uncanny contemporaneity of the prophecies.[8]

It was not until more recent times and the rise of Russia and then the Soviet Union as a major power that the shift of emphasis to Russia as Gog can be seen.

### *The Truman Policy*

Into this morass of confusion and fear, President Harry Truman was called on to formulate a foreign policy that could at once halt Communist advances and restore American prestige abroad. Truman's response, with the considerable aid of his advisors, was what was dubbed "containment." The idea was to contain Communism within its 1947 boundaries and form alliances around the world to facilitate this policy, among them the South East Asia Treaty Organization (SEATO) and, in the Western Hemisphere, the Organization of American States (OAS). NATO, of course, was the flagship alliance, as it would be standing toe to toe with Soviet troops in central Europe. The first test of Truman's resolve was in Greece, where Joseph Stalin was supplying leftist revolutionaries with weapons in an effort to overthrow the government. In response, the United States flooded Greece with an immense amount of military and financial assistance. This move effectively saved Greece from falling to Communism. Although this challenge was decided in favor of the West, in this international game of power politics, it was certain that it would not be the last confrontation.[9]

## The Korean War

Tensions in Korea had been high ever since the Soviet Union had invaded the northern portion of the peninsula as part of a prearranged agreement with the United States near the end of World War II. The Korean Peninsula had been divided at roughly the 38th parallel almost immediately after the end of hostilities with Japan. The northern part of Korea became a brutal Communist dictatorship; the South, a quasi-democratic government that was in fact controlled by ultraconservative politicians kept in power with support from the United States. American aid had in the meantime begun rebuilding the South's economy. Although successful economically, South Korea became increasingly repressive. By late 1949 North and South Korea exchanged harsh words and then gunfire; this proved to be merely the precursor for an imminent Northern invasion. During the summer of 1950 Soviet supplied and armed North Korean forces crossed into South Korea and quickly over-whelmed Republic of Korea (ROK) troops. Within weeks ROK troops were reduced to defending a small corner of the penin-sula with Pusan as the center of resistance.

U.N. troops finally arrived under the command of Gen. Dou-glas MacArthur and began the arduous process of pushing the invaders back. The turning point in the early part of the con-flict was MacArthur's amphibious landing at Inchon, well behind enemy lines and just a few miles from the North Korean border. The result was a helter-skelter retreat of Communist forces back into the North, with the U.N. forces in hot pursuit. MacArthur asked permission to bomb supply routes from China in an effort to choke off Communist supplies. This was refused, but permission was given to reunite the peninsula. As the attacking U.N. troops drove northward, ominous warnings from Communist China were received about its possible entry into the war. It proved to be anything but a bluff.[10]

During the last week of November 1950, four Chinese field armies crossed the Yalu River, the natural boundary between Korea and Manchuria, and joined the battle with their North Korean ideological partners. The American and U.N. troops were quickly overrun and retreated southward to any defensi-ble position they could find. MacArthur now assumed that he would be allowed to use B–29s to bomb Chinese targets inside Manchuria but was, to his disbelief, told this was not the case. Truman feared that carrying the conflict to China would result in a wider war. When MacArthur protested the president's deci-sion, Truman demanded and received his resignation. Thus war was never declared in Korea. The conflict is called a police action, with no clear winner or loser. By the time the frustrating peace negotiations concluded, borders were at approximately the point they had been before the North Korean invasion of the South. The land was divided by an ugly no-man's-land punctuated with barbed wire, land mines, and machine gun nests. Korea was just one of many limited wars that would become distressingly common during the cold war years.

## McCarthyism

What the majority of Americans remember most about the 1950s and the threat of Communism is not so much the war in Korea as the fear of subversion at home. "Red scares" were not uncommon during the twentieth century, as events during 1919–20 and the 1930s attest. One individual who capitalized on the public fear of Communism more than any other was Wisconsin Senator Joseph McCarthy.

To this day the term *McCarthyism* suggests intolerance, political witch hunts, and paranoia about Communism on a grand scale. The period of McCarthyism has been described as a time of shame for a nation holding personal liberty and freedom of thought in high esteem. The hearings and events that ensued forever changed America. From the time of the New Deal and the expansive growth of government to the scandalous Hiss charges—that he was a Soviet agent, a perjurer, and a Communist—Americans of all classes became fearful of what appeared to some a worldwide conspiracy in which members of our own government seemed to be participating. It was not always so, however, as during World War II the USSR had been looked on as an ally and a nation with whom we shared some common political interests. Aside from the vicious purges of Stalinist Russia, there is no question that American Progressivism and Soviet Communism ideologically had some things in common during the New Deal. With the German-Soviet nonaggression pact in 1939, however, the two for the most part went separate ways.[11]

McCarthy tapped that deep-rooted fear. Most of the American public was not able to differentiate between liberals and

Communists and, if McCarthy knew the difference, he did not care to make the distinction clear.[12] In early 1950 McCarthy began his accusations that the State Department had knowingly hired and harbored Communists. The statements caused a firestorm of controversy, as the mass media descended on the story with a vengeance. In the months and years that followed, the Wisconsin Republican attacked and accused a host of individuals of being either outright Communists or at least sympathetic to their goals. When the dust settled, careers had been ruined and reputations badly damaged. Ironically, McCarthy's tactics probably helped any real Communist infiltration more than anything else.[13] After the hearings were finished in 1954 and McCarthy's reputation was in shambles, any accusations of Communist leanings were not taken very seriously. Nonetheless, there were serious problems dealing with internal security and national interests abroad.

### Reports of "Un-American Activities"

As far back as 1945, there had been a raid on the offices of a little-known journal called *Amerasia*. In the process, sensitive documents concerning American interests and intelligence in the Far East were discovered. The big question was how the publisher of this small journal, dedicated to the support of Mao Tse-tung and suspected of being part of a Communist front, came on documents that were clearly of a sensitive nature. Shortly thereafter, in 1948, the famous Alger Hiss case was opened in which the former White House advisor and contributing architect of the U.N. charter was accused of being a Communist agent. The chief witness against Hiss was a former Communist agent himself, one Whittaker Chambers, who provided some very damning testimony. To this day Hiss, now in his nineties, denies spying for the Soviets. The evidence was quite convincing and further increased fears of Communist espionage, which McCarthy used to his advantage. Hiss was convicted of perjury and imprisoned.

The Julius and Ethel Rosenberg case was another headline-grabbing example of spying in the United States. For ideological reasons, the Rosenbergs had passed on vital atomic secrets to the Soviet Union that ultimately boosted that nation's nuclear program. For that reason the couple was executed in the politically charged postwar era.

### Dwight Eisenhower and the McCarran Subcommittee

In the domestic political arena, the United States turned to a nationally known hero to stem the tide against foreign and domestic threats. Both Democrats and Republicans offered Dwight D. Eisenhower the presidential candidacy in their respective political party. Some, including members of the CFR, have suggested that his selection was mainly an attempt to stop Robert Taft's nomination. When Eisenhower took office in January 1953, the heat of anti-Communism was still strong. For instance, the House Committee on Un-American Activities and the McCarran subcommittee continued their investigations of subversive activities. The McCarran subcommittee (Subcommittee on Internal Security, part of the Senate Judicial Committee) seized the records of the Institute of Pacific Relations, the Council on Foreign Relations, and known Communist sympathizers. It was not difficult to prove which way the Institute or the CFR leaned in its views of international relations. What was even more interesting was that both groups had received money from some very large and well-known foundations.[14]

### Foundations and Conspiracy Theory

The use of foundations to shelter the enormous wealth of individuals and families such as the Rockefellers and Fords served two purposes. First, it protected the millions of dollars of the people in question and second, it provided funds for a host of pet projects. One of the ironies conspiracy theorists point out deals with the type of projects funded. Often these foundations made monies available to groups with clearly anti-capitalistic and antidemocratic leanings. Seeing how it is capitalist money making their projects possible to begin with, one has to wonder why these foundations saw fit to fund such questionable enterprises. For instance, one of the projects in the

1950s dealt with a study in how social studies was presented in American public schools. What was advocated in the final report was that quasi-socialistic systems or even global government and the redistribution of wealth be taught in these classes. Again, this begs the question: Why would capitalists fund such seemingly self-defeating projects? Conspiracy theorists suggest that it had to do with a desire of the very wealthy to facilitate social change. Simply put, the wealthy believe in a socialistic system. As Dr. Quigley points out, Round Table groups and financiers did not object to cooperating with Communists as long as it furthered their own goals. Quigley, as conspiracy theorists are quick to point out, was close to many in the Round Table loop and supported their ends.[15]

### Conspiracy Theory, Blacklisting, and Hollywood

As fear of Communism at home and abroad spread, rumors and accusations concerning the loyalties of Hollywood and television stars became even more common than in the 1940s. Some of the biggest names in Hollywood were accused of belonging to Communist groups and were asked to appear before the United States House Committee on Un-American Activities. Lucille Ball, Edward G. Robinson, Eddie Cantor, and Charlie Chaplin were just a few of dozens under suspicion. Although some had in fact joined Communist groups in the 1930s and 1940s, most had done so while quite young or as a sign of solidarity with our then wartime ally, the Soviet Union. Most were not active Communists.

Speaking on behalf of the Screen Actor's Guild, union president Ronald Reagan insisted that he knew of no Communist activity in Hollywood and was certain that few, if any, union members had any interest in helping a monster like Joseph Stalin. In a superb example of how conspiracy theorists will often put liberals and conservatives into the same camp when it comes to politics, Ronald Reagan was and often still is portrayed as a member of the international conspiracy. It is difficult to imagine a more hated man in liberal circles today than

Reagan; yet, if we are to believe the conspiracy theorists, he was cooperating with them.

Another sad accusation during the 1950s had to do with the alleged Jewish control of both the film and fledgling television industries. This control, some conspiracy theorists warned, was a threat to the nation because of perceived Jewish proclivity toward liberal causes, support for the state of Israel, and rumored ties to international banking. As a result, many Jewish actors, directors, and producers were blacklisted simply because of their religion. Such was the general atmosphere during the McCarthy era. Despite what some nostalgic-minded Christian writers tell us, the 1950s were not all *Leave It to Beaver* and *Ozzie and Harriet;* Jews, Blacks (who rode in the back of buses or could not sit at lunch counters reserved for whites), and other minorities certainly had a different experience.[16]

### Ike's Response to the Alleged Communist Threat

In the midst of these problems, President Eisenhower had to deal with the broader issue of what collectively became known as McCarthyism. Joe McCarthy's contention that some 205 Communists were in the State Department drew considerable attention, especially his attacks on Dean Acheson as the most dangerous of the lot; he later reduced the number to 57 "card-carrying" members of the Communist Party. Eisenhower personally found both McCarthy and his charges reprehensible. To make an end run around the Wisconsin senator without splitting the Republican Party, Ike launched his own attack on Communism at home by improving security background checks for government employees. Probably the most famous individual under investigation as a result of the president's new policy was Robert Oppenheimer, a key scientist in the development of the atomic bomb. His reputation was ruined when he was tagged a Communist, or at least a sympathizer, because he turned against nuclear weaponry. Other actions supported by Eisenhower included the passage of the 1954 Communist Control Act, which made membership in the American Communist Party illegal. One of its chief supporters was Democratic Senator Hubert H. Humphrey of Minnesota; a decade later he apologized for contributing his name and support to the law, which by then had been found unconstitutional.[17]

McCarthy's accusations finally reached the point where he lost public support. Never possessing evidence that anyone in the State Department was a Communist, the senator lost all credibility after he accused the U.S. Army of harboring Communists. McCarthy abused witness after witness; finally, an attending attorney reprimanded McCarthy, asking the Wisconsin senator whether he had no shame. The attorney received a rousing ovation for his comment. By late 1954 the Senate finally voted to condemn McCarthy by a sixty-seven to twenty-two margin. He died just four years later in 1957 at the age of forty-eight. His death did not end the fear of Communist infiltration; indeed, few doubted that the Soviets or Chinese were actively trying to do just that. The question was how suspected individuals would be sought out and interrogated. For President Eisenhower, the McCarthy debacle was just one of many challenges facing his administration. Ike found events overseas to be just as challenging.[18]

## International Concerns

The year 1956 was not generally noted for international peace and cooperation. That year the Soviet Union brutally crushed an uprising in Hungary. During the course of the freedom fighters' struggle for independence, participants broadcast pleas to the West, particularly the United States, to come to their aid. Help did not come, and the Soviets succeeded in crushing freedom under tank treads. The policy set forth during the Franklin Roosevelt administration was being upheld by a Republican president: respect for spheres of influence. Besides, with both sides having the awesome power of nuclear weapons, no one wanted to take the chance of starting a nuclear conflagration. Further repression in Eastern Europe did not go without notice, however; Soviet threats against Poland and the Baltic states were chillingly representative of new Premier Nikita Khrushchev's continuation of Stalin's policies. The previous year the Soviets had created the Warsaw Pact, a military alliance between Eastern bloc nations in response to NATO. It was quite apparent that both sides wanted to be certain that they were prepared in the event of a showdown.[19] Strangely enough, there was an unusual degree of cooperation between the ideological opponents that year. These events did not happen in Europe, but in the Middle East, setting the stage for that part of the world to become a major concern to the two superpowers for years to come, as well as a source of conspiracy and prophetic speculation.

### *The Rebirth of the State of Israel*

When the state of Israel was created on May 14, 1948 (the fifth day of Iyar),[20] it created a host of problems. Initially both the Soviet Union and the United States supported the creation of the Jewish state. When David Ben-Gurion and the Israeli government sided with the West, the Soviets dropped their support and backed the Arab nations. The Arab nations surrounding the new Jewish state refused to accept partition and effectively lost most of the areas that would have been given over to them by U.N. vote. After Israel's successful war of independence, Trans-Jordan annexed what is today called the West Bank and renamed itself Jordan. Between 1948 and 1956, relations remained very tense between Israel and her Arab neighbors, at times resulting in bloodshed. When Arab terrorist attacks into Israel from the Gaza Strip increased and Egyptian President Gamal Nasser closed off the Suez Canal and moved to seal off Israeli access to the Gulf of Aqaba and the port of Eilat, the Jewish state was prompted to action. With lightning strikes into Gaza and the Sinai peninsula, Israel Defense Forces (IDF) made it to the Suez Canal zone in time to meet unlikely allies: the British and the French.

Both European powers feared that Egypt's nationalization of the canal could mean a huge increase in fees and restricted access to the Mediterranean Sea from the Indian Ocean. As a result, Britain and France acted in concert with the Israelis to end the threat. Earlier American refusal to help Egypt build the

Aswan Dam on the Nile River was probably one of the major reasons Nasser closed off the Suez Canal and supported terrorism and Arab nationalism. Enraged at the European and Israeli invaders, Eisenhower and Khrushchev demanded that the three armies then actively withdraw from Egyptian territory and return control of the canal to Nasser. The French and British thought the United States was acting in a most inappropriate manner but acquiesced to the demands. The Israelis, too, withdrew from the Sinai and Gaza area. It would be one of the last times the Israelis would withdraw from Arab lands after being attacked. After the Israeli withdrawal, terrorist attacks staged in Gaza by a group known as the Fedayeen escalated. The Jewish state and her political leaders had learned one valuable lesson: Never give up conquered territory without first obtaining something in return.[21] This cooperation between East and West produced something of a euphoria in the American press for a short period of time, but the realities of the cold war quickly squashed the optimism.

### The Acceleration of the Arms Race

Throughout the 1950s there was a new threat for both the Soviet Union and America to ponder. This threat had the potential for destroying civilization and rendering ideological arguments moot. The danger, of course, was the arms race and the rapid development and deployment of bigger and more destructive bombs. After the USSR had developed the atomic bomb, there was a move afoot in scientific and government circles of the United States to build what was being called the "super-bomb," or hydrogen bomb. Edward Teller was among the leading scientists advocating another crash program—like the earlier Manhattan Project that developed the A-bomb—to develop the weapon. In November 1952 the United States succeeded in detonating an H-bomb in the fifteen-megaton range. The atomic bomb was measured in double-digit kilotons, but H-bombs could now produce explosions on a previously unheard of scale. The first test of this super weapon was at Bikini atoll and produced an explosion with more than seven hundred times the destructive power of the bombs that had made rubble of Hiroshima and Nagasaki. Of course this did nothing to stop the Soviets, who immediately embarked on a program of their own to build a bomb of similar capabilities. Just over a year later, the Russians had successfully detonated their own hydrogen bomb. The arms race had begun in earnest.[22]

There was a twist to the arms buildup that had been foreseen as early as World War II when the first V–1 and especially V–2 rockets crashed into London. Space and its use for military purposes had to be considered as a possible threat. The Soviets once again rocked the West when they deployed the Sputnik unmanned satellite in 1957. Although not a military threat, Sputnik came on the heels of successful Russian tests of the first intercontinental ballistic missile system, or ICBM. This meant that the Soviets could conceivably have the ability to deliver their nuclear weapons via missile instead of manned bomber. If these rockets were launched over the polar ice cap, their destructive payload could level cities, military sites, and industrial centers in a matter of half an hour. The United States responded to the Soviet Union's success in space by creating the National Aeronautics and Space Administration (NASA) in 1958 in an effort to catch up. The missile gap—the perceived Soviet lead in technology and in the number of ICBMs, which had been talked about for years—had arrived.[23]

Missile gaps and H-bombs were not the only characteristics of the cold war. One of the oldest games between nations—spying—continued unabated during the nuclear age. The most famous of these episodes involved the shooting down of an American U–2 spy plane, then the most sophisticated in the U.S. arsenal. Pilot Francis Gary Powers was one of the last aviators to fly directly over the Soviet Union to obtain intelligence on the degree of Russian military abilities. Initially incapable of stopping the overflights because of the plane's speed and altitude abilities, the Russians finally shot down the U–2 in the spring of 1960, just before a summit meeting in Paris. An enraged Khrushchev demanded an apology and asked Eisenhower what he would think if the Soviet Union had flown spy planes over the United States. Perhaps what the Soviet premier failed to consider was that had they the technological ability, the Russians would have done just that. The Americans refused to apologize, and the summit broke up early under a pall of uncertainty and tension. President Eisenhower took full responsibility for the flights, and with Eisenhower's presidency at its end, Francis Gary Powers languished in a Soviet prison until a swap was arranged several years later in Berlin. To say that relations between the United States and the Soviet Union were chilly would be a grand understatement indeed.[24]

### Cuba Falls to Communism

The late 1950s were not without other challenges to the United States, some much closer to home. On January 1, 1959, Fidel Castro succeeded in overthrowing the corrupt American-backed dictator of Cuba, Fulgencio Batista. Although resolutely proclaiming that he was not a Communist, when Castro came to power he publicly announced his true ideological leanings and requested that the Soviet Union support his revolution. Needless to say, the Soviets were more than happy to help out and were thrilled at the prospect of having a base of operations only ninety miles from the United States. Hundreds of thousands of Cubans fled the island nation in an effort to obtain freedom from the brutal Communist dictatorship. They have been leaving ever since.

Almost immediately the CIA set about to destabilize the Communist regime, even going so far as to draw up plans for a United States-backed invasion of Cuba using refugees from that island. Although not put into action, the Bay of Pigs operation was planned and the training under way during the Eisenhower administration. The invasion was attempted in 1961 during the Kennedy administration but it failed. This further removed Castro from any kind of contact with his American neighbors.

Castro remains in power to this day, albeit on very shaky ground, with a civil rights record on a par with other Communist nations: abysmal.[25]

### The Kennedy Years

John F. Kennedy, Democratic senator from Massachusetts, was elected president of the United States in 1960, defeating Eisenhower's vice president, Richard Nixon. It was one of the closest races in American presidential election history and marked a turning point of sorts for the young nation: A young president (at forty-three) had a number of new ideas for domestic and foreign policy. Kennedy had accurately stated in his inaugural address that a torch had been passed to a new generation and for millions of Americans he symbolized that transition. Kennedy quickly instituted a number of programs, such as the Peace Corps, but at the same time he increased American military presence in Vietnam. He supported the Bay of Pigs operation and resolutely stood behind military defense of Europe, especially since the building of the Berlin Wall in 1961.

A buildup of American military power continued under JFK, notably in the increase of long-range B–52 bombers and ICBM Minuteman delivery vehicles. American power in the early 1960s was awesome and in fact quickly erased the feared missile gap of the 1950s. The tremendous economic power of the United States was clearly beyond the ability of the Soviets to match, and with it our ability to quickly produce quality weapons systems rendered their most sophisticated systems obsolete. The American capitalistic system, for all of its problems, was a major weapon in the U.S. arsenal, and Kennedy knew it. It was shortly after the Bay of Pigs, however, that both the Cubans and the Russians sought to make a dramatic move to cut into America's increasing advantages. Their plan involved the secret installation of short-range and intermediate-range tactical and strategic nuclear missiles on the island of Cuba. The greatest nuclear threat the world had ever known was about to begin.[26]

If ever there was a miscalculation on the part of Soviet leadership, what became known as the Cuban Missile Crisis was it. Khrushchev, confident he could bully the young president, took a tremendous gamble when he authorized the installation of Russian nuclear missiles in Cuba during the late spring and summer of 1962. Andrei Gromyko, the Soviet foreign minister, had long given assurances to the Americans that no offensive weapons would be introduced into Cuba. Both Eisenhower and Kennedy made pointed warnings about the high price that would be paid should the Russians attempt such a move. Chancing American wrath, the missiles were made operational under as much cover as could be mustered. Kennedy was made aware of the presence of the missiles on October 14, 1962, when a U–2 spy plane photographed some suspicious-looking structures near San Cristóbal, Cuba. Not initially announcing the findings to the Soviets or the American public, Kennedy and his cabinet, as well as the Joint Chiefs of Staff, debated what their plans and options should be. The Joint Chiefs favored an immediate invasion preceded by an enormous air strike on Cuba using nearly every weapon at America's disposal. The problem was that there was no guarantee that air strikes could take out every one of the missiles. It was estimated that the missiles currently in Cuba could hit most of the continental United States and kill approximately eighty million Americans in a matter of thirty seconds to ten minutes.[27] Another option was sought.

President Kennedy finally announced the presence of Soviet missiles in Cuba in a nationally televised speech to the American people. He demanded the dismantling of the missiles and their return to Russia. Moreover, he announced a worldwide priority one alert of American forces and preparations for the blockade and, if need be, invasion of Cuba. During ten days in October, the world stood at the abyss of nuclear holocaust and began to reconsider the massive buildup on both sides of the cold war. Khrushchev backed down in the face of a naval blockade and finally perceived the seriousness of Kennedy's threats. The missiles were withdrawn, and the United States promised to respect Cuba's sovereignty. In addition, the Americans secretly agreed to withdraw aging liquid-fueled intermediate-range missiles already scheduled for removal from Turkey. The United States had survived the first half of the cold war.[28]

## Changes in America

The period between 1945 and 1963 was filled with considerable uncertainty and fear for the American people, to say nothing about those living elsewhere in the world. For a sizable
number of Americans, the failure of the United States to halt
the rapid advance of Communism smacked of conspiracy.
Whether it was working with the Soviets at the end of World
War II or Roosevelt's naive willingness to trust the Russians in
Eastern Europe, the end of World War II was little more than
the beginning of the next conflict as far as conspiracy theorists
were concerned. What frustrated conspiracy advocates most
was their view that the super-wealthy Establishment was selling America out in favor of a one-world system and was in fact
willingly working with Communists toward that end.[29]

During this time of tremendous change in foreign policy during the postwar years, the United States faced dramatic internal changes as well. When millions of veterans returned from
World War II, they found an American nation bustling with
potential in terms of both economic and military power. Return-
ing vets took advantage of the GI Bill and bought homes and
went to college. Despite a minor economic downturn during
the late 1940s, the sky seemed the limit for the United States.
Even with increased tensions with the Soviet Union, American
power and prosperity grew. A person could go virtually anywhere in the world and find the dollar not only accepted but
openly sought. "Sound as a dollar" was a popular saying at the
time. Suburbs grew virtually overnight, population grew
quickly, and highway systems traversed the nation like a system of arteries and veins. This upswing in American prosperity, however, did not extend to all races and classes, and the fact
that some Americans did not share in the good fortune of the
era clearly stands out as an American failure.

Black Americans in particular were subject to economic,
social, and education conditions little better than what they
had experienced at the turn of the century. Many people, among
them conservative Christians, believed that it was sinful to mix
the races. Changes were afoot, however, as important court

decisions began to break the logjam of civil rights abuses. In 1954 *Brown vs. the Topeka Board of Education* was a landmark case that declared that the old doctrine of separate but equal education systems was unconstitutional. Desegregation followed but not peacefully. As the 1950s passed into the 1960s, lunch counters were desegregated, restroom restrictions were lifted, and the remnants of Jim Crow laws were actively dismantled. Leaders such as Martin Luther King Jr., Malcolm X, and Ralph Abernathy led efforts to ensure legal protections of gains made by Blacks. Finally, after nearly a century following the Emancipation Proclamation, steps were taken to fulfill the promise of freedom.

Another area of concern for a number of middle-aged and older Americans (as well as conspiracy theorists and conservative Christians) was the rise of a new music genre with the strange name of "rock and roll." A 1950s street term for having sex, the phrase came to mean a music form that borrowed heavily from blues and rhythm and blues. Musicians such as Elvis Presley combined Delta Blues with rockabilly to form a distinct sound all its own. Other influential musicians in the 1950s included Jerry Lee Lewis, Buddy Holly, and Carl Perkins. Rock and roll was immediately taken to heart by the younger generation and was decried as "the devil's music" from pulpits. Some racist opponents of the music form went so far as to give it the obscene label "nigger music" and warn of the decline of the American way of life.

The next wave of rock and roll came from Great Britain in what has become known as the "British Invasion." Like their American counterparts, British musicians embraced American blues with a passion. When the Beatles arrived in the United States for their first tour in 1964, they indicated that Presley and a Black soul artist named James Brown had greatly influenced their music. Presley everyone knew, but who was Brown? It pointed out the degree to which racism affected the kinds of music people listened to in the States. The Beatles were among the first from another country to make it really big in America. Other groups who would follow changed the style and message of rock music, at times in a negative manner, as when drug use was advocated, for example. A few other British bands helping to define rock music by the late 1960s included the Rolling Stones, the Who, Cream, and Led Zeppelin.

Many of the more conservative members of society were very concerned about the changes they saw happening in the United States; they perceived fundamental changes in the morals of the young as well as widespread social changes involving deseg- regation. Conspiracy-minded individuals tended to paint the whole of the 1950s as something akin to a sellout, perhaps even a planned destruction of America from within.[30]

## What of Conspiracy Theory in This Period?

I do not doubt that there were groups during the period cov- ered in this chapter who actively supported Soviet or Chinese Communist activities, or who sought to change the basic frame- work of American society. This includes average citizens as well as the wealthy and their foundations. The Reece investigations of major corporate foundations showed considerable support given to left-wing causes from a number of foundations rang- ing from Ford to Rockefeller. Still, one must take care not to draw broad conclusions from the actions of a few, albeit wealthy, individuals or foundations. Yes, there were and are people who mean the United States no good and would like nothing more than to see our sovereignty absorbed into a collective world gov- ernment. This does not mean that those so interested are part of the Illuminati or some ideological descendent of it.

It must also be reiterated that there are Round Table groups who have an agenda of their own and seek to put it into place. What we need to ask is simply, what does it matter? There always have been and always will be people seeking to push their political and economic agendas. Above all, to link them to some centuries-old conspiracy with cosmic overtones is, in a word, absurd. What I would love to see is primary source doc- umentation, prima facie evidence, that conspiracy theorists tell us exists. Instead, the researcher or ordinary reader is treated to warmed-over books that continually quote and requote each other without providing some truly impressive primary documentation and proof. One conspiracy advocate once told me that the reason why there are so few pieces of concrete evidence has to do with the great secrecy surrounding the "Plot." Of course, this is an argument from silence. It is tantamount to saying that Jesus in fact was Hindu but that evidence of this has been hidden or lost. Quigley, a favorite author among conspiracy advocates and self-proclaimed insider, does not provide evidence, either. He admits to the existence of Round Table groups and their desire to further the interests of the English-speaking world, but that is a far cry from proving the existence of an all-powerful cabal pulling strings.

The first phase of the cold war merely set the stage for what was to follow. Increased tensions and arms races would punctuate this period—and lead to a frenzy of conspiracy and prophetic speculation.

# The Cold War:
# 1964–1989

The second half of the cold war saw a tremendous increase in both conspiratorial and prophetic writings available to the public at large. Especially among conservative Christians there was an upsurge in publications trumpeting the soon-coming of Jesus. Enemies surrounded Christianity and the United States, and to prophecy advocates all of this looked ominous and was even interpreted as a fulfillment of biblical prophecy. The Soviet Union became to more and more prophecy believers the Gog and Magog of the Book of Ezekiel; the rise of Communist China was interpreted as being the "Kings of the East" of the Book of Revelation; the arms race and profligation of nuclear weapons were a fulfillment of 2 Peter's statement concerning the melting of the elements; and venereal and blood-borne diseases, such as AIDS, were the result of God's wrath on a sinful society.

Conspiracy theory also became more fine-tuned during this period. The international banking conspiracy involving the usual perpetrators became much more tangible as the end of the twentieth century approached. The rise of the Trilateral Commission and the continuance of the Council on Foreign Relations were part and parcel of this. Diplomatic terms, such as the New World Order, suddenly meant much more than merely cooperation. For instance, the late Gary Allen, dean of recent conspiracy writers, commented on the state of the nation and family in his latest book, *Say NO! to the New World Order:*

> The primary objectives of the New World Order which affect the family are as follows: 1.) eliminate the traditional family unit as we know it and 2.) change the value of the traditional family. As would-be dictators, the architects of the New World Order want the complete and unyielding loyalty of their victims for themselves and cannot tolerate loyalty to God, country or family.[1]

More dangerous still to Christian believers was the slow but steady creep of conspiracy theory into prophecy writings. Conspiracy theory tainted a legitimate area of scriptural study and belief in traditional orthodox Christianity. Like just about all conspiracy and modern-day prophecy writings, the origins are in the modern era and in the secular world.

## The 1960s: The End of American Innocence

After that horrible late November 1963 day in Dallas, the United States suddenly found itself without a leader. Political friend and foe alike paid tribute to the fallen president as word of John F. Kennedy's death spread around the world. After his funeral, the nation and world began to adjust to a new head of state in the United States: Lyndon Baines Johnson. Kennedy's vice president was from the Texas hill country near Austin and had a reputation for getting things done in a sometimes gruff fashion. JFK's attorney general, his brother Robert Kennedy, loathed the Texan. The thought of this man taking over for his brother was frankly more than he could stand and ultimately contributed to his decision to seek the Democratic Party presidential nomination in 1968.

The decade of the sixties was one of the most turbulent periods in American history in terms of social change and foreign policy. The death of Jack Kennedy marked the end of an era in many ways: the end of what some have described as America's innocence. In the ensuing years the United States would fight a protracted war in Vietnam, battle for the rights of minorities, and see a generation gap develop that dwarfed any before it. A sizable portion of baby boomers rejected the worldview and values of their parents in favor of a lifestyle and hodgepodge of beliefs collectively known as the counterculture. Although its practice varied greatly from one place to another, the heart of the philosophy appeared to be a rejection of Judeo-Christian teachings of morality, a rejection of the capitalistic economic system in the United States, and general tolerance of anything not in the first two categories: summed up in a platitude of the day, "Tune in, turn on, and drop out." The nation wondered what the tremendous changes meant and just where America was going. For those in the conspiracy circle, there was little doubt.

Conspiracy theory in general views the racial and social upheaval of the 1950s and 1960s as planned chaos by any number of different groups: Jews, international bankers, the Vatican, Communists, or the Council on Foreign Relations. America's seeming retreat from victory in the face of Communism was perceived as part of the signs of the times. How, conspiracy theorists often ask, could so much have gone so wrong so quickly? One conspiracy author of the period, John Stormer, suggested that 1964 was a vital year of decision in the retreat from victory. America's future was in the balance, nothing less than slavery or freedom the issue. Stormer's book, *None Dare Call It Treason,* is in many ways typical of the message of conspiracy books in the 1950s, '60s, and '70s: Urgency, extreme urgency is needed in dealing with the international threat. The fact that this threat had been ignored for so long was apparent in the condition of the world in general and the United States in particular. An old saying among these groups suggests that if only the law of averages was at work, something would go right on occasion; because they saw so much amiss in the world, it simply had to be planned.[2] Active in this conspiracy were said to be the educational system and mass media of the nation. Together, the two were brainwashing the nation into accepting a different interpretation of the role of the nation, family, and individual. This new interpretation, of course, was to conform to the rules of the string pullers, the mysterious "Them" and their quest for world government. Unfortunately for believing Christians, something of a similar worldview began to grow among prophecy writers in the 1960s and 1970s.

### *Prophecy and Conspiracy Theory in the Atomic Age*

One of the hallmarks of prophecy writings in the second half of the twentieth century has been a resolute belief that the technological advances in the area of weaponry is a sure sign of the soon coming of Jesus Christ. Though many would question how in the world these seemingly unrelated events are tied together, authors such as M. R. DeHaan, Charles Taylor, and James Reid all saw the fulfillment of prophecy in the mushroom clouds that formed over detonated bombs. Moreover, there was a firmly held belief that the rise of the computer spelled social, economic, and political control, the creation of nothing less than the feared and anticipated Antichrist system. As pointed out early in this book, since at least 1776 each generation of American Christians has believed that it would be the last. Some Christian writers acknowledge this, but all claim this is the first generation to be truly able to fill the role of the terminal generation. Indeed, Charles Taylor was so sure of it that he stated specific years for the return of Christ. Those mentioned include 1976, 1980, 1988, and 1992. Despite his inaccurate predictions, Taylor remained one of the most respected prophecy teachers in Christian America.[3] In this worldview, Christian and secular conspiracy theorists alike found much on which they could agree.

Civil unrest at home and Communist advances abroad made for a disturbing picture of the work of the ubiquitous hidden hand at work. Although conspiracy theory usually takes a sweeping view of international events, at this time it would zero in on domestic issues, too. The creation of the welfare state under President Johnson was one of those issues.

## The Vietnam War

Lyndon Johnson was faced with a number of domestic and international challenges during his time in office. Supporting

Kennedy's civil rights stand in 1963 and 1964, Johnson helped fulfill part of the late president's social agenda. Johnson, however, had a social agenda of his own that went beyond Kennedy's New Frontier. Johnson's vision was dubbed the Great Society and would be created by a war on poverty in the United States. A series of programs ranging from Head Start to school hot lunches was implemented in an effort to aid society's less fortunate in the most wealthy nation on earth. Immensely expensive, the Great Society might have fared better had it not been for the war in southeast Asia. Johnson faced international challenges in other places, too; all of this put a tremendous amount of pressure on Kennedy's successor.[4]

Following the Berlin crisis in 1961, when the Communist regime in East Germany built the infamous wall to stem the outward flow of its freedom-hungry people, Kennedy had made his well-publicized trip to Berlin where he proclaimed his solidarity with the besieged people of that city. Johnson continued this support of Berlin and opposition to Communism. In fact, there was little variation between the foreign policies of the presidents from the time of Truman through Gerald Ford. Johnson also continued, although with less energy, Kennedy's policy of improving relations with Latin America. This was done primarily through the Alliance for Progress program meant to improve relations between the United States and its neighbors to the south. Unfortunately, American progress in this area was less than impressive. With the rise of an enormously expensive war overseas, interest in Latin America waned. Of course the biggest problem facing President Johnson and the nation was the growing war in Vietnam.[5] For conspiracy theorists, the war was merely a ploy to bleed America's resources further in an effort to weaken us and then absorb us into a world government.

Although John Kennedy had increased the number of military personnel in South Vietnam, it was under Lyndon Johnson that the total number of ground forces would swell to over half a million. By 1964 American forces numbered some twenty thousand "advisors" in that nation, some of whom were flying combat missions on behalf of South Vietnam. In August of that

year, the Gulf of Tonkin resolution was passed in the U.S. Congress. Based on the accusation that North Vietnamese gunboats
had attacked American vessels in the Tonkin Gulf, it essentially
gave the president unlimited power to do what he would to
crush the Communist North. Two days before the passage of
the resolution, American warplanes began bombing North Vietnam. This led to a massive American involvement in Southeast
Asia that split the American people and caused some of the
most serious domestic confrontations in more than a century.
America had entered a conflict it had no idea of how to win and
it was not willing to commit to winning. The war would drag
on through Johnson's administration and into that of his successor, Richard Nixon. The legacy of Vietnam was a divided
nation, nearly sixty thousand dead, and a nation very shy about
being a world leader in the 1970s.[6]

### Nixon and Vietnam

During Richard Nixon's time in office, the Vietnam War
showed no signs of ending. The 1968 Tet offensive was still dis-
proving American estimations of when the war might be over.
Added to this was the American invasion of eastern Cambodia
to clear out Vietcong supply dumps and bases in the Parrot's
Beak region. Intensive bombing of the North, secret wars in
Laos and Cambodia, and the ultimate failure of the American
leadership to properly define military objectives led to massive
demonstrations at home and abroad. Responding to the pressure, Nixon began withdrawal of 140,000 American ground
forces by the end of 1970. The reduction continued, as did what
officials called the "Vietnamization" of the war. It simply meant
turning the conflict over to a better-trained South Vietnamese
army. By any measure, it was a dismal failure.[7]

Realizing that the South Vietnamese were in no position to
win the war, Nixon's secretary of state, Henry Kissinger, engaged
in secret negotiations with Le Duc Tho, his counterpart from
North Vietnam. A cease-fire was arranged on January 27, 1973,
but both sides quickly violated it. The United States responded
with an enormous resumption of bombing, including over

Hanoi. Still, there was no more desire in the American government or public to reintroduce more troops. The result was a continued withdrawal with the full knowledge that the South would collapse as soon as the United States was gone. On April 29, 1975, the last of the American forces left Saigon, then renamed Ho Chi Minh City, and ended the longest war in American history. For the Vietnamese people, it had been a war against outsiders for more than thirty years. Although peace was welcomed and the war won, the Communist regime of Vietnam quickly proved it could do nothing to improve the standard of living of its people.[8]

### *Détente*

In the United States, the war's end was not even on Richard Nixon's watch. The Watergate scandal had caused the collapse of his administration and resulted in the coming to power of Gerald Ford, his vice president. Ironically, Nixon's first vice president, Spiro Agnew of Maryland, had resigned as a result of financial misdealing. Although it was a time of disgrace for Nixon, he had accomplished a few of his foreign policy goals, namely opening relations with the People's Republic of China and the beginning of a policy called détente with the Soviet Union. Relations with the Chinese improved when they saw the U.S. withdrawal from South Vietnam. To show their interest in relations with the United States, they invited an American ping-pong team to compete in the People's Republic. Shortly thereafter, Nixon began negotiations leading to his Peking visit with Chou En-lai and Mao Tse-tung. The fighting on the Chinese-Soviet border helped make improved relations with the Americans more attractive to the Communist rulers, too.[9]

By the end of Gerald Ford's term, *détente* had become a word of derision, with conservative Republicans and some Democrats demanding a change. In 1976, when Jimmy Carter's victory gave the Democrats control of the White House, the cold war only intensified. The Soviets realized that America was in something of a holding pattern in terms of challenging Communism or any outside threat. Besides, Jimmy Carter would prove himself a less than convincing advocate of American power in the world. While the United States was occupied in Vietnam during the 1960s and 1970s, events in another part of the world also demanded American action and leadership. The Middle East, more than any region, would excite opinions both pro and con among conservative Christians and conspiracy theory advocates.

## Strife in the Middle East

The Middle East has been a cauldron of trouble for the peoples in that region and for the two superpowers for decades. After the successful Israeli foray into the Sinai in 1956, the Jewish state found itself the target of increased terrorist attacks from the Fedayeen and then, beginning in 1964, the Palestine Liberation Organization (PLO). Realizing that they could not at that time defeat the Israeli armed forces on the field of battle, Palestinian radicals with Arab support sought out such targets as school buses, nurseries, kibbutzim, and synagogues. Their aim was nothing less than the complete and total destruction of the state of Israel.[10]

Israel is an affront to Islam. By its very existence it suggests that Islam's message of Muslim control of the Middle East is suspect, if for no other reason than that Israel has controlled the Temple Mount since 1967. The conflict in the Middle East is at least as much about religion as it is about territory and a national homeland for the Palestinian Arabs. The post-1964 PLO attacks were led by a number of individuals, but the most influential was Yassir Arafat. Educated in Egypt and a disciple of Gamal Nasser, Arafat believed that nothing less than *jihad*— a holy war—would drive the Israelis into the sea and thus cleanse the region of Jewish control. In early 1967 the surrounding Arab nations agreed with him and decided to try a frontal assault against what they called the "Zionist entity."[11]

Announcing on radio their intentions of wiping Israel off the map with vivid descriptions of the streets of Tel Aviv "running red with Jewish blood," the Egyptian-led Arab nations prepared for an all-out assault on Israel. A few Syrian and Jordanian radio stations even bragged that the displaced Palestinians (as well as Arabs currently living in Israel) could have their choice of the best of Jewish properties. Clearly alarmed at the prospects of a major conflict, the Israelis struck first. After the Israeli air force destroyed the combined air forces of six Arab nations, the Israel Defense Forces quickly moved into Sinai and marched to the canal zone. In the process, the IDF inflicted massive losses of men and materiel on the Egyptian army. Gamal Nasser, the leading Arab figure in the Middle East, was humiliated at the magnitude of defeat.

In the Golan Heights, the high ground from which Syrian artillery shelled the Galilee, the Israelis had a difficult time overcoming the opposition. In the West Bank and especially Gaza, the Jordanians received Israeli warnings to stay out of the conflict—despite King Hussein's funding of PLO attacks from the area. Ignoring the warning, even after the Egyptians had been all but pulverized, Jordan entered the war and was quickly dispatched. It was at this point that the West Bank—what Israelis call Judea and Samaria—was taken over to preclude further terrorist attacks. It seems strange that today one gets the impression from the press that the Israelis simply walked in one day and took over the West Bank and Gaza without provocation. They were repeatedly attacked from the territories and finally took precautions to ensure that no further assaults from the region would occur.

Grand as the taking of Sinai and the West Bank were militarily, nothing compared to the retaking of the Old City, the Jewish Quarter of Jerusalem, site of the Wailing Wall. Judaism once again had access to its most holy site, long denied to Jewish worshipers. Interestingly, the Israelis never closed the Dome of the Rock to Muslim believers, nor holy sites to Christians as the Jordanians had. Indeed, the Jordanians had gone out of their way to desecrate Jewish cemeteries and synagogues, using many of them as public rest rooms. Israel had returned to the Temple Mount as a nation for the first time since the Roman forces under Titus had destroyed Herod's magnificent structure. Jerusalem was under Jewish control after nearly two thousand years. The

1967 war, which the Israelis were not supposed to win, was over in less than a week, earning it the name Six-Day War.[12]

### The Significance of the Middle East in Prophecy

The successful recapture of Jerusalem in 1967 marked an important date on the prophetic calendars of many conservative Christians. Millions of prophecy believers immediately saw the significance of the event in terms of Daniel's prophecy concerning Jerusalem being under control of the Gentiles until their time was up. In short, it meant that another prophesied event could be checked off the list of necessary happenings before the coming of Jesus. The recapture of the Old City set the stage for the next prophetic event, the rebuilding of the third temple on Mount Zion. The existence of the Dome of the Rock on the same site did not seem to deter any of those insisting that it was only a matter of time before construction would begin. Rumors were rampant in the next few years after 1967 that orders were in to American granite quarries from Israeli companies set to reconstruct the holy site, a strange idea given the amount of quality stone in Israel. As recently as 1992, a book entitled *Ready to Rebuild: The Imminent Plan to Rebuild the Last Days Temple* was published. This book detailed much the same plan for the third temple. Depending on your particular interpretation of prophecy, a person could begin counting down the "last generation" (see Matthew 24) from either 1948 or 1967. If 1948 is your benchmark, a generation (forty years) has already passed; if 1967, when the Israelis took control of East Jerusalem, a generation will not pass until 2007. When the year 1988 came and went, counting from 1948 quietly went out of vogue in Christian circles. It is worth mentioning that in the autumn of that year some Christian believers held forth the idea that sometime between Rosh Hashanah and Yom Kippur the end would come.[13]

### The War of Attrition and the Yom Kippur War

The conclusion of the Six-Day War and the recapture of Jerusalem did not end the state of war between Israel and her

Arab neighbors. Between 1967 and the 1973 Yom Kippur War there was a conflict called the War of Attrition. This war was essentially a stepped-up terrorist campaign on the part of an increasingly fractionalized PLO, Egypt, and Syria. On constant alert, the Israelis responded with air strikes and counterterrorist tactics.[14] At the same time, hundreds of thousands of Jewish immigrants made their way to Eretz Yisrael, with more than 90 percent settling in the pre-1967 border area. Others settled in the occupied territories on the theory that terrorist attacks from these areas would be much more difficult with a permanent Jewish presence. Attack and counterattack were the order of the day during this difficult period, but this time also saw remarkable growth in the relationship between Israel and the United States. The two nations had been on cordial terms since 1948, but during the 1967 war when the Soviets were supporting the Arabs, the Americans came down firmly on the side of the Jewish state.

All did not go well, however, as the sinking of an American intelligence-gathering vessel called the *Liberty* demonstrated. Mistaking it for an Egyptian ship of similar capabilities, the Israelis repeatedly attacked the ship before discovering their mistake.[15] Some have suggested, particularly anti-Israeli elements in the United States, that the attack was deliberate and calculated. If so, the reason behind the Israeli action was to prevent any information concerning troop movements and air attacks from inadvertently making their way to the Egyptians via the Americans. Still, it is a strange argument to make, that the Jewish state was willing to sacrifice American goodwill and aid in the interests of sinking a ship. The Israelis apologized and America accepted the explanation of events. It would be one of a number of times when the friendship between the two powers would undergo a considerable test.

The next major confrontation between Israel and her Arab neighbors was what became known as the Yom Kippur War. Anwar Sadat, Nasser's successor, launched an attack from Egypt and her Arab allies on the holiest day of the Jewish year. The Israelis were caught flat-footed, in part because of their fear of negative world press. In the previous conflict, the Israelis had been accused of launching an attack without proper cause. The October War of 1973 was the probable cause. Egypt swept into the Sinai, overrunning Israeli positions and forcing a general retreat. Tel Aviv was bombed, as were portions of Jerusalem. Israel's prime minister, Golda Meir, pleaded with Secretary of State Henry Kissinger and President Richard Nixon for help in repulsing the attack. The Americans responded with a massive shipment of M–60 tanks and Phantom jet fighter-bombers. Within a few weeks of receiving the materiel, the Israelis drove the invaders back and once again reestablished control of Sinai, Gaza, the West Bank, and now the Golan Heights. The Arabs again lost billions of dollars in equipment and tens of thousands of casualties. Enraged Soviet leader Leonid Brezhnev then put the Red Army on alert, making motions that he intended to send Russian forces into the Middle East. In response, Nixon put U.S. forces on worldwide alert, signaling the Soviets that a move on their part would be met with a massive American response. The Soviets backed down. The Yom Kippur War was over but it had three noteworthy outcomes: an extremely costly Israeli victory, much closer Israeli ties to the United States, and the OPEC (Oil Producing and Exporting Countries or Cartel) imposition of an oil embargo against nations supporting Israel. Nonetheless, there were signs of hope. Against great odds there was finally a meeting between Israel and Egypt to discuss peace.[16]

During the term of Jimmy Carter, a most unusual and even unexpected event took place: the meeting at Camp David of Carter, Israeli Prime Minister Menachem Begin, and Egyptian President Anwar Sadat. After considerable debate—shouting matches in some cases—the parties emerged with a peace treaty. In exchange for recognizing Israel as a legitimate nation, the Egyptians would have the Sinai returned to them. Israel also promised to begin to look into a permanent settlement of the Palestinian issue. It was a time of euphoria in the diplomatic world, but the agreement had earned enemies for both sides, especially for Mr. Sadat. In 1981 the Egyptian president was the victim of a PLO and Islamic fundamentalist-sanctioned assassination for what they saw as betrayal of their cause. Although the peace treaty remained in effect, it was essentially a cold peace, with neither side doing much to solve some of the broader issues in the region. For some in the Christian community, the peace treaty was a great hazard to Israel and instigated by none other than Satan himself. Some Christians feared it was the "final peace" or its harbinger before the coming of Antichrist.[17]

### Questionable Christian Prophecy Teachings on the Middle East

Wim Malgo, a Dutch-born Christian writer, was the founder of Midnight Call Ministries and Beth Shalom Association for Bible Study in Israel. Malgo was an ardent supporter of Israel, as are many conservative Christians, and published periodicals reflecting this outlook. *News from Israel* and *Midnight Call* contained articles with prophecy-laden messages warning of the soon-coming of Jesus Christ. One of Malgo's most passionate booklets, entitled "Begin with Sadat," offered pleas for the Israelis to reject the peace process and for Christians to enter into prayer on behalf of the Jewish state. Some of the arguments offered were less than compelling, especially when punctuated with photographs of Begin holding a napkin folded in the shape of Israel's borders and Sadat wearing a tie with a swastika on it as proof of God's warning.[18]

Another Christian writer who feared for Israel's safety was Mary Stewart Relfe, whose books *When Your Money Fails* and *The New Money System* became best-sellers among Christians in the early 1980s. Relfe contended that Sadat could possibly be the Antichrist himself and that, despite his assassination, was still the closest thing to the Antichrist yet. With statements like "I maintain Sadat is History's nearest prototype of the Jewish false Messiah!"[19] the author leaves little room to maneuver. Like Malgo, Relfe used some of the strangest bits of information as evidence of the fulfillment of prophecy. Some of the items offered as proof were such things as the existence of an October 6 avenue in Cairo (date of the Yom Kippur War) and the fact that Sadat visited Israel six years after the Yom Kippur War on October 6, on a ship with "666" painted on the side.[20]

Apparently the appearance of the number 6 was enough to excite some into seeing the Antichrist system in everything from an address to license plates.

One of the more common occurences among prophecy teachers during the postwar period was the relative lack of any formal theological education. For instance, Hilton Sutton, Salem Kirban, and Jack Van Impe operated ministries as individual enterprises. Others, such as Tim LaHaye, attended Bob Jones University and subsequent to that began a widespread topical ministry—centering on prophecy and conspiracy theory.[21] Paul Boyer, in a magnificent overview of American prophecy belief, states the following:

> Far from apologizing for their lack of credentials or denominational standing, these writers offered it as evidence for the trustworthiness of their message. The genre exuded suspicion of the mainstream Protestant establishment with its formal hierarchies. . . . In novels such as Dan Betzer's *Beast,* the learned ministers of fashionable churches invariably express contempt for the Rapture, only to repent bitterly when the event actually occurs.[22]

As for the Jewish state itself, it had chilly relations at best with the Egyptians, mostly over Israel's insistence on taking action against any perceived threats to its national security. Israel would be criticized for this from many quarters, but in 1981 the outrage was worldwide.

### Israeli Foreign Policy in a Culture of Prophecy

One of the broader misunderstandings of Israeli foreign policy has been what many Americans see as a gratuitous use of force. A point in question was the Begin government's decision to bomb the Iraqi nuclear facility called Osirak near Baghdad on June 7, 1981. Fearing that the Iraqis were nearing the capability of building a nuclear weapon, Begin authorized an air strike to destroy the French-built nuclear plant. The attack effected near complete destruction on the reactor in a textbook case of a surgical air strike. Undoubtedly, the Iraqis had planned on building a nuclear device and using it on Tel Aviv—as Saddam Hussein had himself proclaimed. There was a blast of negative public opinion over the attack, but secretly the Israelis were admired for the professionalism of the attack and, in the words of some, the necessity of dealing with a threat. When the United States and its allies were at war with Iraq ten years later, they had the Israelis to thank for Baghdad's lack of atomic weaponry. Little or no attention was paid to this fact, however.[23]

Despite Sadat's death, the peace treaty has held between Israel and Egypt. There have been some very difficult periods. Probably the most serious test of the peace was Israel's invasion in 1982 of southern Lebanon in an attempt to rid itself of terrorist attacks into Galilee once and for all. Code-named Operation Peace for Galilee, the attack force quickly struck into Lebanon and was joined by Israel's Christian Lebanese allies. Seizing enormous stocks of weaponry, some of which were not part of the PLO arsenal, the Israelis drove the PLO into Beirut, where some of the worst scenes of the war took place. The basic premise of the attack as envisioned by Prime Minister Begin was to destroy the PLO without entering Beirut; under pressure from Ariel Sharon, Minister of Defense, the goals changed. Western media has seldom been kind to the Israelis in recent years, but in the wake of the Peace for Galilee attack they became positively rabid. Editorials on network news accused the Israelis of trying to do with military might what they could not do domestically through diplomacy.

Since the Israeli withdrawal from Lebanon and the creation of the Christian militia security zone, the main concern about the Arab-Israeli conflict has to do with what is called the Intifada, or uprising. The Intifada began as something of a groundswell of small, local uprisings in the Gaza Strip and the West Bank among average Palestinians walking the streets of Jericho, Nablus, and Gaza. The PLO, having proven that tactics ranging from Olympic terrorism to head-to-head conflict with the IDF in south Lebanon were not gaining any ground, quickly seized on a movement actually outside of their planning. It is entirely possible that this tactic will be the harbinger of change in the Middle East quagmire, leading to negotiations and eventually a Palestinian homeland in the occupied territories. While not yet in sight, the creation of this Palestinian homeland (something that was rejected in 1948) could provide a degree of stability in the world's most turbulent area.[24] The February–March 1994 outrage over the murder of twenty-nine Palestinian Muslim worshipers was just one expression of the extremely deep feelings among both Jewish and Islamic fundamentalists regarding the issue of the land and the religious implications thereof. So, too, was the late 1995 murder of Yitzak Rabin, the Israeli Prime Minister, by a religious Jewish zealot against the land-for-peace idea. As with most things in the Middle East, there are no easy answers.

### Conspiracy Theorists and Events in the Middle East

It is with regard to the Middle East, particularly Israel, that contemporary conspiracy theorists find much to criticize and attack. To many of this mind-set, Israel is the icon of the conspiracy. "Zionists" are targeted as the chief source of trouble with American foreign policy over the last several decades. To many in conspiracy circles, U.S. policy is controlled by some unidentified Jewish conspiracy with aid to Israel as the bottom line. Little or nothing is said about Arab terrorism, the PLO's general acceptance of the *Protocols of the Learned Elders of Zion* as truthful history, and the PLO's desire to drive Israel into the sea. The reason for U.S. support of Israel, according to conspiracy advocates, is to have a center of operation outside the United States for the Rothschilds and others. The Jewish invasion of Palestine would make this possible. Indeed, some conspiracy writers believe the United States is so far gone that America is nothing less than a nation under Zionist political occupation (or Zionist Occupational Government—ZOG). These same people also either deny outright that the Holocaust happened or minimize it. The anti-Israel, anti-Semitic conspiracy theorists are among the chief supporters of the Arab nations surrounding the Jewish state. These ultra-right-wing supporters of the Arab states found themselves on the same side as the Soviet Union, a strong supporter of the Arab states. This seems to be a contradiction, since most conspiracy theorists hate Communism and what it stands for. It seems that hatred of Jews has united what would otherwise be diverse groups.[25]

### Jimmy Carter's Middle Eastern Woes

With the Carter administration's abject failure in foreign (and domestic) policy, the nation once again looked to another leader to change the direction in which America was going. The hostages in Iran and the Soviet invasion of Afghanistan presented Jimmy Carter with a couple of major league crises; unfortunately, Carter and his advisors, such as Cyrus Vance and Warren Christopher, were perceived to be handwringers at a loss for answers. In fairness to Carter, much of what happened in those two foreign policy debacles was beyond his ability to foresee. In the case of the Iran hostage situation, Carter allowed the Shah of Iran to enter the United States for cancer treatment, seemingly oblivious to the possible repercussions. True, the CIA did not anticipate the Iranian reaction of the Ayatollah Khomeini; on the other hand, it was during the Carter administration that the intelligence community had its budget slashed and was then blamed for its shortcomings.

Despite perceived ineptness as our nation's chief executive, Carter is best remembered among conspiracy advocates for his membership in a branch organization of the CFR known as the Trilateral Commission. The creation of David Rockefeller in 1973, the commission had as its stated goal the fostering of better relations among the United States, Japan, and the European Common Market. Zbigniew Brzezinski reportedly drafted the charter for the organization, which was openly advocating a global agenda. Membership numbers were smaller than the CFR, but the group had a significant impact during the 1970s and 1980s in guiding and advising policy makers in a variety of areas of common interest between these powers. The Trilateral Commission still exists and still provides presidents with advice and personnel for important trade or foreign policy posts. Nonetheless, it is for his abysmal foreign policy and economic fiasco (21 percent interest rates and over 20 percent inflation), not the Trilateral Commission, that the former Georgia governor was shown the White House door in favor of Ronald Reagan. Carter was perceived to be an honorable man but not entirely up to the role as leader of a great power.[26]

## The Reagan Years

Ronald Reagan ushered in what has been known as the Conservative Revolution. Reagan had been California's chief executive during the 1960s, when he continued to make a name for himself as a staunch anti-Communist and fiscal conservative. A supporter of Barry Goldwater in the 1964 election, Reagan was also remembered as the head of the Screen Actors Guild during the 1950s, when accusations were flying fast and furiously about Communist infiltration in the entertainment industry. As an actor, Reagan had appeared in a few memorable films, such as *Where Is the Rest of Me?* and *The Knute Rockne Story*, in which he played George Gipp. The nickname "Gipper" stuck with Reagan during his political career.[27]

To many Americans Ronald Reagan represented something of a return to the confidence America had possessed in the post-war years. Reagan was often quoted as saying that in international affairs he was not so interested in whether the United States was liked or not, but that we were respected. During the 1980 campaign, much as during his bid in 1976, the former California governor ran on a platform of strong national defense, tax cuts, an end to what he saw as a one-sided détente policy, and the cutting back of an increasingly intrusive government into the lives of Americans. When the dust had settled in November 1980, Reagan had buried Jimmy Carter in a landslide. The Reagan Revolution had begun.[28]

Despite his seemingly unimpeachable conservative credentials, members of the extreme right have always been suspicious of Ronald Reagan. Many of the ultra-rightists holding conspiracy views deemed Reagan little more than an active participant in the Plan whose rhetoric fell far short of any true conservative actions. Most of these views go back to the time of

Reagan's Hollywood days when he defended members of his profession (while at the same time taking a hard line against Communism). Conspiracy theorists watched his rise to power and prominence first as governor of California and eventually as president with a knowing smirk. He was one of "Them," a puppet of his CFR masters; to make matters worse, Reagan was also a Mason. The combination of the two made his presidency little better than that of Johnson, Nixon, Ford, or Carter. This is one of the hallmarks of the conspiracy mind-set: It matters not who is elected or what the circumstances; everything has been planned. A statement attributed to FDR is often quoted among these circles and is a summary of their worldview: "If things in politics happen in a certain manner, you can be sure they were planned that way."

What conspiracy theorists see as the major strikes against Reagan, and every president since FDR, is the large number of Council on Foreign Relations members in his administration. The CFR, you will recall, is often referred to as the hub of the American Illuminati among conspiracy advocates. It is true that many administrations have tapped the CFR for qualified State Department personnel; the major reason would appear to be that this invitation-only organization comprises some of the most brilliant and capable individuals in the field. There are Democrats and Republicans in the CFR, conservatives and liberals, some sharing world government views, others against them. Reagan set the record for having the most CFR and Trilateral Commission members in his government until the election of George Bush, and conspiracy theorists have never forgotten it.[29]

### The Bilderberger Group

Another organization that has figured highly in conspiracy literature over the last forty years or so is a semisecret group known as the Bilderberger group. Named for a hotel in Belgium where they first met, the group comprises some of the most wealthy and powerful people in the Western world. Banking houses represented by the Rockefellers and Rothschilds are generally in attendance at the annual meetings. The agendas

at these get-togethers are, of course, secret, but many have speculated about the nature of the topics. Conspiracy groups, such
as Liberty Lobby—the publishers of the rabidly anti-Semitic,
anti-Israel paper *Spotlight*—published a booklet containing all
that was in their archives concerning the Bilderberger group.
What emerges is clear-cut evidence that the organization does
indeed exist (something one needn't be a conspiracy theorist
to recognize) and that it has met under varying degrees of
secrecy since the 1950s. Judging from the limited amount of
material on this cryptic organization, its concerns are chiefly
in economic affairs, especially as it concerns the free world.
Since Liberty Lobby is already predisposed to assign conspiracy to international banking, its logic merely follows a predictable end: The group is meeting to order the world's affairs,
especially economic ones. The Bilderbergers may indeed have
world economic and even political unity in mind, but we really
do not know. The argument stating this as fact, therefore, tends
to be based on speculation rather than documentation.[30] As for
Ronald Reagan, his personal involvement in these groups is
difficult to nail down. The only sure thing is that he made many
appointments of individuals with ties to the CFR.

### Reagan's Fiscal Policy as the Basis
### of Later Conspiracy Theory

Reagan's first term in office saw recession rebound into the
fastest growing economy since World War II, due largely to the
tax cuts pushed through Congress. Unfortunately, Reagan left
America with another legacy that threatens to seriously impair
our economy unless steps are taken to correct it. Entering office,
Reagan was horrified over the $60 billion deficit under the
Carter administration's last year in office; by the time Reagan
left the oval office in 1989, the national debt had topped $3 tril-
lion. The tax cuts, which nearly doubled tax receipts, were off-
set by the inability of Congress to match them with spending
cuts. The result was that deficits yearly added to the debt, rolling
like a river with the power of compounding interest. By 1989
the interest on the national debt had reached the point where

it was one of the largest budget items. Bad as the budget situation was during the 1980s, George Bush would set the new administration record with deficits of $153.5 billion, $220.5 billion, $268.7 billion, and in his final year in office, nearly $400 billion. America now had an outstanding national debt of nearly $5 trillion—on budget. The off-budget items would approximately double this amount, setting the stage for what could possibly cause a depression.[31]

Although Ronald Reagan won another landslide victory over his Democratic opponent Walter Mondale in 1984, his presidency was crippled as a result of illegal activity coming out of the National Security Agency. Adm. John Poindexter, Col. Oliver North, and a number of others masterminded a highly controversial secret policy. In their effort to obtain freedom for the hostages held in Lebanon, these men and others arranged for arms shipments to Iran in exchange for the release of the hostages. The cash paid for the arms was then used to fund the anti-Sandanista Contras of Nicaragua. The operation was uncovered and the American people witnessed a nationally televised congressional hearing into the whole affair. Special prosecutor John Walsh found neither Reagan nor his vice president, George Bush, guilty of wrongdoing. North was acquitted on appeal as well and even ran and lost a bid for a Senate seat in his home state of Virginia in 1994.[32]

The end of Reagan's two terms in office presented mixed results in terms of his conservative agenda. The worst of the 1980s probably had to do with the deepening national debt and the inability or lack of concern of American political leaders to do anything about it. The next election, in 1988, saw yet another Republican come to power. George Bush, even more than Ronald Reagan, was looked on as a tool of the Establishment.

## George Bush

George Bush was by any measure a consummate Washington insider. He had an unsuccessful run for the U.S. Senate in 1964, when he was defeated by Democratic incumbent, Ralph

Yarborough. Two years later, in 1966, Bush ran for the Seventh District seat in the House of Representatives and won. As an ambitious young Republican, he began to attract the attention of the Republican National Committee. In 1970 Bush again ran against Yarborough and was defeated a second time. Although Yarborough did not have the support of an incumbent president in 1970, he did have the support of Governor John Connally, possibly the most powerful politician in Texas at the time. Despite this defeat, Bush went on to represent the United States in the United Nations during Nixon's first term. Although lacking in diplomatic experience, Bush was perceived to be a star on the rise and served with distinction in the international body. When the Nationalist Chinese were expelled from the United Nations in favor of Communist China representation, Bush was furious over the betrayal of a valued friend. Strangely enough, Bush and the Chinese Communists would cross paths again, albeit on better terms. Bush would be designated the U.S. ambassador to China in 1974.[33]

Before George Bush would go to China, however, he had the highly difficult job of Chairman of the National Republican Committee. Bush's job was unenviable because his tenure occurred during the Watergate fiasco, doubtless one of the Republican Party's most difficult periods since its founding in the 1850s. Bush did his best to push the Republican agenda.

When Gerald Ford took over after the Nixon resignation, he sought to reward Bush with a diplomatic position of his choice. The future president immediately responded by asking for the China post. Prior to leaving for his diplomatic mission in Peking, Bush understood that he was also to shortly thereafter take over the directorship of the Central Intelligence Agency.[34] Bush was nominated and passed congressional investigation to become the head of the CIA in early 1975. Many within the agency considered him a political appointment and, as such, not worthy of the respect normally given a career intelligence employee. Bush again served with distinction until he was replaced after the 1976 presidential victory of Jimmy Carter. The Texas oilman stepped down and pondered his next political move. He didn't have to think too long about what course of action to take.

In 1979 George Bush announced himself a candidate for the office of president of the United States. Having an initial good showing in Iowa, it soon became apparent that the choice of the majority of Republicans was Ronald Reagan. Although there were differences of opinion between the two, Reagan and Bush mended fences after Reagan won the nomination, and Bush became the Gipper's running mate. The size of their 1980 victory seemed to indicate public satisfaction with both Reagan's policies and his selection for vice president.

As in his previous posts, Bush served with distinction as a vice president. The most serious problem he faced had to do with the Iran-Contra affair; throughout the investigations he maintained that actions taken were without his knowledge or consent. It did not hurt him politically, for in 1988 he obtained his party's nomination for president of the United States. He was running against the tide of history, however, as no sitting vice president had been elected president since Martin Van Buren succeeded Andrew Jackson. In yet another landslide victory, the Bush camp defeated a poorly run Dukakis campaign. One of the most unusual aspects of the whole campaign had to do with the Bush running-mate selection of Dan Quayle of Indiana. A young, good-looking candidate for the position, Quayle had solid conservative credentials but lacked experience.

During George Bush's first year in power, a truly remarkable series of events took place in Eastern Europe that would forever change the nature of East-West relations. In late 1989 and early 1990 Communism, that seemingly intractable force holding the peoples of the Soviet bloc captive, simply fell apart. From the uprising in Romania and execution of their bloodthirsty dictator to the Velvet Revolution of Czechoslovakia, there was no doubt that times had changed in the Communist world. Probably the most symbolic event of the fall of Communism, however, was the demolition of the Berlin Wall and the reunification of Germany. Western ideas, always popular among the young in the old Soviet bloc, now were voiced freely. Nation after nation in Europe threw off the yoke of Communism and entered the testy waters of free market economies and democracy. The Soviet Union itself broke into republics under the leadership of Mikhail Gorbachev. Although today the old Soviet Empire lies in ruins, the world is faced with new dangers. The revival of nationalism in places like Russia, the Ukraine, and Georgia indicate a troubled road ahead for the new nations.

In the minds of conspiracy theorists, the end of the cold war paved the way for the arrival of the New World Order. Incredible as the fall of Communism was in 1989, events in the Middle East would once again dominate headlines and the attention of policy makers.

### *Desert Shield and Desert Storm*

Without a doubt, the greatest challenge facing the Bush administration was the Middle East crisis in the Persian Gulf. This part of the world has proven to be a headache for American presidents from Truman to Clinton. During the summer of 1990, however, events in that troubled region took a very definite turn for the worse when Iraq invaded its neighbor to the south, Kuwait. Claiming that British and French division of the Middle East had robbed the Iraqis of some of their territory (Kuwait), Iraqi dictator Saddam Hussein sent in his enormous army into the virtually defenseless Arab state. Fearful of a wider war, the United States convinced the House of Saud that Hussein had designs on the Arabian oil fields. Reluctantly acquiescing to American military intelligence, the Saudis allowed the buildup of American troops in Arabia during the late summer, fall, and early winter 1990. Called Desert Shield, the initial operation was to prevent any further Iraqi invasion. By October, the buildup had reached the point where the United States and her allies were clearly intent on driving the Iraqis from Kuwait altogether.[35]

On the night of January 16, 1991, the United States and her allies unleashed an air assault against Baghdad and other targets with nearly every weapon in their air arsenal. Among those joining the traditional American allies were the Syrian and Gulf

State forces. The new Stealth fighter-bomber began the attack, reaching the Iraqi capital undetected. This was followed by an onslaught of Tomahawk cruise missiles launched from battleships and submarines in what is now remembered as a famous display of technological firepower. The destruction was thorough and sustained. In fact, sorties continued until the ground war began. It was the most impressive display of air power against an entrenched foe in the history of warfare. And, as if the fighter attacks were not enough, American B–52s engaged in sustained attacks against the elite Iraqi Republican Guard forces in Kuwait. To say Iraqi forces were demoralized would be a grand understatement.[36]

Before the ground war began, there were some extremely nervous moments in keeping the American-led alliance together. The Iraqis, true to their word, began launching Scud missile attacks against Israel. Going against every human instinct to strike back, the Israelis did not respond militarily against Iraq in deference to American requests. Instead, the United States engaged in seek-and-destroy missions against the mobile Scud launchers in western Iraq. Israeli pilots nonetheless maintained round-the-clock vigilance and preparation for an all-out assault on their Iraqi foe. The Israelis brought out their intermediate-range ballistic missiles in plain sight to send a message to Hussein. These missiles in all likelihood contained nuclear warheads and would most certainly have been launched had chemical weapons been used in the bombardment against the Jewish state. Happily, this did not happen and Israeli Prime Minister Yitzak Shamir did not have to make an enormously weighty decision.[37]

The ground war portion of the conflict was almost anticlimactic by comparison. Initial estimates of tens of thousands of American dead were far off the mark. The actual campaign took approximately one hundred hours and presented a watching public with some remarkable scenes of mass surrender by the highly vaunted Republican Guard. The worst damage was probably environmental. Saddam Hussein ordered the polluting of the Persian Gulf and the dynamiting of hundreds of oil wells. Originally it was believed that it would take up to a decade to put out all of the fires; it required only eighteen months. No march on Baghdad took place, and almost as soon as the allied forces returned home the Iraqi dictator resumed his genocide of the Kurds in the north of Iraq and the slaughter of Shiite Muslims in the delta swamp regions between the Tigris and Euphrates Rivers. In a strange footnote, George Bush's political career did not survive the 1992 election, and he went into retirement. As of this writing, Saddam Hussein is still in power.[38] Conspiracy theorists see this war as the "test case" for the use of UN forces to enforce and maintain world government.

## The Rise of Financial Conspiracy Theories

Since the Gulf War and the election of Bill Clinton, the world is still a very dangerous place. Regional conflicts, such as that in Bosnia, bear testimony to this sad fact. Whether or not the United States continues to bear the lion's share of world leadership remains to be seen; there are definitely some in the Clinton administration who favor a much more active international role for the United States in the future. The impact of such a policy is questionable at best. Most Americans, I believe, would not favor surrender of any national sovereignty to the United Nations or any international collective.

Although America has faced serious foreign policy issues since World War II, it has also carried with it a society that has undergone enormous change. The metamorphosis is so pronounced, so overwhelming, that it is something akin to a quantum leap in perception, of mind-set if you will. It is metaphysical yet quite tangible. The Age of Aquarius has arrived.

# Conspiracy and the Age of Aquarius

In this two-century overview of American conspiracy theories we now come to one current movement that many have labeled a conspiracy. I am referring, of course, to the New Age movement. Interest in mysticism and the occult has always been around, but in the 1960s and early 1970s the counterculture helped to spur and revive study of non-Western beliefs. This popular cultural uprising was just one root of the Aquarian tree; other far more intellectual and spiritual taproots include a variety of mystical and philosophical schools of the nineteenth century. Esoteric groups such as the Theosophy Society provided important philosophical underpinnings common in today's New Age dogma. What was once merely a colorful and unusual lifestyle typified at Haight-Ashbury, Big Sur, or any number of other counterculture centers has now donned the garb of respectability and entered mainstream America. The curiosity of yesterday has become a movement today; some see it as a challenge to orthodox Christianity in America that cannot be ignored. It is, in a sense, westernized Hinduism. This sociological and spiritual groundswell is the topic of this chapter and has in it much more of the traditional attributes of conspiracy than anything yet explored.

## "New Age" Origins

During the last half of the twentieth century some of the greatest social, political, military, and religious changes in world history have taken place. Perhaps never before has there been as rapid a shift in worldview among a nation's population as what the United States has experienced since the early 1960s; some see cultural changes as great as those in the Persian Empire after Alexander the Great's conquest, or the transition from paganism to Christianity in the Roman world. To many conservative Christians, it appears that the United States is on a cultural and historical cusp from which there is now no retreat. There has been a paradigm shift in general consciousness.[1]

The Judeo-Christian tradition, which had provided our nation and Western civilization with its moral underpinnings, has now come under both direct and surreptitious attack. To a great extent this tradition has been replaced with apathy, amoralism, political correctness, and in some limited cases a renewal of ancient mystery religions and occult practices. For those who see the emerging worldview and religion as a form of salvation, it is welcomed with open arms; for those who treasure traditional Western values, it is perceived as a time of difficult adjustment and in some cases, danger. The New Age movement is not a phenomenon that simply popped out of the 1960s counterculture or even the mystical schools of the nineteenth century. To trace its origins, we need to go back to the mystery religions of the ancient Near East. For the sake of providing a brief historical overview, I will present some of the beliefs from the distant past before delving into more contemporary roots of neopaganism.

### The Same Old Lie

To begin with, the reader must understand that the term *New Age* is a misnomer. There is nothing new about the belief system. Boiled down to its essentials it is really nothing more than what orthodox Judaism and Christianity's Scriptures describe as the first and greatest lie: "Thou shalt be as gods." New Age beliefs teach that all of the human race are essentially gods on their way up the spiritual ladder. Through the cleansing of reincarnation one eventually reaches enlightenment and merges with the impersonal godhead.[2] Because New Agers believe there are many paths to God, it doesn't matter which one you choose to follow. What matters most is that we all ultimately show up at the celestial trophy ceremony in the end. There are therefore no absolutes, no right or wrong, only what the individual chooses at any given moment. Traditional Christians see this view as potentially dangerous; indeed, some have described such a philosophy as chillingly similar to Nazi or Communist beliefs: If my will and desire clash with yours, neither of us is truly right or wrong. The person with the will or power to have it his way will come out on top: It is essentially a doctrine of might makes right. If there is no standard, no absolute on which we measure behavior, all things are permissible. The person with the power to obtain what he or she wants wins. The person on the losing end has no recourse because, after all, the loss is relative.

Such a philosophy could even justify such moral outrages as the Holocaust; if there are no moral absolutes, no one can condemn the Nazis for any of their crimes. One does not have to go far in history to see examples of such a worldview. Mao Tsetung, Joseph Stalin, and Adolf Hitler carried the philosophy to its logical conclusion. For millennia philosophies of this nature have existed and exerted their influence in governments and societies. They are, in fact, quite ancient. For a glimpse at conservative Christianity's interpretation of the origins of this philosophy, we only need consult a work as familiar as the Book of Genesis.

### *The Nimrod Legend in Conspiracy*

According to some ministries dealing with the New Age phenomenon, any explanation of the contemporary movement needs to consult ancient, scriptural sources for answers: Indeed, some beliefs depend on legend and myth for explanation. According to the Genesis account, after the great flood, Noah and his family landed on the Mountains of Ararat, where they disembarked to begin a new life. The Genesis author, presumably Moses, tells us that God had destroyed the Earth in the deluge for a host of apparently gross spiritual infractions, most of which boiled down to the average human being seeking absolute, unfettered freedom of action and responsibility for his or her actions: in short, seeking personal deification. In this atmosphere, some postulate, it is possible that an organized "man as God" religion grew up, resulting in divine judgment. After the flood, one of Noah's grandsons, Nimrod (son of Cush), became a powerful leader.

Noted for his ability as a hunter, Nimrod became a spiritual as well as political personage of importance. Legend has it that he married a woman named Semiramis, said to be a woman of incredible beauty—and also Nimrod's own mother. Sometime after the consummation of this incestuous relationship, unknown persons assassinated Nimrod. Given the growth of his power and spiritual authority, it has been speculated that Nimrod was disposed of out of fear of a return to the mystery (man as God) religions that had existed prior to the flood. Remember, it was during Nimrod's reign that the famous Tower of Babel was built—a building that was supposed to reach God himself. The structure was probably a ziggurat that symbolized man-initiated efforts to attain deity. Nimrod's death, however, did not end the revival of the quest for self-deification.[3]

### The Semiramis Legend in Conspiracy

According to this legend, Nimrod's wife, Semiramis, gave birth to her late husband/son's child and named him Tammuz. She immediately proclaimed the baby to be Nimrod reborn: a reincarnated version of the now dead king. What is striking about Semiramis's proclamation and doctrine is how quickly it spread beyond the Fertile Crescent. Over the course of centuries the image of Semiramis with Tammuz at her breast would appear again and again on coins, pottery, and statues. As Tal Brooke, president of the conservative Christian think tank Spiritual Counterfeits Project, states in his book, *When the World Will Be as One*, "The secret wisdom of Babylon is a direct ancestor of India's mystical system, from its hidden wisdom of man's inner divinity and its priestly class, to its gods and goddesses."[4] This legend has persisted, although it has been given different names in different cultures. For instance, in ancient—and contemporary—India, mother and child have become Shakti; among the Greeks Semiramis became Artemis or Diana; with the Romans she was Cybele, wife of Jove. Her names have changed over time and place, but there she is: Whether she is called Europa, Minerva, or Ishtar matters not. She is the same deity adapted for different cultures and presenting the same message: "You shall be as gods." The identity of the messenger changes, but not the message.[5]

### The Babylonian Dance

According to some Christian scholars, the message of ancient Babylonian religion was the root for virtually every mystery religion that would follow. During Greek and Roman times, there was a proliferation of mystery cults, such as those honoring Bacchus and Mithras. During the Middle Ages in Europe, what is today identified as New Age philosophy could be found in a number of quarters, among them a collection of writings known as the *Kaballah*. Essentially a collection of Jewish mysticism, the *Kaballah* provided the basis for a host of mystery-oriented philosophies. The *Kaballah* is best remembered for an emphasis on numerology, or the belief that by assigning letters and words spiritual significance one can obtain a deeper meaning from Scripture. Although the *Kaballah* passed out of popularity several hundred years ago, it is enjoying something of a revival with the rise of Aquarian philosophy.

The underlying premise of any mystery religion is that man can become God. For a long time India was the primary place a person had to go to see evidence of this. No longer. The United States and Canada and other places around the world have witnessed the rise of the New Age movement and its revived ancient mystery religion. The age-old doctrine of personal deity has not lost its appeal with the passing of years; if anything, it provides the ultimate high for a generation perpetually seeking an ever greater thrill. What could be more intoxicating, more seductive, than power of this magnitude and potential? Nonetheless, for the average American the historical background of this belief system escapes notice or comprehension. To quote Brooke again, it is the same temptation repeated over the course of history: "Mystery Babylon dances through history, but her garments and dance remain the same. It is the forbidden fruit that men and women crave: sensual fulfillment and godhood, a hard combination to beat."[6]

Hard to beat, indeed. In the late twentieth century, there has been a move toward mysticism that is nothing less than phenomenal. Ranging from President Clinton's participation in New Age seminars to Nancy Reagan's belief and utilization of astrology, Aquarian mysticism knows no political ideology, cares not for national borders, and most alluring of all, promises godhood. If one considers the similarities, what is striking is how the seeming goal—what New Ager Marilyn Ferguson calls the "Aquarian Conspiracy"[7]—is for unity in both the tangible and metaphysical worlds. This unity is spiritual yet advocates economic and political unity as the natural outcome of the New World Order. It is interesting indeed how so many conspiracy theories over the previous two centuries were about those who sought political and economic control but lacked anything resembling networking or interactive planning. It is for this reason (among many others) that conspiracy theorists have not been taken seriously. Oddly enough, now, in the form of a spiritual movement, there are for the first time some elements of classic worldwide interaction, although not yet in the political and economic spectrum.

So what exactly do Christian prophecy and conspiracy theory believers believe the Aquarian Conspiracy holds for the world in general and the United States in particular? That depends to a great extent on the degree that it is able to win the allegiance of the people. Many Christians believe we are virtually at the threshold of the New World Order, what the Book of Revelation calls the "Whore of Babylon." It would in my opinion be necessary for something catastrophic to happen to trigger global acceptance of this faith.[8] The slow and continued growth of the

Aquarian Conspiracy to the point where it is the dominant worldview could also bring about the New World Order, but that could take decades, if indeed such an Eastern worldview would ever be universally accepted at all. There is also an obvious point to consider that many conspiracy believers fail to take into account: The whole New Age movement and Aquarian Conspiracy could turn out to be no more than a passing fad. How then did we come to a place where increased numbers of people have embraced an entirely different mind-set and cosmological view? Part of the answer can be seen in the story of a nineteenth-century organization called the Theosophy Society.

### Theosophy and New Thought

Helena Petrovna Blavatsky (1831–91) founded the Theosophy Society in 1875. The daughter of German immigrants to Russia, Blavatsky showed a proclivity toward mysticism and the occult. Her attraction for the hidden arts took a decided turn in 1848, when during a trip to Asia Minor she was rumored to have met Paulos Metamon, a conjurer of some renown. Never on terribly good terms with her family, she had left, in 1848, her parents and a husband considerably older than herself. According to some stories told about Blavatsky, she had married on a dare at the age of seventeen; the marriage lasted all of three months. Shortly thereafter she moved to London, where she became involved in many spiritually and even politically revolutionary groups. During this period HPB, as her friends called her, was alleged to have become increasingly interested in what has been called "The Great White Lodge," a secret society said to rule the world. This period, between 1848 and 1858, was kept veiled by Blavatsky, who refused to divulge much if any information about her life. It has been suggested that she traveled widely, perhaps to India, Mexico, and the United States. None of this is certain, of course, as much myth and legend—some originating from Blavatsky and the Theosophy Society—shrouds her travels.

One of many stories has HPB meeting an opera singer in Russia during a return trip to her homeland in 1858. Shortly thereafter she took up with the singer, Agardi Metrovich, and again left for an extended period of travel. According to some sources, Metrovich died in a boating accident in 1871 while the pair were en route to Cairo, Egypt. After arriving in Cairo, Blavatsky established an occult organization that acted as a precursor to the Theosophy Society. In any event, her new organization, the Société Spirite, was essentially just one of many worldwide groups involved in spiritism.[9] Again, it should be pointed out that tales of Blavatsky's pre-Theosophy Society life are numerous and often conflicting. Perhaps hoping to construct an impressive spiritual history, either Blavatsky or her later followers may have embellished her past to make for a more awe-inspiring personal history. Whatever the case, the history and teachings that eventually became theosophy grew in the telling.

Summarizing the goals and creeds of theosophy is difficult, for it takes in a number of mystical schools. In an abbreviated manner, the philosophy can be explained as follows: (1) Seek a universality and brotherhood of the human race; (2) advocate extensive study of world religions to help facilitate goal 1; and (3) harness the latent psychic and spiritual power in all of us for the ultimate goal of reaching deity. Theosophy is thus a conglomerate of largely Hindu and Buddhist worldviews sometimes superficially dressed in Christian garb. But make no mistake, the teachings also include occult philosophy and doctrine. Theosophy was the nineteenth-century New Age movement and so it is not surprising that it continues to provide inspiration for today's Aquarian Conspiracy.[10]

Of course, the New Age movement of today has extended far beyond the Theosophy Society. Ranging from the work of Annie Besant and later Alice Bailey and the Lucis (Lucifer Publishing Company) Trust to a host of other "New Thought" groups, Aquarianism lived on and grew slowly until the 1960s. The movement is not a monolithic entity; it is made up of thousands of groups with their own beliefs and dogmas. What makes the New Age movement appear to many to be a conspiracy is the active networking among a myriad of diverse groups to reach a common goal: spiritual unity. A far smaller number go further still and hope for possible economic and political unification.[11]

## Aspects of the New Age Conspiracy

Having said this, clarification must be made. Although there is an Aquarian spiritual "conspiracy" involving like-minded individuals, there is not a conscious, planned overthrow of world governments. It is a revolution of ideas, of spiritual enlightenment that New Agers seek. Any change in the economic and political world will take place as a result of individuals opening up to cosmic consciousness, not planned political changes in smoke-filled back rooms. Over the past decade or so, when New Age thinking came to the attention of the greater Christian community, some writers created unnecessary concern by seriously overstating the power and abilities of the Aquarian conspirators. To be sure, there are people and organizations who would like nothing better than to see an end to organized Christian and Judaic faiths and to have them replaced with a generic mystical belief structure; these groups, however, currently lack the power or ability to implement their agenda.[12]

### New Ageism in Public Schools

How exactly could a revolution of the magnitude of the New Age movement possibly make the kind of inroads some are suggesting is possible? In America today the most effective place to introduce Aquarian ideas is in public schools, as well as universities. It isn't difficult to reason that if a generation of children today can be indoctrinated to at least question traditional values, they will within a few decades be running society based on a different worldview. Many conservative Christians believe that the problems in public education can in part be attributed to the introduction of valuefree viewpoints. Even the most ignorant American adult, I assume, is aware that many schools struggle to provide even the most basic education. It is for that reason, among others, that home-schooling and private religious schools have flourished across America in recent years. In the values vacuum found in public schools, educators fear to tell a student that a given action is morally wrong; instead, wrongdoing is reduced to mere rule breaking. During the last two decades or so, America has watched her public schools become cesspools of permissiveness and drug and alcohol abuse, with intellectual achievement on the decline. Many also see the United States as being in a position where a generation (or two) has been raised incapable of performing simple academic tasks, much less being able to understand why being a virtuous person is important. Although these problems no doubt exist, the reason for their plaguing the nation is a source of considerable debate. A minority of Christians believe the spread of New Age ideas and philosophies is to blame.

An example of this can be seen in the increasing number of Christian leaders who believe that students are taught in school to conjure up images or "spirit guides" to teach them important spiritual and temporal truths. Johnny may not be able to read or write, they say, but he may well obtain training in contacting his inner self and learn the importance of being able to say yes to his desires, whatever they may be. This trend is reminiscent of the occult credo "Do what thou wilt shall be the Whole of the Law."[13] We are left with an increasingly large number of students who will tolerate no infringement on their personal gratification but wouldn't know the history of their nation if it were read to them. In the perception of many in the Christian right, we have a generation on the rise in both the city and countryside who have no real hope for the future, who despise the present, and who cannot fathom the past. Conservative Christians rightly point out that despite misapplications and abuses over the course of history, the Judeo-Christian tradition has nonetheless given the West a standard of living that is a goal for the world. It has also produced a spirit of philanthropy that is the most generous in the world.[14]

If this perceived assault on the values he or she holds dear were not bad enough to the conservative Christian observer, there is another movement on the rise that, according to some interpretations of Scripture, points to the sureness of Christ's soon return—the popularization of the occult.

## *Occult and Satanic Ritual Abuse*

In the world of conspiracy and end-time prophecy, few areas are attracting as much attention among Christians as the occult. Stories of abductions by occultists abound, and black-robed or sky-clad (nude) figures in the moonlight are said to have been seen in rural and urban sites in recent years. The result has been increasing fear among many in the Christian community that this seemingly widespread rise of the occult is yet another sign of the soon return of Jesus. Entire ministries have been based on the exposure of Satanism and Wicca (witchcraft) in American society. Bob Larson's Denver-based organization and nationally broadcast radio show *Talk Back* is a noteworthy example. Others have included Tom Wedge and Jack Johnston, both holding highly fundamentalistic interpretations of Satanism. Perhaps none have been as visible—and now infamous—as Mike Warnke. Ever since the publication of his *The Satan Seller* in 1972, Warnke had been seen as an expert on Satanism and the occult. A superb book based on an earlier article in the journal *Cornerstone* exposed the outright falsehoods in Warnke's story of being a one-time Satanic high priest.[15]

The willingness of Christians to believe Warnke's stories set up many believers, who lacked understanding and simple facts, to stereotype and pass rumors. According to some Christians, thousands of American and Canadian children are being abducted each year and used in horrible rituals, some ending in sexual abuse and even human sacrifice. As with charges or claims of conspiracy, we need to ask just how widespread this problem is. Undoubtedly, occult activity and even Satanism exists, but how common is its more horrific side? Christians have to a considerable degree overreacted to the worst reports, thereby branding occult activity of any kind as "Satanism." It is my opinion that like conspiracy theory in the political world, so too have theories of "Satanic ritual conspiracy" become increasingly accepted among the Christian public based on less-than-compelling evidence.[16]

Strictly speaking, the word *occult* means hidden. The idea is that the knowledge found therein is esoteric, hidden from the public at large. This definition provides a twofold purpose: One, it gives the adherent a sense that he or she is the recipient of special restricted knowledge; and two, it is hidden from the unbeliever because of that person's unworthiness. The basic premise is really no different from the mystery religions of ancient Greece. Occult teachings are sometimes purposely shrouded in terminology known only to the participants or at least individuals familiar with the topic. Because the occult is a widely varied arena of creeds with a host of different practices, Christians today often assume that all that we know as the occult is essentially the same. There is in fact an enormous variation of beliefs under the occult umbrella, some diametrically opposed to each other. These can range from nature worship of Wiccans to Left-Hand Path (Satanist) practitioners, to crystal and I Ching advocates; the point is that the occult cannot be neatly pigeonholed into any one category. Most Christians I have encountered, however, are unable (or unwilling) to perceive any difference whatsoever. Moreover, if you were to ask a Wicca practitioner his or her opinion of occult works such as the *Necronomicon* or Aleister Crowley's *Equinox* journal, that person would most likely express disapproval but cautious tolerance. What we have then is a classic example of failure to define our terms correctly, to understand that occultism is quite varied; so we ultimately draw conclusions based on misinformation, ignorance, fear, or rumor.[17]

Of course, involvement in the occult in any form is strictly forbidden to the Christian and Jew, at least according to their shared Scriptures. According to Levitical law, consultation of mediums, fortune tellers, or spell casters is way beyond the realm of acceptability.[18]

Through the ministries of men such as Bob Larson and the now fallen Mike Warnke, many in the Christian community have come to believe that occultic practices—even Satanic sacrifices—are or have become commonplace in America. Appearing on the formidable Christian television and radio media, the "I survived satanism" stories became hot topics. Unfortunately, a number of dishonest promoters of what has been called "Satanic Panic" have arisen. These include Lauren Stratford, who claimed to be a "breeder" for Satan and the victim of ritual abuse at the hands of her parents; Rebecca Brown, who claimed to have ministered to persons involved in Satanism; and the infamous John Todd, who toured the Christian circuit espousing a Satanic and Illuminati-conspiracy theory message. The falsehoods of all three have been publicly exposed, due in part to the excellent work of evangelical Christian journalists and apologists affiliated with organizations such as Christian Research Institute of Southern California and *Cornerstone* magazine in Chicago.[19] The point I hope to get across is that like conspiracy theory, unreasonable fear of the occult serves no good purpose and only helps to perpetuate the stereotype of Christians as ignorant followers willing to believe the most outlandish rumor.

### The Diversity of New Ageism

Just as the occult is so difficult to categorize, the same is true of what we have come to know as New Age beliefs. Aquarian philosophy is difficult to define precisely because it has interwoven itself with a host of other movements that more or less share in its overall goals of spiritual transformation. Nonetheless, there are shared beliefs that can be pointed out. Although some in the various and sundry suborganizations dispute it, the New Age movement can correctly be defined as a religion. By nearly any definition, including that found in a dictionary, Aquarian philosophy is fundamentally religious in nature. Mystical experience seems to be key to the New Ager, placing spiritual experience above any measure of whether or not the experience is valid or believable, much less something to which one should commit time, money, and life. Although most Mormons would be quite opposed to the Eastern teachings of the New Age, their own "burning in the bosom" doctrine for positive justification of the teachings of Joseph Smith is not qualitatively different.[20] For that matter, there are adherents of the Word-Faith teachings of Kenneth Hagin, Kenneth Copeland, or Charles Capps within the Christian charismatic movement who have themselves given a great deal of credence to personal revelation. Regardless of whether these revelations are said to have been given to ministries or to individuals, far too many Christian believers are willing to accept them as "gospel truth" equal to Scripture. It should come as no surprise, then, that from time to time there are embarrassing reminders that not all "revelations" are of God, regardless of the vessel pronouncing them. For the New Ager it goes well beyond that. The mysticism into which the adherent is introduced takes him or her into an ancient belief system that, while originating in ancient Babylon, ultimately takes one to India.[21]

The New Age movement has produced its share of mystical practices. This revival of ancient pagan ritual has included a host of practices in a number of categories. Some of the more common involve mind control, professional (business) guidance, holistic medicine, New Age oracles, channeling, and of course, globalism.[22] New Ageism involves practices such as visualization, meditation, acupuncture, pyramid energy, crystal energy, homeopathy, Rolfing, astrology, aura therapy, I Ching, tarot card readings, and dream interpretation. As stated earlier, the New Age movement is so massive, includes so many different interest groups, that it is difficult to do justice to all of the many spiritual ideas. The same can be said about the leadership of the so-called Aquarian Conspiracy.

### New Age Leaders . . . of Sorts

Probably the best known but less than spiritually or intellectually impressive leader of the New Age movement is actress Shirley MacLaine. An active participant in the "human as god" trend, this talented actress made a name for herself in mysticism primarily through her book and television miniseries, *Out on a Limb*. MacLaine has gone on to publish other works, hold workshops and seminars, and even offer videotape presentations to aid the seeking soul to find the proper Hindu paths.[23] Taking some of her ideas from Theosophy, MacLaine draws on the teachings of Helena Blavatsky, Alice Bailey, and Annie Besant. MacLaine borrows heavily from a number of other sources as well. The New Age movement has certainly had its share of original thinkers.

Other contemporary leaders include the late Pierre Teilhard de Chardin, a French Jesuit whose writings have long been considered heresy in the Catholic church. This formidable thinker and writer has been considered something of a New Age godfather. Virtually everyone in the Aquarian conspiracy heaps praise on the Jesuit as an early pioneer of the new spirituality. Other twentieth-century leaders include Elisabeth Kübler-Ross, death and dying expert; Ruth Montgomery, a famous psychic known for automatic writing; Jane Roberts, the channeler through whom someone called "Seth" spoke and wrote; Robert Muller, assistant secretary-general of the United Nations; David Spangler, the philosopher and educator who was active in both the Findhorn Foundation and Planetary Citizens; and Marilyn Ferguson, author of *The Aquarian Conspiracy*, a volume that triumphantly announced the nearly completed New Age conquest.

There are also a host of institutions and organizations pushing the Aquarian gospel. One of these is the Findhorn Foundation, a 1962 Peter and Eileen Caddy creation, founded to encourage reverence for all forms of life, including plants. Others include Apollo 14 astronaut Edgar Mitchell's Institute of Noetic Sciences, Robert Muller's Planetary Citizens, and Donald Keyes's Planetary Initiative for the World We Choose. Virtually all of these groups have their roots in Eastern philosophy and religion and at the very least are questioning Christian beliefs. In fact traditional orthodox Christianity and its cosmology is especially hated by most New Agers.

### Views of Orthodox Christianity

Not everyone in the New Age movement is rabidly anti-Christian; indeed, some adherents are clergy of various denominations who claim to love the faith while at the same time adopting either pseudo- or anti-Christian positions. The tone in many New Age publications goes far in explaining why many conservative Christians distrust Aquarianism, aside from obvious doctrinal differences. Few outside the church, however, try to hide their open disdain for the cardinal doctrines that have historically defined Christianity. The basic Christian doctrines Aquarians find objectionable include the following: Christ was not one of many avatars, but the unique Son of God—God in flesh, in fact; the Bible is the sole written scriptural authority; and belief and submission of one's life to Christ as Savior is the only path to eternal life. There are other Christian beliefs that New Agers find objectionable, but Christianity's exclusive claims of being the only path to God is what really causes many of them to grind their teeth in angst.[24] What we now need to explore are some of the individual goals of this vast movement and just how feasible they are. In short, is the Aquarian Conspiracy really a threat or merely a fad?

### New Age Messiah?

When I was a Ph.D. candidate in history at the University of New Mexico in Albuquerque, I had a daily habit of picking up either the *Los Angeles Times* or *USA Today* to read with my morning cup of coffee. One fine April day in 1982, when I went through my usual routine, my eyes were met with a full-page ad proclaiming, "The Christ is Now Here." This was a startling proclamation to be sure, and one that at the time left me somewhat bemused. If Christ had returned, I was puzzled that his arrival had escaped my attention. The ad, under the sponsorship of the Tara Center, stated in no uncertain terms that the long-awaited world avatar was here at last and would soon meet the press and field questions. I found myself wondering how "Christ" would handle questions from Sam Donaldson.[25]

Of course "Christ" did not appear. The leader of the Tara Center, Benjamin Creme, suggested that the time was not yet right for a public appearance because of apathy or perhaps lack of faith. Media interest quickly died and the story became something of an embarrassment for New Agers who genuinely thought their messiah would appear. The name used among New Agers for this messiah was Maitreya, a personage taken from myth and legend surrounding Buddha. Maitreya is the "Buddha of the future," who will live in a modern country, be familiar with the world's problems, be endowed with extraordinary spiritual powers, and unite the world under his leadership.

### *Mother Meera: Ancient Avatar in the New Age*

In one of my own recent encounters with Eastern religion, I had the opportunity to see for myself the impact it can have on individual lives. A good friend of mine recently told me that his wife had become a devotee of an East Indian avatar named Mother Meera. My friend's wife delved into the Divine Mother aspect of Hinduism as once taught by Sri Aurobindo and his aide, a woman who became known as "Sweet Mother." Both Aurobindo and Sweet Mother have since died, but an increasing number of people in India, Europe, and now the United States believe that Mother Meera, a beautiful Indian woman in her thirties, is the present embodiment of the Divine Mother. Whatever Meera represents, it is not anything really new. "Ma," or the mother concept, is immensely old in Indian religious tradition. Avatars have come and gone, their teachings and followers ultimately still empty when the ride is over. I believe that we will hear more of Mother Meera in years to come as her Western audience grows. It is a shame she will deceive people frustrated with their past and present and who are unsure of the future. As is true with many such avatars, she demands absolute spiritual surrender, effectively becoming the father and mother figure for those seeking such authority and assurances in their lives. Still, Meera does not represent the New Age movement as much as she does aspects of classic Hinduism.[26] Sadly, Meera is just one of thousands making such claims. For some in conspiracy camps, it is all part of a wider plan hatched in the mind of a fallen Lucifer.

## The New Age Movement and the End Times

As with all conspiracy theories or end-time scenarios, a thinking person has to critically judge the events going on in the world about him or her. After all, there have been multitudes of false

"Christs" over the past two and a half millennia; just because a new one comes along with a better public relations department does not mean that he or she is the real McCoy. What is different about, say, Creme's Maitreya, is the enormous psychological, spiritual, and social changes that have preceded and followed the newspaper announcement. Moreover, the Aquarian conspirators boast of new and powerful (albeit strange) means of spreading the message. Called SPINs (Segmented Polycentric Integrated Networks), the networked organizations are said to pick up energy that in turn is multiplied many times over through the various participating groups. The message and transformation thus takes on increases of an exponential nature. Although each group is independent and supposedly self-sufficient, it can draw on the power that comes from an enormous collective or network. Ultimately the SPIN theory sounds very like societal change as seen in the old hundredth monkey story, which says that a behavior adopted by one monkey will be copied by others until it becomes common in the group.[27]

A skeptic at this point would rightly point out the weakness in the Aquarian Conspiracy argument: For a nationwide or worldwide New Age conspiracy to exist would necessarily mean a degree of interaction and precognition currently unheard of. It would assume near omnipresence or omniscience on the part of the conspirators; it would also assume a near omnipotent ability to move and influence a vast array of social, religious, and political machinery. For Aquarian conspirators, that is very close to the mark in terms of their outlook of the world being shaped about them: Cosmic forces are working toward some end that will, when complete, cause a quantum leap in cosmic consciousness. It is a process and an event looked to with great anticipation. It will be a paradise, a new millennium filled with hope and potential. Christians have for two thousand years written about such a movement and series of events. The traditional word used to describe it is simply tribulation, and the New Age messiah, Antichrist. A good many Christians today believe that it is this New Age movement that will usher in these end-times events.[28]

### *"The Sky Is Falling" Mentality*

Along with Constance Cumby, probably the most prominent proponent of the New Age as Antichrist system is Texe Marrs. Marrs, a former U.S. Air Force officer who taught in aerospace studies at the University of Texas at Austin some years ago, contends that there are no ifs, ands, or buts about it: The New Age movement is the vehicle that will serve as the harbinger of the Antichrist. His books attack the New Age movement, something not surprising given the differences in theology between Christianity and Aquarian philosophy. Marrs goes far beyond apologetics, however, and provides in nearly every book, video, and audiotape he has produced "proof" of conspiracy using some of the most questionable sources imaginable. Secular conspiracy theory sources are routinely used, such as the works of Des Griffin, whose Emissary Publications publishes anti-Semitic writings of the ilk of Henry Ford's *The International Jew* and the infamous *Protocols of the Learned Elders of Zion*. These hateful books and pamphlets do not seem to faze Marrs, who continues to use works from publishing houses and authors who hold highly questionable interpretations as though they were the Scripture itself. It is one thing to oppose New Age philosophy on theological grounds; it is quite another to use Fascist, racist, and anti-Semitic sources to make your point. Further evidence of this is Marrs's use of such rabidly anti-Semitic sources as Liberty Lobby's *Spotlight* newspaper and the earlier mentioned Nesta Webster, alleged British Fascist Party member during the 1920s. This mixing of obscene, racist sources with traditional prophecy belief is unfortunately common in Marrs's books and tapes.[29] Though I do not doubt the authenticity of the author's belief in Christ, I certainly do question Marrs's willingness to use the sometimes hate-filled sources to "prove" his point.

Another Christian author who makes liberal use of secular conspiracy theory researchers and writers is Gary Kah. His 1992 book, *En Route to Global Occupation,* uses some of the worst sources imaginable to back his claim that there is a coming world government.[30] Many are taken from the John Birch

Society—an extreme right-wing conspiracy theory group head-
quartered in Appleton, Wisconsin—others from Emissary Publications. Most of these secondary source conspiracy works are
known to any historian or sociologist familiar with the anti-
Semitism, scapegoating, and just plain fearmongering making
the rounds over the past two centuries. What is particularly dis-
heartening is that Kah uses these works as believable sources,
authorities whose word is valid and historically correct. Like
Marrs, Kah relies on Nesta Webster, as well as the writings of
Lady Queensborough (Edith Starr Miller). The latter's *Occult
Theocracy* was published in the 1930s and is filled with horror
stories of conspiracy and international intrigue. Though some
of the items are worth notice, most are based on worldviews
most Christians would find offensive. For instance, in the index
of this source Kah apparently deems worthy of citation is a list
of topics or subjects on those who are of Jewish background.
They are marked with a small Star of David alongside their
names. Although not as vulgar as the *Protocols* or *Mein Kampf*,
Lady Queensborough's book draws upon similar viewpoints.
The fact that Kah would then use it to supposedly bolster his
contention for conspiracy is, to say the very least, questionable.
I like to give Kah, Marrs, and other Christian conspiracy theorists the benefit of the doubt and suggest that they were or are
unaware of the nefarious and anti-Semitic nature of some of
their sources.[31] If so, they certainly need to be much more careful in their research and writing in the future. At the very least
it calls into question among nonbelievers the worldview of those
calling themselves Christians.

## Potential Impact of the New Age Movement

What we have here in late twentieth-century America at least
is a clash of worldviews. By its nature, the Judeo-Christian
worldview is exclusive and New Ageism (Hinduism, for the
most part) is all-inclusive. Should the latter come out on top,
it would destroy the former by eliminating its uniqueness, its
exclusivity. We are now potentially on the historical transitional

cusp where traditional Judeo-Christian views of the universe are being replaced with a values system that will threaten to bury them. Should this happen, the world we leave our children and grandchildren will be an immensely different place from what we have experienced. It would doubtless be a place where the beliefs and values orthodox Christians hold dear will seem strangely out of place.

### Is the New Age Movement a True Conspiracy?

Before we close this chapter, we must address one issue that is often brought forth as a primary example of why a cosmic conspiracy cannot exist. I have used the same arguments myself in tracing this mind-set in the previous chapters. Simply put, it is this: How would it be possible? For a cosmic conspiracy to come about some important things must first occur, one of which is that a person of the highest intellect and understanding of world affairs must come into leadership. Some believe this person to be the mysterious Maitreya or some other New Age avatar. The only way this or any conspiracy could come off successfully would be for someone of immense ability to lead it, and even then there would be titanic problems. For orthodox Christians, this sounds ominously familiar; it is also a source of potential problems in interpreting current events as "end times."

Over the centuries, traditional Christianity has taught that in the latter days there would arise a person of tremendous power who would be the embodiment of Satan himself. In much the same way that Christians see Jesus as God in flesh form, so would this end-time leader be the embodiment of a fallen Lucifer. Moreover, this Antichrist is said to have a high sense of mission, an urgency stemming from his sure knowledge that his time is very limited. His motivation would be simply hatred of Christianity, Judaism, anything reminding him of God's love for the human race. Although presenting himself as savior of the human race and initially succeeding in his efforts, conservative Christianity teaches that he would ultimately be seen for the unmitigated deceiver he is: a pathetically poor substitute for the Deity he rejected and sought to replace.

The irony of the whole New Age conspiracy, at least as concerns this book, is that although conspiracies have come and gone with little or no evidence suggesting a Great Plan, there is in Aquarianism an element missing in other conspiracies: a spiritual component with the power to make global change, one person at a time. If the New Age movement is the prophesied Antichrist system, and I am by no means convinced it is, the change would not initially be oppressive; indeed, it would be welcomed as the answer to the world's problems. Still, prophecy and pronouncements that this or that movement or belief system is the Antichrist system can be dangerous and embarrassing speculation. The history of Christianity is littered with those making such bold pronouncements who later proved to be woefully inaccurate. Speculation on a belief system different from our own in the area of prophecy is best left unformulated.

# The New World Order

As we near the end of the twentieth century and the second millennium since Christ, both the secular and Christian worlds are being inundated with publications, video- and audiotapes, and pamphlets proclaiming the coming of a world government. Although conspiracy theory is nothing new, it has become considerably more popular in recent years among Christian writers and ministries who specialize in prophecy. The unholy melding of eschatology with this dubious view of the past is the focus of this chapter; I hope it will serve as a warning to readers to avoid ideologies with questionable roots. Some of these core beliefs within secular conspiracy theory include anti-Semitism, Fascism, and bigotry. Although I do not doubt that most ministries and individuals believing this false message are unaware of the wellspring from which they draw their ideas, it is my hope that those ministering to the body of Christ will take a closer look at the ideology they are propagating. Just a few contemporary ministries specializing in conspiracy, prophecy, or financial conspiracy theory are those led by Texe Marrs, Jack Van Impe, Grant Jeffrey, Jeffrey Baker, William Still, Gary Kah, Don S. McAlvaney, Jack Chick, Larry Burkett, and even Pat Robertson.

The basic premise that these ministries have in common with each other and with secular conspiracy theorists is that they say there are groups, organizations, and secret societies that are in fact the true string pullers in the world today. Using Dr. Carroll Quigley's massive tome *Tragedy and Hope*[1] as something of a conspiracy Bible, advocates contend that conspiracy groups are known by many names, but the most common to surface are the Illuminati, the Council on Foreign Relations, the Trilateral Commission, the Bilderbergers, the Council of 300, the Rockefeller family, the Rothschild banking house, and even the Vatican. These ministries proclaim to be against violence, but many of their ideas about the groups they oppose were and are believed by people who are willing to use violence against the New World Order, however they interpret that phrase. There is no question that prophecy plays an important role in historical, orthodox Christianity: Conspiracy theory, on the other hand, does not. Speculation about when the end times are to come is not unusual, but many have gone so far as to state as fact that current conspiracy-related theories are the fulfillment of prophecy. Those making such statements certainly do not know this for fact and will, in the process of proclaiming it, bring disrepute on Christianity as the harbor of crackpots and extremists.

## Post–Cold War Era Scapegoating

Secular conspiracy theorists have long predicted the coming of a world government. When former President George Bush used the phrase "New World Order" to describe the post–cold war world, believers in this view of history were alarmed. To the average listener, "New World Order" was simply diplomatic jargon used to describe an increasingly global approach to the world's myriad problems. Whether the users of such a phrase mean specifically world government of some sort demanding subjugation of nationalism is debatable; some undoubtedly meant just that. Still, what we see in the world today is not so much a new world order as the ruins of the old world order, the flotsam and jetsam of the cold war. Despite this, some insist that a faceless collective is about to enslave the world. Secular conspiracy theorists believe it to be tantamount to a modern Illuminati; some Christians see the Antichrist system. Ultimately, both groups see dire times ahead. Some authors have also suggested that the United States is in danger of imminent economic collapse as a result of debt load, declines in American education and moral standards, or the rise of the New World Order. Whatever the viewpoint, conspiracy theorists and prophecy writers have had much to say of late.

### Fiscal Doom and Gloom Conspiracies

Although Russia at present is no longer much of a military threat to the United States, our nation does face a formidable foe, according to a few secular and Christian economic writers. According to these writers, notably Harry Figgie, Larry Burkett, and Larry Bates, the enemy is of our own making and is symptomatic of deeper problems facing our nation and society as a whole. The enemy is the accumulated national debt. For decades, but particularly since 1979, the United States has spent well in excess of its revenues. At first, deficit spending did not appear to be much of a problem. After all, in the 1960s the United States had the most powerful economy on the planet, and the actual debt being incurred was a very small percentage of the gross national product. We easily handled the debt at the time, despite growing commitments to the Vietnam War and Lyndon Johnson's Great Society programs. As we entered the 1970s and the government became increasingly demanding of funds from taxpayers, our yearly deficits still rose. By the last year of the Carter administration, the nation had spent some $60 billion more than it received in taxes.[2]

When Ronald Reagan came to office in 1981, he brought with him an economic philosophy that had many questioning its feasibility. Reaganomics is the theory that if tax breaks are provided to the middle and upper classes, huge sums of money will be unleashed for reinvestment in an ailing American economy. Lambasting the plan as a tax cut for the rich, Democratic opponents claimed it would simply deprive the government of much-needed revenue and make the overall debt situation worse. To the amazement of Reagan's critics, revenues did in fact rise with the corresponding cut in taxes. The problem, however, was that Republicans and Democrats alike spent the excess monies on any number of pet projects instead of paying the debt. The result was that after eight years as president, Reagan left office with the United States $3 trillion in debt. Reaganomics got the blame, Congress waxed sanctimonious, and both political parties shook their collective heads over how awful it was that interest payments were consuming so much of the yearly budget.[3]

By 1992 the massive amount of debt required the United States to pay out $250 billion a year in interest alone to simply service the debt; that is, keep it current while not actually reducing the amount owed. Whether or not you believe the gloomy statements of Burkett or Figgie, it is sobering to consider the enormous amount of good that could be accomplished with money otherwise disappearing into the interest payment abyss: college grants and loans, job training, Head Start, housing, and so on. The frightening rise of debt during the 1980s provided the backdrop for the increased borrowing of the 1990s and with it jeremiad pronouncements of doom and destruction soon to befall the United States.

In Larry Burkett's *The Coming Economic Earthquake* and its updated version, the author suggests that just when everyone thought the budget problem could not get any worse, along came the Bush and Clinton administrations. Admittedly, both administrations proved their ability to spend money like drunken sailors. Just as appalling, political leaders of both parties didn't seem to mind shelling out the huge sums of money for interest—so long as it also bought them votes. Other politicians just didn't consider it much of a problem at all. For example, Bush made it quite clear that his first love was foreign affairs and he did not care that much for domestic concerns. During his four years in office, the Texas oil man saw yearly deficits increase to the point where by 1992 they totaled $1 trillion. It had taken Ronald Reagan nearly six years to reach that point, but Bush exhibited a cavalier attitude about the whole topic. The rise in the national debt did not go unpredicted, how-

ever, as during the Reagan administration a special commission had been assembled to study the debt problem and come
up with solutions.[4]

The group of distinguished bipartisan business and political
leaders assembled at President Reagan's request in 1984 was
officially known as the President's Private Sector Survey on Cost
Control but was known in the press as the Grace Commission
for its leader, Peter Grace. The commission took its job very
seriously and provided the president and future administrations with some shocking statistics pertaining to the direction
of the national debt. Its projections for the remainder of the
Reagan administration were relatively accurate, as were their
debt predictions for his successor. One member of the commission was Harry Figgie, a wealthy businessman with financial interests in sporting goods. Figgie and co-author Gerald
Swanson, Ph.D., wrote the fearsome *Bankruptcy 1995* based on
the research conducted in the 1980s and early 1990s and concluded that the United States would effectively spend itself into
insolvency by middecade. This was a shocking premise, to be
sure, and one that immediately gathered hundreds of thousands of supporters.[5]

If we use Figgie and Burkett's figures and logic, sometime
between 1995 and 2000 deficit spending will cause us to spend
100 percent of our tax income on interest payments alone. If
these scenarios are correct, it would leave nothing for defense
or social programs. At that point, at least according to Larry
Burkett, the government would have no choice but to do one
of three things:

1. Be honest with the American people and our creditors (80
   percent of the debt is owed to American citizens) and seek
   renegotiations or forgiveness of the debt. This would mean
   a massive cut in social and military spending across the
   board.
2. Repudiate the debt and let the chips fall where they may.
   This choice would doubtless result in retaliation from
   nations to whom we owe money.

3. Monetize the debt. This option would mean simply printing more money to pay our bills. Any Economics 101
   student can tell you that such action would result in
   hyperinflation.[6]

If Burkett's assessment of the economy's direction is right, I
would agree with him that our government would opt for choice
number three. The operative word here is *if*. Unfortunately,
Burkett does not see any possibility other than massive economic collapse as evidenced in his chilling statement, "It is not
a matter of if, but when."[7]

It is at this point where traditional conspiracy theory and
these most recent economic doom scenarios come into agreement. Both groups believe that by hook or crook the powers
that be have led us to a situation where the nation will be
brought to its knees through economic mismanagement.
Some go so far as to suggest that the coming economic collapse is in fact part of a grand master plan to bring the United
States into some sort of world government. For Christians
believing in the nearness of the second coming, such theo-
rizing ties into some beliefs concerning the Antichrist and a
unified, reborn Roman Empire. Among those holding similar
secular conspiracy views is the John Birch Society's John
McManus. His book, *Financial Terrorism: Hijacking America
under the Threat of Bankruptcy*, is the quintessential financial
doom and gloom position so popular of late. Unfortunately,
Larry Burkett is not immune to such radical positions, either.
In his 1991 novel, *The Illuminati*, Burkett writes a fictional
account of the financial collapse of the United States and how
it was essentially engineered by a strange, faceless "Them."
The purpose of the collapse as presented in this book is the
absorption of America into a global government—exactly as
the John Birch Society and other conspiracy theorists have
long taught. Although Burkett does not introduce these conspiratorial ideas into his nonfiction work in this same outright fashion, one has to wonder if his predictions are not
based on them.[8]

## Masonic Conspiracies

Other Christians have also bought into the international conspiracy theory in recent years. Some believe wholeheartedly that a contemporary version of the Illuminati is at work with nothing less than the overthrow of the American government and Christianity as its goal. With little or nothing to back their contentions, these authors, many well known in Christian circles, have published books advocating conspiracy and melding it into more traditional eschatology.

William Still's *New World Order: The Ancient Plan of Secret Societies,* for example, is a two-hundred-page polemic claiming there is a "hidden hand" that has been at work for centuries, even millennia. It is, for the most part, based on the same documentation secular conspiracy theorists have used for decades. In an interesting twist, Mr. Still claims that some Anasazi ("Ancient Ones"), Native American structures in the Desert Southwest, may in fact have been Indian Masonic lodges. As a historian with Native American history as my specialty, I can assure you that this is a false—indeed, ridiculous— assertion. It is nonetheless an example of how far some will go to try to prove that there is an ancient conspiracy at work. Still's statement is not that far off from declaring Native Americans to be the survivors of the struggle between the Nephites and Lamanites as told in the Book of Mormon. I do not doubt that Still would oppose the Latter Day Saint interpretation, but his claim about Indian Masonic lodges is no less ridiculous. The rest of the New World Order is a collection of rehashed conspiracy theories common among secular groups of like mind—especially those who are wont to see Masonic conspiracies behind every tree or under every bed. Like a few other Christian authors, Still falls into the trap of using as authoritative some publications of highly questionable authenticity, not to mention truth. In a similar vein but much less alarmist in tone, respected Christian leader and head of the Christian Broadcasting Network Pat Robertson dedicates a couple of chapters in his book, also entitled *New World Order,* to the premise that the Illuminati, CFR, and Trilateralists are the driving force behind the New World Order.[9] Unfortunately, they are not alone in the Christian community.

### The Conspiracy from Marrs

Another noteworthy Christian author who has utilized the idea that there is an unseen "Other" out there pulling strings to bring about the New World Order is Texe Marrs, whose books, audiotapes, and videotapes state ad infinitum that an international conspiracy exists. His ministry seems to be based on this conspiracy thesis: A glance at his "Intelligence Examiner" and any accompanying order form bear this out. On one of Marrs's audiotapes, he goes so far as to insult any who disagree with his conspiracy theory interpretation of history and, by extension, prophecy interpretation. "Ladies and Gentlemen," Marrs piously intones, "if you have a friend who says he does not believe in conspiracy, look him straight in the eye and tell them that they are ignorant. 'I love you brother, I love you sister, but you are stupid . . .'" Marrs goes on to pontificate that those denying conspiracy theory are unlearned, have not studied the topic, and simply don't know what they're talking about.[10]

According to one of Texe Marrs's latest contributions, *Circle of Intrigue,* the world is essentially controlled through the conspiring of ten men who comprise what the author calls the "Inner Circle" of the Illuminati. The Texas-based prophecy/conspiracy minister contends that a combination of the Rothschilds and Rockefellers, among others, are in fact calling the shots. The book is in essence a reiteration and expansion of Marrs's earlier work, *Dark Majesty.* As is the case in his earlier works, Marrs uses other conspiracy theory literature to "prove" his point. Stretching this "proof" even further, his January 1996 *Flashpoint* leads with the headline "Bible Prophecy Confirms Revelations in Circle of Intrigue." Texe Marrs thus uses the Bible as evidence to support a book he authored: Somewhat less than objective, wouldn't you say?[11]

If this were not enough, Marrs also had a guest on his *World of Prophecy* radio program pertaining to the topic "The Secret Power of Foundations" who contended that nearly every bad social change to come down the pike has been funded through the Rockefellers and their foundations. Incredibly, some of the items included in these "bad" changes were publications that were later used to encourage the *Brown vs. The Topeka Board of Education* Supreme Court decision! On the same tape Marrs goes on to attack other organizations, such as the Parliament of World Religions, a group also receiving Rockefeller Foundation money. In addition, Marrs mentions Michael Novak and Billy Graham and the questionable nature of their receiving monetary awards ("Progress in Religion" category) from the PWR.[12] One has to wonder: If these awards are funded through the Rockefeller Foundation, and Marrs and others deem this family to be part of the world plot, are they also suggesting that award recipient Billy Graham is in on the "fix"?[13]

There is an unsettling arrogance about the sort of statements emanating from Texe Marrs's Living Truth Ministries and other organizations of its sort. The inference seems to be that theirs is the final word in eschatology and historical interpretation. A pseudospiritual air is taken on that suggests that those rejecting their view of prophecy or history are deceived. I beg to differ: Conspiracy theory is not the spiritual equivalent of prophecy! I refuse to recognize as authoritative some of the people in these ministries who apparently feel they hold special status or have a special revelation from God. To borrow an old A. W. Tozer phrase, I refuse to recognize in these ministries a "second prophet from Nazareth." Marrs even had militia supporter and highly decorated former Green Beret Bo Gritz as a guest on his *World of Prophecy* short-wave radio program on November 4, 1995. I don't understand how a Christian ministry can stoop to having such spokespersons. On another occasion, Marrs and Gritz verbally affirmed each other as they blasted Israel and Zionism and accused the Jewish state of murdering many thousands of Arab prisoners of war.[14] (Although Marrs and Gritz have since had a falling out, their conspiracy views at one time were virtually identical.) Still, even this isn't the most bizarre proclamation coming from Marrs's ministry.

On one of Marrs's taped releases from his *World of Prophecy* radio program, the Austin-based minister had as his guest a per-

son introduced as simply "René." The content of this tape, entitled "NASA's Space Program—Hoaxes and Deception" involves
a discussion between Marrs and René about the latter's insistence that the space program was a hoax. The guest openly states
that the moon landings were all staged in a studio to rip off the
American public. Of course, to these two it is all part of the international conspiracy with Illuminati fingerprints all over it.
Marrs, who is a retired career Air Force officer and one-time
assistant professor at the University of Texas at Austin, incredibly gives credence and substance to this fantasy.[15] For Marrs
and his conspiracy theory view of history, it appears that it will
get only more extreme as time goes by; one can only hope that
his views will mellow and he turns from what is a patently false
interpretation of history, not to mention of prophecy.

Other prophecy writers also buy into the conspiracy theory
interpretation of history and prophecy, albeit much less arro-
gantly than does Marrs. Some of these include Grant Jeffrey,
who states in his *Prince of Darkness* that there are forces at work
that have both political parties under their control.[16] Given the
high praise these books have received from major Christian
ministries (Jack Van Impe Ministries, Dan Betzer of Revival
Time Ministries, and Jerry Rose of the National Religious
Broadcasters, among others), it suggests far too much acceptance of conspiratorial ideas. David Allen Lewis also throws in
his views of the ties between prophecy and conspiracy theory.
In his *Prophecy 2000*, he dedicates a short chapter to the international conspiracy in which he holds forth that organizations
such as the Council on Foreign Relations and the Trilateral
Commission are part and parcel of a general anti-Christian
world takeover. To his credit, Lewis does tone down his earlier
statements made in 1979 about the conspiracy and states that
his first impressions might have been oversimplifications.[17]

### More Conspiracy Madness

Conspiracy belief is not limited to Christian writers whose
forte is prophecy, either. Books such as Michael Coffman's *Saviors of the Earth?* brings conspiracy theory into the environ-

mental debate. And Constance Cumby, in her book *Hidden Dangers of the Rainbow,* launches into one of the most bizarre treatises I have ever read. Although not specifically dealing with groups like the CFR or Trilateral Commission, she nonetheless exhibits some of the most frantic and fearful pronouncements imaginable about New Age tactics.[18] Cumby even goes so far as to accuse a number of fellow Christians as being part of the New Age plot. A few she has targeted include the late and highly respected cult expert Dr. Walter Martin of the Christian Research Institute, the leadership of Spiritual Counterfeits Project of Berkeley, California, and even Pat Robertson of CBN, who she seems to feel may in fact be the Antichrist![19] Indeed, in recent years the trend has been away from the more blatant 1970s game of guessing the Antichrist's identity to concern about conspiracy.

## America in the Post–Cold War Era

The year 1989 will in all likelihood go down in history as one of the century's most important. Especially as it affected the members of the Eastern bloc and the Warsaw Pact, powers and desires long under Communism broke into the open with a crash. After throwing off the shackles of Communism, the recently liberated countries found themselves exposed to consumerism in a manner they had never imagined possible. Although freed from the tyranny of Communist control, they were now faced with a multitude of new challenges. The chief of these would be the transformation from a tightly controlled economy to one under the supply and demand principles of a free market. Also of critical importance was how many of these nations, under Communism for so long, would do in an emerging democratic revolution. Most had little or no experience in self-government. It was and is for that reason that so many of America's former foes looked to us for advice and financial assistance. The United States, the last remaining superpower on the planet, was asked to lead the way for an emerging political system. Sadly, our nation can no longer provide the help it gave during the Marshall Plan years. The question remains: If we cannot help, who will?

There are, of course, a host of problems about the emerging New World Order that have to be answered. Conspiracy theorists visualize the New World Order to be nothing less than the early stages of a blossoming world government and see emerging questions and problems in quite a different light. First of all, a world government would necessarily have to be a truly international body with significant enforcement powers. The United Nations in its present form can't protect its troops in Bosnia or meet its budget, let alone rule the world. If this sort of power were centered in a revamped world organization, imagine the problems that would confront America: Our economic policy would no longer truly be our own; our foreign policy would be subservient to an international body; basic guarantees of freedom of religion, press, and assembly could be curtailed. Any thinking person, whether he or she believes in conspiracy or not, would find such a dictatorial government odious. The question to be asked, however, is how likely this is to happen.[20]

## Conspiracy and Prophecy after the Cold War

Henry Kissinger recently described the New World Order as certainly far short of the euphoria surrounding its presentation in the wake of the Gulf War.[21] My own judgment concerning the possibility of a world government is that we are decades away from anything so pervasive, if it could be formed at all in the foreseeable future. Given the differences in culture, religion, society, and politics, the obstacles are truly enormous. After all, incorporation of a world system of the sort conspiracy theorists predict would mean the surrender of virtually all national sovereignty. Christian writers have joined secular conspiracy theorists on this bandwagon, too. Some have gone so far as to suggest that it will be the rapture of the church that will precipitate this demand for world order, others see an economic collapse, and still others see the threat of nuclear war. Whatever it is that will act as the predicted catalyst, it has yet to happen. We doubtless live in a time of great uncertainty; the sometimes wild speculation among Christians and non-Christians alike is testimony to this fact. It is just this uncertainty that requires all of us to exercise a great deal of caution before we draw any conclusions. Secular writers are, of course, aware of this uncertainty, too. One of Jimmy Carter's former cabinet members has written a number of books and articles dealing with just this problem. Despite the fact that conspiracy theorists consider him to be an insider of the Great Conspiracy, his views are well worth considering.

Zbigniew Brzezinski's *Out of Control* is a brilliant assessment of the late-twentieth-century world political conditions in the wake of the cold war. Brzezinski suggests that the world has gone from a place of generally understood events to one where change is happening so fast that it endangers our ability to react to it. In short, history has become condensed to the point where we lack the ability to properly deal with world situations as they arise. Our worldview, the author argues, is often based on outdated information, ideas, or philosophies—or misconstrued by new views that are erroneous.[22] That is essentially where we are today in the world—we lack the ability to see events around us in proper context.

In the West this problem is a deep one indeed. The ability of the United States to act as some sort of moral authority and guide in these uncertain times has eroded to the point of nonexistence. America has fallen by degrees into a philosophy of relativism that by its nature lacks compassion. A strong sense of right that even our enemies respected has given way to a new absolute: self-indulgence. It is precisely this hedonistic view of life that is most counterproductive in a world increasingly needing moral guidance. America is now in a most unenviable position: Rightly or wrongly, the world still tends to see us as a moral guidepost at a time when we lack the authority to dispense guidance. This again leaves a question: If the United States does not (or cannot) lead, will some world organization step in?

Despite the many uncertainties facing the United States and the world today, there is reason for hope, even optimism. Never before in the history of the world has there been so much potential for advances to be made in the world at large. Whether one considers scientific, medical, space research, agriculture, the thirst for democracy, or of course, the inner hunger for religious truth, there is reason to be hopeful. It is therefore necessary for the United States to once again find its moral bearings, to shed the patently false notion that all truth is relative. Without this sort of leadership, we would be little better off than moral Neanderthals having to deal with space-age problems. Remember, Nazi Germany was among the most technologically advanced nations on earth in the 1930s and 1940s: Its contributions in the arts, sciences, and any other field of endeavor did not save that nation from falling into the moral abyss.

In sum, the New World Order could turn out to be a number of things. It is possible that nothing at all will result from the efforts of those backing global government. Moreover, the very term *New World Order* may in time become obsolete, causing us to wonder a few years from now what all the fuss was about. If there is a world government on the horizon of the sort conservative Christians fear, I believe that there is danger of oversimplifying complex issues to fit prepackaged prophecy viewpoints.

## Prophecy, Millennialism, and Conspiracy

The nearness of the year 2000 has had many prophecy writers feverishly straining to put contemporary events into the context of Bible prophecy in anticipation of the coming of Christ and the establishment of his millennial kingdom. The belief in Christ's literal reign on earth for a one-thousand-year period is not a new one, nor is it the only interpretation of the millennial kingdom; indeed, at least two other interpretations have been around for a very long time and have been offered as possible explanations of biblical prophecy. Of course, this is to the chagrin of some in the Christian community who have their feet in theological cement when it comes to acceptance of contrary views of most anything outside of their belief system. This writer knows of many Christians (as doubtless the reader does, too) who refuse fellowship on the basis of something as minor as when they believe the rapture will occur—or not occur.[23] If beliefs surrounding such a topic—or for that matter whether or not you read the King James version—can separate believers, it should surprise no one that millennial interpretations can do the same. As has been shown with previous movements (Miller, Pitts, Baldwin, and others), belief in the premillennial coming of Jesus has taken many shapes over the course of American church history and is not, despite what some prophecy teachers tell us, the single monolithic view universally accepted since the time of the early church.[24] The other interpretations of Scripture references to the millennium fall into two basic camps: postmillennial and amillennial.

Postmillennial belief, simply stated, holds to the view that Christ's return will be at the end of the thousand-year period, which will in essence be the culmination of continued improvement in the world via conversion. Evil is not eradicated but reduced greatly as a result of continuous improvement of society and the healing of various and sundry social evils. When this is accomplished, Christ will return and judge the living and the dead. It should be pointed out that postmillennialists do not necessarily believe that the millennial period will be exactly one thousand years in length. According to many of this viewpoint, the thousand-year period could be symbolic.

Amillennialists hold to a somewhat similar view. According to this interpretation, the earth is constantly undergoing a battle between good and evil, which will ultimately result in the victory of good through conversion to Christianity. Like postmillennialists, amillennialists contend that all of earth's myriad problems will be eradicated through conversion to Christianity and that Christ will then return. Both views hold to the ultimate victory of Jesus and Christianity but in quite a different context than premillennialists present. Adherents of a non-premillennialist view have been among the most vocal critics of the more popular interpretation, and few more strident in their criticism than writers such as Gary North and R. J. Rushdoony, both of whom hold to what has been referred to as Kingdom Now or Dominion Theology.

One may well disagree with the postmillennial or amillennial positions from a theological point of view, but it is difficult to deny the many (and embarrassing) pronouncements that Christians have made concerning the coming of Jesus. Those holding to postmillennial or amillennial beliefs, whether one agrees with them or not, have not engendered the lunacy and anticipation common to the premillennial view concerning the return of Jesus. Indeed, there is little sense of urgency in either of these views.

The premillennialist view, however, predicts the soon, indeed, almost immediate return of Jesus to earth to mete out punishment or reward. Some prophecy ministries have gone so far as to declare anything other than a premillennial view as heresy and they attack it with great zeal.[25] Some even demonize those holding other views as deluded of Satan or perhaps even willfully propagating heresy.

While premillennial prophecy writers are legion, few writers of this genre are as well-known as Hal Lindsey. Like others in contemporary prophecy ministries, Lindsey also holds to some conspiratorial interpretations of history and eschatology.

### Hal Lindsey

In 1970 the Zondervan Publishing Company released a most influential book on prophecy entitled *The Late Great Planet Earth*. Its author, Hal Lindsey, had been a student at Dallas Theological Seminary and fine-tuned his work into a soon-to-be best-seller. In truth, Lindsey's writings did not unveil anything really new in the way of end-time revelation, but despite the voluminous amount of prophecy writings already out there, Hal Lindsey became the authority on the topic for millions of Christians. *The Late Great Planet Earth* kicked open prophetic doors to millions who had been ignorant (or initially uninterested) in prophetic teachings and presented prophecy to them in an easy-to-read style. Although Lindsey's book contained some disturbing predictions, of the millions of people who read it, many adopted the author's view of the future. It ushered in

the century's last prophecy frenzy, a phenomenon that continues to this day.[26]

While Lindsey was among the first and best known of the
"modern" prophecy writers, he is not without his detractors.
One area of his prophecy in particular that caused a stir was
Lindsey's emphasis on Israel as a time clock for end-time events.
Of course this was nothing new; prophecy writers decades and
even centuries earlier had suggested as much. Lindsey found
himself the subject of criticism when he postulated that a single generation would not pass away from the time of the reestablishment of Israel as a nation to the second coming of Christ.
Since Israel was (re)founded in 1948, Lindsey speculated that
by 1988 Christ could return. A generation in Scripture is thought
to be approximately forty years. The idea of Israel's connection
to this comes from the idea that Scripture uses the fig tree as a
symbol for national Israel. In Matthew 24:32–34, Jesus used the
parable of the fig tree when he stated that "this generation will
by no means pass away until all these things take place." The
"all things" according to Lindsey speaks of the context of the
conversation: signs of the end. Since 1988 came and went without the predicted end, Lindsey and many other writers sub-
scribing to this view came into varying degrees of disrepute. In
fairness to Hal Lindsey, it must be pointed out that he never
insisted that the end had to happen by 1988. He used the year
as a possible frame of reference. Still one has only to look at
Lindsey's publications and videotapes to see conspiracy theory
rear its ugly head; true, it's not anywhere close to the rabid, foam-
ing at the mouth sort, but it's there nonetheless.

A few examples of Lindsey's willingness to use conspiracy
theory ideas can be found in his *Plant Earth: 2000 A.D.* and a
number of his videos available through his ministry offices.[27]
Granted, Lindsey is not anywhere near the most radical proponent of these conspiracy ideas, but like Jack Van Impe, he
taps into them to make his point concerning what he sees as
the end of the age. This is unfortunate, especially since so many
anti-Semitic groups spout the same drivel. It is also ironic as
well as indisputable that Hal Lindsey is one of the staunchest
supporters of Israel and any number of Jewish causes in con-

servative American Christianity. It could well be that Mr. Lindsey is simply unaware of the unsavory source of much of conspiracy theory's ideology and literature.

If Lindsey blazed a path for other writers to follow, it was no
guarantee that subsequent books would be of any great quality. A few fringe books of the 1970s included Salem Kirban's
666, a fictionalized account of the coming of the Antichrist and
how it would change the world. It is, to put it kindly, a less-
than-compelling treatment of the topic. Unfortunately, so too
were his later works. Another book playing on the seemingly
endless Christian appetite for prophecy literature was Edgar
Whisenant's immensely popular 88 Reasons Why the Rapture
Will Be in 1988. While it is true that most prophecy teachers
are loathe to set dates for the second coming and would criticize Whisenant for doing so, the popularity of the book makes
a statement in and of itself.[28]

### Jack Van Impe, Charles Taylor, John Hagee, and the Lalondes

Other noteworthy writers and speakers include Jack Van
Impe of Michigan, who has been on the prophecy circuit for
decades and has been warning of the soon coming of Jesus
throughout his career. During 1994 Van Impe made open
prophetic suggestions pertaining to the year 2007 as a date to
watch; the reader will recall that increasing numbers of Christian writers adopted the Israeli taking of the Old City of
Jerusalem during the 1967 Six Day War rather than 1948 as a
point where the end times began. During the spring of 1995 the
Michigan prophecy teacher offered a revised version of Charles
Taylor's book proclaiming King Juan Carlos of Spain as the
Antichrist. Taylor is perhaps the most prolific date-setter for
the return of Christ. Although well meaning, his consistently
inaccurate proclamations would rival the most daring Jehovah
Witnesses. Van Impe has also been increasingly bold in his use
of Nostradamus as at least a somewhat authoritative source for
proving his end-time theories. Anyone who has read the writings of the French seer immediately recognizes the ambiguous

nature of his verse. It certainly is a less-than-reliable source on which to base one's interpretation of prophecy.[29]

Other recognizable but not original theories of Jack Van Impe include the "Six-Day—Six Thousand Year" teaching. This teaching asserts that just as a thousand years are like one day to God, so, too, should our count be concerning the last days. Since Adam was supposedly created around 4000 B.C., we are near A.D. 2000: Therefore, the "six days" are about up and Christ will soon establish his millennial kingdom on earth. Perhaps even more disturbing is Van Impe's suggestion that the Great Pyramid of Giza may be a "Bible in Stone," to borrow a phrase from the infamously inaccurate Southwest Radio Church. Van Impe was not the first to suggest this, nor was David Webber, one-time Southwest Radio Church minister. Dr. Gene Scott of Los Angeles is another advocate of this Pyramid theory.[30]

Van Impe has also gone on to dedicate more than one segment of his weekly television program to the fear of conspiracy increasingly common in Christendom, especially in the wake of the Oklahoma City federal building bombing in 1995. Van Impe holds to certain conspiracy ideas himself but differentiates his ideas from the much more radical sort that inspires terrorism. Indeed, Van Impe has gone so far as to lend verbal support to the Michigan militia as God-fearing men and women who would give no thought at all to causing harm to others. And, for the sake of clarity, I must clearly state that Van Impe is against violence of any sort and has spoken out against it on many occasions. Still, some of his views on world conspiracy are dangerously close to the radical fringe who are given to carnage. Although I support the right of the Michigan-based minister and others of like mind to speak their opinions, there is danger in how all of this is perceived in the minds of average Christian believers. A great misfortune is that many other Christian leaders agree with this world and prophecy view.[31] What is missing in this interpretation is a sound sense of history when it comes to conspiracy theory.

Another notable preacher/prophecy teacher is the inimitable Pastor John Hagee of the Cornerstone Church in San Antonio, Texas. Hagee is the quintessential fire and brimstone pastor, right down to his predictable pronunciation of glory as "glow-RAY!" The Texas-based minister has recently published a book dealing with the end times in which he predicts the end of Israeli independence as a result of giving up the Golan Heights and then signing a treaty with the Antichrist. Titled *Beginning of the End,* this Thomas Nelson publication will doubtless sell by the hundreds of thousands. It rehashes old premillennial prophecy themes and like an increasing number of such ministries, throws conspiracy theory into the mix.[32] The book unfortunately is just one more of a series of tired conspiracy-tainted prophecy monographs so common these days; there is scarcely an original idea to be found between its covers. The reader is "treated" to sensationalistic predictions about the Israeli State and the nearness of Christ's return based on conspiracy and closet date-setting. Hagee is not alone on the TBN airwaves making conspiracy allegations about the second coming.

The Niagara Falls–based Lalonde ministry and its chief outlet, *This Week in Bible Prophecy,* also engages in prophecy, interpretation of current events, and conspiracy theory. Peter Lalonde's books are replete with examples of how the "New World Order will soon descend on the planet and usher in the reign of Antichrist." To the ministry's credit, they state they do not know when Jesus will return, but one comes away with the distinct impression that if it isn't soon, it will definitely be a grand disappointment. Like Hal Lindsey and Jack Van Impe, Lalonde has a weekly program on the Trinity Broadcasting Network. From this platform, Lalonde insists that the end times are upon us and has his announcer close the weekly broadcast by saying, "Unless the Lord comes in the next seven days, we will see you next week."

The Lalonde ministry has published a number of videos and books on just this theme of the nearness of Christ's return. The most recent is *Left Behind,* written for those who will be literally left behind after the rapture. It is a sort of survival guide for those who are not fortunate enough to be taken up with Christ at the great "snatching away." This book was even used as a premium at TBN for the month of February 1996 for those who would send in support to the ministry.[33]

Unfortunately, most students of prophecy appear to be ignorant of the fact that every generation since the time of Christ has assumed that theirs would be the one to see his return. Indeed, the church has been subjected to sometimes outlandish, even weird, explanations of why the end of the world must happen in the immediate future. In the text of this book, I have listed only a very few. Still, when it comes to truly outlandish interpretations, few prophecy teachers of this genre have been able to outdo Jack Chick.

### Jack Chick

There have been few writers in the American Christian community who have more openly adopted a combined conspiracy/prophecy slant than Jack Chick of Chino, California. Owner and founder of Chick Publications, Chick is known worldwide for his comic-book-style tracts such as "This Was Your Life!" In recent years, however, Chick has given increased time and effort to exposing what he sees as the Antichrist system: the Roman Catholic Church. Based for the most part on the life of Alberto Rivera, an allegedly one-time Jesuit, Chick has distributed millions of tracts and comic books "exposing" Catholicism as the biblical Whore of Babylon. Rivera's story and claims of being a Jesuit spy, having inside knowledge of some sort of international Vatican plot, and now, since his conversion, having his life in danger, are suspect at best. Despite the evidence pointing to the fraudulent nature of Rivera's claims, Chick continues to cling to his belief in them and the implications: that Catholicism is un-Christian, and worse still, is involved in a worldwide plot to gain spiritual, economic, and political control of the planet. The Illuminati is even mentioned in a few "Alberto" comics where Rivera claims knowledge of Jesuit attendance at high-level black masses. The leader at one of these masses, Rivera claimed, was a member of the London branch of the Illuminati. With comics and some tracts like this, it should surprise no one that Chick Publications has compromised its credibility and become a hotbed for anti-Catholic bigotry.[34]

Of course, not all Christian prophecy writers fall into this trap. The danger is nonetheless there and must be guarded against. It is imperative that the church be on the alert for the sometimes subtle incursion of bigotry and conspiracy explanations of prophecy as the final word on the topic. Anti-Semitism is simply the easiest example to use: As shown above, bigotry can and does enter the church in any number of ways. Stereotyping and hatemongering have no place in Christianity and should be rejected, regardless of any pious wrapping covering them. In these days when believers are under attack from the secular press and in some cases the government for simply exercising their faith, the last thing the church needs to do is to provide ammunition to nonbelievers who already hold bigoted views of Christianity.

## Conclusion

In this short book I have attempted to provide something of an overview of conspiracy theories and prophecy belief as they have existed in recent decades. In taking on such a task, it was apparent from the beginning that I would have to be selective in my examples. I hope that my choices provide the reader with the gist of my thesis: Conspiracy theories and talk of the end of the world have been going on for centuries and have been believed just as passionately as any held today. What therefore needs to be exercised is a good deal of caution when combining traditional eschatological beliefs with conspiracy theory. There is a very real danger that Christians could pick up some extra spiritual baggage in their understandable zeal to recognize the "signs of the times."

Because we live in an increasingly complex world, it is not surprising that people look to unusual sources for explanations of why things have changed so quickly. As the pace of change picks up speed, you can expect to see more people grabbing onto any number of answers as to why things are as they are. Christians need to take care not to step outside of the bounds set in Scripture when trying to tie spiritual meaning to it all.

Dealing with a modern world and then trying to apply ancient texts to explain it (at least in the literal sense) can open the way for some outlandish ideas. As mentioned earlier, there is a growing sense of expectancy as we near the end of the twentieth century and the beginning of a new century and millennium. Expect to see even more of this "sign-reading" in the months and years to come. You will see them in the area of economics, politics, and religion. All will tend to be highly apocalyptic; some will be conspiratorial in content and tone. Caution, again, must be the watchword for Christians.

Finally, besides faith and the Holy Spirit, the bottom line in deciding if conspiracy theories are true, the accuracy of prophecy interpretation, or any area of theology or philosophy is one's own thought and decision-making process. Simply put, think for yourself! Just because a respected or recognized Christian leader makes pronouncements does not necessarily mean it is so. It is perfectly natural for Christians to look for and anticipate the return of Jesus, but this should not be the core of the Church's worldview. The Person coming, not the event itself, is the important element.

# Selected Bibliography of Conspiracy Theory

What follows is a list of just some of the material I read while researching this book. I have included it here for those who wish to conduct further research. Resources are organized by categories for the reader's convenience. The materials listed under a particular heading may express views in favor of or against the topic. For example, some of the works listed under "Anti-Semitism" are offensively anti-Semitic in content or tone. Most, however, are filled with questionable interpretations. This is especially true pertaining to conspiratorial works dealing with Jewish history, conspiracy theory, and, sadly, Christian views of the end times. This bibliography is by no means comprehensive but is intended to provide the scholar and the curious with a place to start.

## Mainstream Historians against Conspiracy Theorists

Barker, William E. *The Aryan Nations: A Linkage Profile*. William E. Barker, 1986.

Bell, Daniel. *The Radical Right*. Garden City, N.Y.: Doubleday, 1963.

Berlet, Chip, and Matthew N. Lyons. *Too Close for Comfort: Right Wing Populism, Scapegoating, and the Fascist Potential in U.S. Politics*. Boston: Southend Press, in press.

Clabaugh, Gary K. *Thunder on the Right: The Protestant Fundamentalists*. Chicago: Nelson Hall, 1974.

Coates, James. *Armed and Dangerous: The Rise of the Survivalist Right*. New York: Noonday Press, 1987.

Cohn, Norman. *The Pursuit of the Millennium: Revolutionary Millenarians and Mystical Anarchists of the Middle Ages.* New York: Oxford University Press, 1970.

Conway, Flo, and Jim Siegleman. *Holy Terror: The Fundamentalist War on America's Freedoms in Religion, Politics and Our Private Lives.* Garden City, N.Y.: Doubleday, 1982.

Crawford, Alan. *Thunder on the Right: The "New Right" and the Politics of Resentment.* New York: Pantheon, 1980.

Curry, Richard O., and Thomas Brown, eds. *Conspiracy: The Fear of Subversion in American History.* New York: Holt, Rinehart, and Winston, 1972.

Davis, David Brion. *The Fear of Conspiracy: Images of Un-American Subversion from the Revolution to the Present.* Ithaca, N.Y.: Cornell University Press, 1971.

Donner, Frank J. *The Age of Surveillance: The Aims and Methods of America's Political Intelligence System.* New York: Vintage, 1981.

Erlinger, Robert. *The Conspiracy Peddlers.* Mason, Mich.: Loompanics Unlimited, 1981.

Finch, Phillip. *God, Guts, and Guns—A Close Look at the Radical.* New York: Seaview/Putnam, 1983.

Hofstadter, Richard. *The Age of Political Reform.* New York: Vintage, 1955.

———. *The Paranoid Style in American Politics and Other Essays.* Chicago: University of Chicago Press, Phoenix, 1979.

Johnson, George. *Architects of Fear: Conspiracy Theories and Paranoia in American Politics.* Los Angeles: Jeremy Tarcher, 1983.

Jorstad, Eric. *The Politics of Doomsday: Fundamentalists of the Far Right.* Nashville: Abingdon Press, 1970.

Jorstad, Erling. *The Politics of Moralism: The New Christian Right in American Life.* Minneapolis: Augsburg, 1981.

Kornhausser, William. *The Politics of Mass Society.* New York: The Free Press, 1959.

Lipset, Seymour Martin, and Earl Raab. *The Politics of Unreason: Rightwing Extremism in America, 1790–1977.* 2nd ed. Chicago: University of Chicago Press, 1978.

Lowenthal, Leo, and Norbert Guterman. *Prophets of Deceit.* New York: Vintage Press, 1949.

Marsden, George M. *Fundamentalism and the American Culture: The Shaping of 20th Century Evangelism, 1870–1925.* New York: Oxford University Press, 1970.

Myers, Gustavus. *History of Bigotry in the United States.* New York: Random House, 1953.

**Conspiracy Theory**

Aarons, M. Loftus. *Unholy Trinity.*
Agee, P. *Dirty Work.*
———. *Inside the Company.*
———. *On the Run.*

Allen, Gary. *None Dare Call It Conspiracy.*
———. *Rockefeller: Campaigning for the New World Order.*
———. *The Rockefeller File.*
———. *Say "NO!" to the New World Order.*
Alterman, E. *Sound and Fury.*
Armstrong, Judge George. *Rothschild Money Trust.*
Baker, Jeffrey A. *Cheque Mate: The Game of Princes.*
Bates, Larry. *The New Economic Disorder.*
Beaty, John. *The Iron Curtain over America.*
Beckman, M. J. *Walls in Our Mind.*
Benson, Ezra Taft. *A Nation Asleep.*
Bramley, William. *The Gods of Eden.*
Brewton, Pete. *The Mafia, CIA, and George Bush.*
Carr, William G. *Pawns in the Game.*
———. *Red Fog over America.*
Carroll, Gerald A. *Project Seek.*
Case, P. F. *The Great Seal of the United States, Its History, Symbolism and Message for the New Age.*
Chomsky, Noam. *Necessary Illusions.*
Cobb, W. H. *The American Challenge.*
Coleman, John. *Conspirators' Hierarchy: The Story of the Committee of 300.*
Collier, Kenneth, and James Collier. *Votescam: The Stealing of America.*
Constable, Trevor James. *The Cosmic Pulse of Life.*
Cooper, William. *Behold a Pale Horse.*
Daniel, John. *Scarlet and the Beast,* 3 vols.
Daraul, Arkin. *A History of Secret Societies.*
DeLove, Sidney. *The Quiet Betrayal.*
Deyo, Stan. *The Cosmic Conspiracy.*
———. *The Vindicator Scrolls.*
Eakman, B. K. *Educating for the New World Order.*
Eden, Jerome. *Scavengers from Space.*
Elleston, Roger C. *The Highlights of the Power of Parameters of Money.*
Emory, Dave. *UFO Phenomenon and ET Myth.*
Emry, Sheldon. *Billions for Bankers, Debts for People.*
Epperson, Ralph. *The Unseen Hand.*
Eringer, Robert. *The Global Manipulators.*
Farrell, James. *The Judas Syndrome.*
Garett, Garet. *The People's Pottage.*
Gill, Stephen. *American Hegemony and the Trilateral Commission.*
Golitsyn, Anatoly. *New Lies for Old.*
Griffin, Des. *Descent into Slavery?*
———. *Fourth Reich of the Rich.*
Hargis, Billy James. *The Real Extremists—the Far Left.*
Hieronymous, Robert. *America's Secret Destiny.*
———. *The Two Great Seals of America.*
———. *The 200th Anniversary of America's Great Seal.*
Hoffman, Michael A. *Secret Societies and Psychological Warfare.*

Holmes, Donald. *The Illuminati Conspiracy.*
House, Col. Edward. *Phillip Dru.*
Howard, Michael. *The Occult Conspiracy.*
*It's a Conspiracy!* A Compilation.
Jeffrey, Grant. *Apocalypse.*
———. *Messiah.*
———. *The Prince of Darkness.*
Jurjevich, Ray. *Aliens and American Strategy.*
Kah, Gary. *Demonic Roots of Globalism.*
———. *En Route to Global Occupation.*
Kaplan, Louis. *The Damned Universe of Charles Fort.*
Keith, Jim. *Black Helicopters over America.*
Keith, Jim, ed. *Casebook on Alternative 3: UFO's, Secret Societies and World Control.*
———. *The Gemstone File.*
———. *Secret and Suppressed.*
Kincaid, Cliff. *Global Bondage: The U.N. Plan to Rule the World.*
King, John L. *Chaos in America.*
Kirban, Salem. *How the Money Manipulators Keep You Poor!*
———. *The Illuminati.*
———. *The Power Seekers: The Bilderbergers and the CFR.*
———. *The Trilateral Commission.*
Knuth, E. C. *Empire of the City.*
Lillie, Dean. *America: Liberty or Tyranny.*
Linington, Elizabeth. *Come to Think about It.*
Manion, Dean. *Let's Face It.*
Marrs, Texe. *Circle of Intrigue.*
———. *Dark Majesty.*
Martin, Len. *The Attack on Gordon Kahl at Medina (ND).*
———. *The Feds Lose Big.*
Martin, Malachi. *The Keys of This Blood.*
McAlvany, Donald S. *Toward a New World Order.*
McCarthy, Joseph. *America's Retreat from Victory.*
Monk, Maria. *Awful Disclosures.*
Mullins, Eustace. *The Curse of Canaan.*
———. *Murder by Injection.*
———. *The Rape of Justice.*
———. *Secrets of the Federal Reserve.*
———. *The World Order.*
———. *A Writ for Martyrs.*
Noebel, David A. *Communism, Hypnotism, and the Beatles.*
———. *The New Americanism.*
Oliver, Revelo P. *All America Must Know That the Terror Is upon Us.*
Perhoff, James. *Shadows of Power.*
Ramsey, Captain A. H. M. *The Nameless War.*
Ravenscroft, Trevor. *Spear of Destiny.*
Ripplinger, G. A. *New Age Versions (of the Bible).*

Rivera, David Allen. *Final Warning: A History of the New World Order.*
Roberts, Archibald E. *The Most Secret Science.*
Robertson, Pat. *The New World Order.*
Robison, John. *Proofs of a Conspiracy.*
Russell, Dean. *Government and Legal Plunder.*
Sklar, Holly. *Trilateral Commission and Elite Planning for World Management.*
Skousen, Cleon. *The Naked Capitalist.*
———. *The Naked Communist.*
———. *To Seduce a Nation.*
Spear, Robert K. *Living under the New World Order.*
———. *Surviving Global Slavery.*
Spenser, Keith. *Cult of the All-Seeing Eye.*
Springmeier, Fritz. *The Top 14 Illuminati Bloodlines.*
Stormer, John H. *None Dare Call It Coincidence.*
Sutton, Anthony C. *America's Secret Establishment.*
———. *The Best Enemy Money Can Buy.*
Thomas, Harold, ed. *World Power Foundation: Its Goals and Platform.*
Turner, Capstan, and A. Jay Lowery. *There Was a Man: The Saga of Gordon Kahl.*
Vankin, Jonathan. *Conspiracies, Cover-ups and Crimes.*
Vankin, Jonathan, and John Whalen. *Fifty Greatest Conspiracies of All Time.*
Warner, Ken. *Give U.S. a King.*
Webster, Nesta. *Boche and Bolshevik.*
———. *The French Revolution.*
———. *Secret Societies and Subversive Movements.*
———. *Socialist Network.*
———. *Surrender of an Empire.*
Weishaupt, Adam. *An Apology for the Illuminati.* (1787)
———. *An Improved System of the Illuminati.*
———. *A Picture of the Illuminati.* (1786)
Welch, Robert. *The Blue Book.*
———. *A Brief Introduction to the John Birch Society.*
Wickstrom, James. *The American Farmer: 20th Century Slaves.*
Wilgus, Neil. *The Illuminoids.*
Wilson, Robert Anton. *Cosmic Trigger I: Final Secret of the Illuminati.*
———. *Cosmic Trigger II: Down to Earth.*
———. *The Illuminati Conspiracy: The Sapiens System.*
———. *Illuminati Papers.*
———. *Masks of the Illuminati.*
———. *Right Where You Are Sitting Now.*

## Anti-Semitism

Bakony, Istvan. *Chinese Communism and Chinese Jews.*
———. *The Fifth Column in Japan.*
———. *The Jewish Fifth Column in India.*
———. *The Jewish Fifth Column in Islam.*

————. *Jews Want to Dominate Negroes.*

————. *Paranoid Judaism.*

————. *What Is Judaism?*

Belloc, Hilaire. *The Jews.*

Benson, Ivor. *The Zionist Factor.*

Bergmeister, Karl. *The Jewish World Conspiracy—the Protocols before the Court in Berne, Switzerland.*

————. *My Farewell to Israel, Thorn in the Middle East.*

Bex, Bryan. *The Hidden Hand.*

Bey, Major Osman. *The Conquest of the World by Jews.*

Bielsky, Louis. *The Soviet-Israeli Claw Strangles the Arabs.*

Brenner, Lenni. *Zionism in the Age of Dictators.*

Brown, Bruce. *The World's Greatest Trouble-Makers.*

Bujak, F. *The Jewish Question in Poland.*

Burton, Sir Richard. *The Jew, the Gypsy, and El Islam.*

Butz, Arthur. *The Hoax of the 20th Century.*

*The Cause of Anti-Jewishness in the United States.*

Cherep-Spiridovich, Major General. *Jews and the Catholic Church.*

Chomsky, Noam. *The Fateful Triangle: The US, Israel, and the Palestinians.*

————. *Pirates and Emperors: International Terrorism in the Real World.*

Coleman, Dr. John. *Conspirators' Hierarchy: The Story of the Committee of 300.*

Combs, James. *Christian Sheep and Satan's Wolves.*

————. *Who's Who in the Zionist Conspiracy.*

Connor, J. E. *Christ Was Not a Jew.*

Coughlin, Father Charles. *Persecution—Jewish and Christian and Let Us Consider the Record.*

Cuddy, Dennis L. *Israel and the New World Order.*

Curtis, Richard S. *Stealth PAC's: How Israel's American Lobby Took Control of US Middle East Policy.*

Day, Donald. *Onward Christian Soldiers.*

DePoncines, Leon. *Judaism and the Vatican.*

Dilling, Elizabeth. *The Jewish Religion.*

Eckhart, Dietrich. *The Red Dragon and Black Shirts—How Italy Found Her Soul.*

Edmondson, Robert E. *The Damning Parallels of the Protocol "Forgeries."*

Elmhurst, Ernest. *The World Hoax.*

Faurisson, Robert. *Faurisson on the Holocaust.*

Feeney, Rev. Leonard. *The Judaizing of Christians by Jews.*

Field, A. N. *Today's Greatest Problem—the Jews.*

Findley, Rep. Paul. *They Dare to Speak Out.*

Fisher, Paul. *Their God Is the Devil.*

Flynn, John. *The Smear Campaign.*

Ford, Henry. *The International Jew.*

Freedman, Benjamin. *Facts Are Facts.*

Fry, L. *An Analysis of Zionism.*

————. *Waters Flowing Eastward.*

Gabler, Neil. *An Empire of Their Own: How the Jews Invented Hollywood.*
Ginn, Gordon L. *The Late Great Road to Holocaust.*
Goebbels, Joseph. *The Truth about Stalin.*
Goff, Kenneth. *The Jewish Power.*
———. *Still 'Tis Our Ancient Foe.*
Good, O. B. *The Hidden Hand of Judah.*
Graham, O. J. *The Six-Pointed Star.*
*The Great Jewish Masque.*
Griffin, Des. *Anti-Semitism and the Babylonian Connection.*
Halsell, Grace. *Prophecy and Politics: Militant Evangelists on the Road to Nuclear War.*
Harwood, Richard. *Six Million Lost and Found.*
Higger, Michael. *The Jewish Utopia.*
*Historical Fact #1: Did Six Million Really Die?*
Hitler, Adolf. *Mein Kampf.*
*Hitler's Last Testament—The Hitler-Bormann Documents.*
Hoffman, Michael A. *The Great Holocaust Trial.*
*Holy Book of Adolph Hitler.*
*The Holy See and the Jews.*
Hoskins, Richard Kelly. *Our Nordic Race.*
Jensen, B. *The Palestine Plot.*
John, Robert. *Behind the Balfour Declaration.*
Jurjevich, Ray M. *The Fear of Jews Syndrome in America,* 2 vols.
Klein, Henry. *A Jew Exposes the Jewish World Conspiracy.*
———. *Zionism Rules the World.*
Koestler, Arthur. *The Thirteenth Tribe.*
Kotler, Yair. *Heil Kahane.*
Lease, Arnold. *Bolshevism Is Jewish.*
———. *Devilry in the Holy Land.*
———. *Gentile Folly: The Rothschilds.*
———. *Jewish Ritual Murder.*
———. *Jewish War for Survival.*
Lenski, Robert. *Holocaust on Trial: The Case of Ernest Zuendel.*
Leuchter, Paul. *The Leuchter Report.*
Luther, Martin. *The Jews and Their Lies.*
Malcolm, James A. *Origins of the Balfour Declaration.*
Marsden, Victor. *Jews in Russia.*
Marsden, Victor, ed. and trans. *The Protocols of the Elders of Zion.*
McLaughlin, Michael. *Death of a City.*
Mullins, Eustace. *New History of the Jews.*
O'Beaty, Dr. John. *The Iron Curtain over America.*
O'Brien, Lee. *American Jewish Organizations and Israel.*
Pickney, George. *Jewish "Anti-Communism."*
Pike, T. W. *Israel: Our Duty, Our Dilemma.*
Pinay, Maurice. *The Plot against the Church.*
Pool and Pool. *Who Financed Hitler?*
Prainatis. *The Talmud Unmasked.*

Rassinier, Paul. *The Holocaust Story and the Lies of Ulysses.*
———. *The Real Eichmann Trial or the Incorrigible Victors.*
Ravage, Marcus Ely. *The Real Case against the Jews.*
Reed, Douglas. *The Controversy of Zion.*
———. *Far and Wide.*
———. *Somewhere South of Suez.*
Rittenhouse, Stan. *For Fear of the Jews.*
Rokach, Lavia. *Israel's Sacred Terrorism.*
Roques, Henri. *The "Confessions" of Kurt Gerstein.*
Rullman, Hans Peter. *Victim of the Holocaust.*
Samuel, Maurice. *Your Gentiles.*
Schrieber, Haviv. *Holy Land Betrayed.*
The Sisson Report. *The German-Bolshevik Conspiracy.*
Smith, Gary. *Land of ZOG* (Zionist Occupational Government).
Staeglich, Judge Wilhelm. *Auschwitz: A Judge Looks at the Evidence.*
Stoddard, Lothrop. *A Gallery of Jewish Types.*
Swift, Wesley. *Was Jesus Christ a Jew?*
Tenny, Jack B. *Anti-Gentile Activity in the United States.*
———. *Jews in the Russian Revolution.*
Thompson, H. K., and Henry Strutz. *Doenitz at Nuremberg.*
Wagner, Richard. *Judaism in Music.*
Warburg, Sidney. *Hitler's Secret Backers.*
Warner, James. *The Real Hate Mongers.*
Williams, Robert H. *The Anti-Defamation League.*
———. *The Ultimate World Order.*
Winrod, Gerald. *Adam Weishaupt—A Human Devil.*
———. *The Jewish Assault on Christianity.*
———. *The Truth about Protocols.*

**Freemasonry**

Allsopp, Fred W. *Albert Pike: A Biography.*
Ankerberg, John, and John Weldon. *Bowing at Strange Altars.*
———. *The Secret Teachings of the Masonic Lodge.*
Ankerberg, John, John Weldon, Jack Harris, et al. *The Masonic Lodge: What Goes on behind Closed Doors.* (Transcript from the John Ankerberg Show)
Brophy, Edward. *Brotherhood Religion—Is It Christian?*
Burman, Edward. *The Templars: Knights of God.*
Burns, Cathy. *Hidden Secrets of the Eastern Star.*
Cagliostro, Comte de. *Cagliostro's Secret Ritual of Egyptian Rite Freemasonry.*
Carrico, David. *Lucifer, Eliphas, Albert Pike, and the Masonic Lodge.*
———. *Manley P. Hall. The Honored Masonic Author.*
———. *The Masonic/Egyptian/Satanic Connection.*
———. *The Occult Meaning of the Great Seal of the United States.*
———. *The Pentagram, Freemasonry, and the Goat.*
Cook, Benjamin. *Freemasonry Condemned from Its Own Sources.*
*Egyptian Mysteries: An Account of an Initiation.*

Evans, Henry R. *History of the York and Scottish Rite.*
Jouin. *Papacy and Freemasonry.*
Knight, Stephen. *The Brotherhood: Secret World of Freemasonry.*
Lang, R. Ossian. *The Comacine Masters.*
Mackey, Albert G. *Encyclopedia of Freemasonry,* 2 vols.
Maria y Rodriguez, Cardinal José. *Mystery of Freemasonry Unveiled.*
McReavy, Lawrence. *Forbidden and Secret Societies.*
Morgan, Captain William. *Freemasonry Exposed.*
Pike, Albert. *Liturgies of the Ancient and Accepted Scottish Rite of Freemasonry.*
————. *Liturgy of the Blue Degrees.*
*Rituals of the Swedenborgian Rite of Masonry.*
Ronayne, Edmond. *Freemasonry at a Glance.*
Schnoebelen, William. *Beyond the Light.*
Shaw, Jim. *The Deadly Deception.*
Storms, E. M. *Should a Christian Be a Mason?*
*The Textbook of Advanced Freemasonry.*
*Three Distinct Knocks.*
Wagner, Martin. *Freemasonry: An Interpretation.*
Waite, Arthur E. *Brotherhood of the Rosy Cross.*
————. *The Templars: Knights of God.*
Woodrow, Ralph. *Babylonian Mystery Religion: Ancient and Modern Dissertations and Theses Relating to Freemasonry.*

**UFOs, Physics, and Conspiracy**

Adamski, George. *Inside the Flying Saucers.*
Amdahl, Kenn. *There Are No Electrons.*
Andrews, George C. *Extraterrestrials among Us.*
————. *Extraterrestrial Friends and Foes.*
Barker, Bill. *The Complete Schwa Kit.*
Beckley, Timothy G. *The UFO Silencers.*
Bennett, Virginia. *A UFO Primer.*
Bernard, Raymond. *The Hollow Earth.*
Cathie, Bruce L. *The Bridge to Infinity: Harmonic 371244.*
————. *The Energy Grid: Harmonic 695.*
————. *The Harmonic Conquest of Space.*
Chatelain, Maurice. *Our Cosmic Ancestors.*
Childress, David Hatcher. *Extraterrestrial Archaeology.*
————. *The Fantastic Inventions of Nikola Tesla.*
————. *The Free-energy Device Handbook.*
Childress, David Hatcher, ed. *Anti-Gravity and the Unified Field.*
————. *Anti-Gravity and the World Grid.*
————. *The Anti-Gravity Handbook.*
Commander "X." *Nikola Tesla: Free Energy and the White Dove.*
————. *Underground Alien Bases.*
Constable, Trevor James. *The Cosmic Pulse of Life.*
Cooper, William. *Behold a Pale Horse.*

Crandall, B. C., ed. *Nanotechnology*.

Curran, Douglas. *In Advance of the Landing: Folk Concepts of Outer Space*.

Cyr, Donald., ed. *America's First Crop Circle*.

———. *Crop Circle Secrets*.

Dannelley, Richard. *Sedona UFO Connection*.

Deavereaux, Paul. *Earth Lights Revelation: UFOs and the Mystery Light*.

Delgado, Pat, and Colin Andrews. *Circular Evidence*.

de Meos, James. *The Orgone Accumulator Handbook*.

Deyo, Stan. *The Cosmic Conspiracy*.

———. *The Vindicator Scrolls*.

Dione, R. L. *God Drives a Flying Saucer*.

Edwards, Frank. *Flying Saucers—Serious Business*.

Fawcett, Lawrence, and Barry Greenwood. *Clear Intent: The Government Coverup of the UFO Experience*.

Friedman, Stanton. *Crash at Corona*.

Fuller, John G. *The Interrupted Journey*.

Gaddis, Vincent. *Mysterious Fires and Lights*.

Godwin, Joscelyn. *Arktos: The Polar Myth*.

Green, Gabriel. *Let's Face the Facts about Flying Saucers*.

Greene, Vaughn. *The Six Thousand Year-Old Space Suit*.

Greenfield, Allen. *Secret Cyphers of the UFOnaughts*.

Gribben, John R., and Stephen H. Plagemann. *The Jupiter Effect*.

Grossinger, Richard. *Planetary Mysteries*.

———. *Waiting for the Martian Express*.

Guthrie, Kenneth Sylvan. *The Pythagorean Sourcebook*.

Hamilton, William F. III. *Cosmic Top Secret*.

Hansen, Brad and Sherry. *Super Scientists of Ancient Atlantis and Other Unknown Worlds*.

Harrison, C. G. *The Transcendental Universe*.

Hayes, Jeffrey. *Tesla Technology: Series*, vol. 2.

Heinerman, John. *People in Space*.

Hendry, Allan. *The UFO Handbook*.

Hoagland, Richard. *The Monuments of Mars*.

Hynek, J. Allen. *The UFO Experience: A Scientific Inquiry*.

Jacobs, David M. *Secret Life: Firsthand Accounts of UFO Abductions*.

———. *The UFO Controversy in America*.

Kalton-Minkel, Walter. *Subterranean Worlds*.

Kaplan, Louis. *The Damned Universe of Charles Fort*.

Keith, Jim. *Casebook on Alternative 3*.

Keyhoe, Major Donald. *Aliens from Space*.

———. *Flying Saucers from Outer Space*.

Knap, George. *Spaceship Conspiracy*.

Lindemann, Michael. *UFO's and the Alien Presence: Six Viewpoints*.

Lorenzen, Coral E. *Flying Saucers*.

Lyne, William T. *Space Aliens from the Pentagon: Flying Saucers Are Man-Made Electrical Machines*.

Mack, John E. *Abduction: Human Encounters with Aliens*.

McDaniel, Stanley. *The McDaniel Report.*

Menzel, Donald H., and Ernest H. Taves. *The UFO Enigma: The Definitive Explanation of the UFO Phenomenon.*

Montgomery, Ruth. *Aliens among Us.*

Nichols, Preston N. *The Montauk Project: Experiments in Time.*

Nichols, Preston N., and Peter Moon. *Montauk Revisited.*

North, Carolyn. *Crop Circles: Hoax or Happening?*

O'Leary, Brian. *Exploring Inner and Outer Space.*

———. *The Second Coming of Science.*

Randle, Kevin D., and Donald Schmitt. *UFO Crash at Roswell.*

Randles, Jenny. *From Out of the Blue.*

———. *UFO's and How to See Them.*

Ruppelt, Edward J. *The Report on Unidentified Flying Objects.*

Sanderson, Ivan T. *Invisible Residents: A Disquisition upon Certain Matters Maritime, and the Possibility of Intelligent Life under the Waters of This Earth.*

Schellhorn, G. Cope. *Extraterrestrials among Us.*

Schonberger, Martin. *The I-Ching and Genetic Code.*

Screeton, Paul, and Donald Cyr. *Seeks of the Linear Vision.*

Steiger, Bielek. *The Philadelphia Experiment and Other UFO Conspiracies.*

Tesla, Nikola. *The Fantastic Inventions of Nikola Tesla.*

———. *Tesla Technology*, vol. 1.

Thomas, John. *Anti-Gravity: The Dream Made Reality.*

Thompson, Richard L. *Alien Identities.*

———. *Vedic Cosmology and Astronomy.*

Trinkaus, George. *Radio Tesla.*

———. *Tesla: The Lost Inventions.*

———. *Tesla Coil.*

Turner, Karla. *Taken: Inside the Alien-Human Abduction Agenda.*

*UFO Encyclopedia. Apogee Books.*

Vallee, Jacques. *Forbidden Science.*

Vesco, Renato, and David Hatcher Childress. *Man-Made UFO's, 1944–1994.*

von Daniken, Erich. *Chariots of the Gods?*

———. *Gods from Outer Space.*

Watts, Alan. *UFO Quest.*

Williamson, George H. *Other Tongues, Other Flesh.*

Wood, David, and Ian Campbell. *Geneset: Target Earth.*

Zindler, Frank. *The UFO of Bethlehem.*

### UFO-Related Videos

Unless noted, all videos are available from Adventures Unlimited, Inc.

*Etheric Weather Engineering,* with Treavor James Constable.

*Eye of the Storm,* with Stan Deyo.

*The Montauk Project Tour,* with Preston Nichols.

*Nikola Tesla.* Nikola Tesla Museum, Belgrade.

*Stan Deyo in Conference.*

**New Age Movement**

Achad, Frater. *The Egyptian Revival.*
Agrippa, H. C. *Fourth Book of Occult Philosophy.*
Albrecht, Mark. *Reincarnation.*
Amberston, Celu. *Blessings of the Blood.*
Anderson, Bill. *Life Cycles: The Astrology of Inner Space.*
Anderson, Red. *The Healer's Manual: A Beginner's Guide to Vibrational Therapies.*
Andrews, Ted. *Dream Alchemy, Shaping Dreams.*
———. *How to Uncover Your Past Lives.*
———. *The Occult Christ.*
Ankerberg, John, and John Weldon. *The Facts on the New Age.*
Aurobindo, Sri. *The Mother.*
Bacon, Francis. *New Atlantis.*
Baer, Randall. *Inside the New Age Nightmare.*
Bailey, Alice. *The Destiny of Nations.*
———. *Education in the New Age.*
———. *The Externalization of Hierarchy.*
———. *The Problems of Humanity.*
———. *The Reappearance of the Christ.*
Baron, Will. *Deceived by the New Age.*
Bartley, W. W. *Werner Erhardt: The Transformation of a Man: The Founding of EST.*
Basil, Robert, ed. *Not Necessarily the New Age.*
Benares, Camden. *Common Sense Tarot.*
Bernbaum, Edwin. *The Way to Shambala.*
Bernstein, Henrietta. *The Crone Oracles.*
Berwick, Ann. *Essential Holistic Aromatherapy.*
Bloom, William. *Devas, Fairies, and Angels.*
Bobgan, Martin, and Diedre Bobgan. *Hypnosis and the Christian.*
Boss, Judy. *A Garden of Joy.*
———. *In Silence They Return.*
Breaux, Charles. *The Way of Karma.*
Brooke, Tal. *Lord of the Air.*
———. *Riders of the Cosmic Circuit.*
———. *When the World Will Be as One.*
Bruyere, Rosalyn. *Wheels of Light.*
Burt, Kathleen. *Archetypes of the Zodiac.*
Campanelli, Dan, and Pauline Campanelli. *Circles, Groves, and Sanctuaries.*
Campbell, Bruce. *Ancient Wisdom Revived: A History of the Theosophical Society.*
Campbell, Joseph. *The Hero with a Thousand Faces.*
———. *The Inner Reaches of Outer Space: Metaphor as Myth and as Religion.*
Campbell, Joseph, and Bill Moyers. *The Power of Myth.*
Carroll, David. *The Magic Makers.*
Case, Paul F. *The True and Invisible Rosicrucian Order.*

Castaneda, Carlos. *The Teachings of Don Juan.*
Castleden, Rodney. *The Making of Stonehenge.*
Clow, Barbara H. *Chiron: Rainbow Bridge between the Inner and Outer Planets.*
Circle Network. *Circle Guide to Wicca and Pagan Resources.*
———. *Magickal Contacts: An Updated Supplement to the 1981 Circle Guide to Wicca and Pagan Resources.*
Coffman, Michael. *Environmentalism: Dawn of the Age of Aquarius.*
———. *Saviors of the Earth?*
Conway, D. J. *Ancient and Shining Ones.*
Corydon, Bent. L. *Ron Hubbard—Messiah or Madman?*
Creme, Benjamin. *The Reappearance of Christ and the Masters of Wisdom.*
Crisp, Tony. *Dream Dictionary.*
Culling, Louis. *The Pristing Yi Ching.*
Cunningham, Scott. *Encyclopedia of Crystal, Gem and Metal Magic.*
———. *Encyclopedia of Magical Herbs.*
de Chardin, Teilhard. *Building the Earth.*
———. *The Heart of the Matter.*
———. *How I Believe.*
———. *Human Energy.*
———. *Hymn of the Universe.*
———. *The Phenomenon of Man.*
Denning, Melita, and Osborne Phillips. *Astral Projection.*
———. *Creative Visualization.*
Devereaux, Paul. *Earth Memory: Sacred Sites—Doorway into Earth's Mysteries.*
Donnelly, Ignatius. *Atlantis: The Antediluvian World.*
Eadie, Betty J. *Embraced by the Light.*
Faivre, Antoine. *Access to Western Esotericism.*
Ferguson, Marilyn. *The Aquarian Conspiracy.*
Flowers, Stephen. *Fire and Ice: Magical Teachings of Germany's Secret Occult Order.*
Frawley, David. *Gods, Sages, and Kings: Vedic Secrets of Ancient Civilization.*
Fuller, Buckminster. *The Critical Path.*
Gamache, Henri. *Master Book of Candle Burning.*
Gardener, Martin. *New Age: Notes of a Fringe-Watcher.*
———. *Urantia: The Great Cult Mystery.*
George, Llewellyn. *The New A to Z Horoscope Maker and Delineator.*
Glass-Koentop, Pattalee. *The Magic in the Stones.*
Goodwin, Joscelyn. *The Chemical Wedding of Christian Rosenkreutz.*
Gordon, James S. *Channelling into the New Age: The "Teachings" of Shirley MacLaine and Others.*
———. *Golden Guru: The Strange Journey of Bhagwan Shree Rajneesh.*
Gray, William. *Thinking Critically about New Age Ideas.*
Green, Jeff. *Pluto: The Evolutionary Journey of the Soul.*
———. *Uranus: Freedom from the Known.*
Groothius, Douglas. *Revealing the New Age Jesus.*
———. *Unmasking the New Age.*
Gunther, Bernard. *Energy Ecstasy and Your Seven Vital Chakras.*

Guttman, Ariel, and Kenneth Johnson. *Mythic Astrology.*
Haraldsson, Erlendur. *Modern Miracles: An Investigative Report on Psychic Phenomenon Associated with Sathya Sai Baba.*
Harding, Elizabeth. *Kali: The Black Goddess of Dakshineswar.*
Harold, Edmund. *Focus on Crystals.*
Harvey, Andrew. *Hidden Journey.*
Heady, Joseph, and S. L. Cranston. *Reincarnation: The Phoenix Fire Mystery.*
Henderson, C. William. *Awakening: Ways to Psycho-Spiritual Growth.*
Hexham, Irving, and Karla Poewe. *Understanding Cults and New Religions.*
Hodson, Geoffrey. *The Brotherhood of Angels and Men.*
Holzer, Hans. *Directory of the Occult.*
Howard, Michael. *Incense and Candle Burning.*
Hubbard, Barbara M. *The Revolution.*
Hughes, John. *Self Realization in Kashmir Shaivism.*
Hulse, David A. *The Key of It All,* 2 vols.
Hunt, Dave. *America: The Sorcerer's New Apprentice.*
———. *Beyond Seduction.*
———. *Cult Explosion.*
———. *Peace, Prosperity, and the Coming Holocaust.*
———. *The Seduction of Christianity.*
Hyatt, Christopher. *Secrets of Western Tantra.*
Illion, Theodore. *Darkness over Tibet.*
International Cooperation Council. *Directory for a New World: A Planetary Guide for Cooperating Organizations.*
Jochmans, J. R. *Rolling Thunder: The Coming Earth Changes.*
Johari, Harish. *Numerology: with Tantra, Ayurveda, and Astrology.*
Joseph, Frank. *Destruction of Atlantis.*
Judith, Anodea. *Wheels of Life: A User's Guide to the Chakra System.*
Kaser, R. T. *I Ching.*
Kasturi, N. *Sai Baba.*
Ketch, Tina. *Candle Lighting Encyclopedia,* 2 vols.
Keys, Donald. *Earth at Omega: Passage to Planetization.*
King, Teri. *Love, Sex, and Astrology.*
Klimo, Jon. *Channeling: Investigations on Receiving Information from Paranormal Sources.*
Knight, J. *I Am Ramtha.*
Korem, Danny. *The Fakers.*
———. *Powers.*
Kraig, Donald M. *Modern Magick: Eleven Lessons in the High Magickal Arts.*
Krishnamurti. *Think on These Things.*
Krystal, Phyllis. *Sai Baba: The Ultimate Experience.*
Larson, Bob. *Straight Answers on the New Age.*
Lash, John. *The Seeker's Handbook: The Complete Guide to Spiritual Pathfinding.*
Lawhead, Alice, and Stephan Lawhead. *Pilgrim's Guide to the New Age.*
Lebar, James J. *Cults, Sects, and the New Age.*
Levi. *The Aquarian Gospel of Jesus the Christ.*

Levine, Roz. *Palmistry.*
Lewis, James R., and J. Gordon Melton. *Perspectives on the New Age.*
Lindholm, Lars B. *Pilgrims of the Night: Pathfinders of the Magical Way.*
Lone Wolf Circles. *Full Circle: A Song of Ecology and Earthen Spirituality.*
Lyle, Jane. *Secrets of the Zodiac.*
Mann, A. T. *Millennium Prophecies: Predictions for the Year 2000.*
McCoy, Edain. *Witches Guide to Faery Folk.*
McEvers, Joan. *Astrological Counselling: The Path to Self-Actualization.*
———. *Planets: The Astrological Tools.*
MacLaine, Shirley. *It's All in the Playing.*
———. *Out on a Limb.*
Marrs, Texe. *America Shattered.*
———. *Big Sister Wants You.*
———. *Dark Secrets of the New Age.*
———. *Fascist Terror Stalking America: Did Our Corrupt Federal Government
    Slaughter the Innocents in Oklahoma?*
———. *Mystery Mark of the New Age.*
———. *New Age Cults and Religions.*
———. *Ravaged by the New Age.*
———. *The Secret Brotherhood and the Magic of "A Thousand Points of Light."*
———. *Unmasking the Plot to Destroy Our Families and Our Country.*
Martin, Walter. *Kingdom of the Cults.*
———. *New Age Cults.*
Mead, G. R. S. *The Divine Pymander of Hermes Trismegistus.*
Meera, Mother. *Answers.*
———. *Writings.*
Mehr, Farhany. *The Zoroastrian Tradition.*
Melton, J. Gordon. *Encyclopedic Handbook of Cults in America.*
Meredith, Lynn. *Vultures in Eagle's Clothing.*
Michael, Russ. *Finding Your Soul Mate.*
Mickelsen, Johanna. *The Beautiful Side of Evil.*
———. *Lambs to the Slaughter.*
Miller, G. H. *The Dictionary of Dreams.*
Monroe, Robert. *Far Journeys.*
———. *Journeys Out of Body.*
Moody, Raymond. *Life after Life.*
Moon, Margaret, and Maurine Moon. *The Jupiter Experiment.*
———. *Wedge: The Extraordinary Communications of an Earthbound Spirit.*
Morgan, Keith. *Easy Astral Projection.*
Muir, Ada. *Healing with Herbs and Health Foods of the Zodiac.*
Muller, Robert. *New Genesis.*
Murphet, Howard. *Sai Baba: Man of Miracles.*
Norbu, Namkhai. *Dream Yoga and the Practice of Natural Light.*
Oakland, Dennis. *Your Planetary Personality.*
Parry, Robert. *In Defense of Astrology.*
Paulson, Genevieve. *Kunalini and the Chakras.*
Pennick, Nigel. *Rune Magic.*

Perschell, Lisa. *A Practical Guide to Runes: Their Uses in Divination and Magick.*
Phillips, Phil. *Turmoil in the Toybox.*
Ramakrishna. *Sayings of Ramakrishna.*
Regardie, Israel. *The Middle Pillar.*
———. *The Philosopher's Stone.*
Reuchlin, Abelard. *The True Authorship of the New Testament.*
Rieder, Marge. *Mission to Millboro.*
Ressier, P., T. Ressier, and John Weldon. *New Age Medicine.*
Rodriguez, Birgitte. *Glimpses of the Divine.*
Romney, Dr. Rodney R. *Journey to Inner Space: Finding God in Us.*
Sandweiss, Samuel. *Sai Baba: The Holy Man and the Psychiatrists.*
Schulman, Arthur. *Baba.*
Scott-Elliot, W. *Legends of Atlantis and Lost Lemuria.*
Shah, Inries. *The Sufis.*
———. *Sufi Thought and Action.*
Shepherd, Joseph. *Elements of the Bahai Faith.*
Sherwood, Keith. *Chakra Therapy.*
Sjoos, Monica, and Barbara Mor. *The Great Cosmic Mother.*
Spangler, David. *Explorations: Emerging Aspects of the New Culture.*
———. *Festivals of the New Age.*
———. *Reflections on the Christ.*
———. *Revelation: Birth of the New Age.*
Spiritual Counterfeits Project. *TM in Court.*
Smith, Warren. *The Light That Was Dark.*
Stern, Jess. *Edgar Cayce.*
Strohmer, Charles. *What Your Horoscope Doesn't Tell You.*
Sui, Choa Kok. *Prantic Healing.*
Sutphen, Dick. *Past-Life Regression.*
———. *Rapidly Develop Psychic Ability.*
Thompson, Keith. *Angels and Aliens.*
Tringpa, Chogyam. *Shambala: The Sacred Path of the Warrior.*
Tyl, Noel. *Analysis and Prediction.*
———. *Astrology, Mundane, Astral and Occult.*
———. *Exploring Consciousness in the Horoscope.*
Waley, Muhammad Isa. *Sufism: The Alchemy of the Heart.*
West, John Anthony. *Serpent in the Sky.*
Wilcock, John, and Elizabeth Pepper. *Magical and Mystical Sites.*
Wilson, Dr. Joyce. *The Complete Book of Palmistry.*
Wilson, Robert Anton. *Ishtar Rising.*
Zukav, Gary. *The Seat of the Soul.*

### New Age/East Indian Videotapes

Baba, Sathya Sai. *Aura of Divinity.*
———. *Compilation: Advent of the Avatar, The Endless Stream, The Early Years, and Darshan.*

————. *Darshan with Sai Baba.*
————. *The Universal Teacher.*
*Gods of the New Age.*
*Lost Years of Jesus.* 2 tapes.
*The Pagan Invasion* (Gods of the New Age, II).
*Sadhus: India's Mystic Holy Men.*
*Secret Garden Trilogy: Tantric Massage; In Sensual Ceremony; Sacred Orgasms.*
*Tantra: The Art of Loving.*
*Tantra of Gyuto: Sacred Rituals of Tibet.*

## Occult and Paranormal

Adler, Margot. *Drawing Down the Moon.*
Alan, Todd, and Lady Pythia. *Earth Magick.*
Alba, De-Anna. *The Cauldron of Change.*
Alexander, Brooks. *The Occult.*
Anderson, Ken. *Hitler and the Occult.*
Anglebert, Jean-Michael. *The Occult and the Third Reich.*
Ankerberg, John, and John Weldon. *The Coming Darkness.*
————. *The Facts on the Occult.*
Aquino, Michael. *The Crystal Table of Set.*
Aylsworth, Thomas. *The Story of Witches.*
Bainsbridge, William. *Satan's Power: A Deviant Psychotherapy Cult.*
Barton, Blanche. *The Church of Satan.*
Baskin, Wade. *Dictionary of Satanism.*
Black, S. Jason, and Christopher Hyatt. *Pacts with the Devil.*
Boar, Roger, and Neil Brundell. *The World's Most Infamous Murders.*
Bounds, E. M. *Satan: His Personality, Power, and Overthrow.*
Buckland, Raymond. *Buckland's Complete Book of Witchcraft.*
————. *Practical Candleburning Rituals.*
Bunson, Matthew. *Vampire Encyclopedia.*
Carlson, Shawn, Gerald Larve, and Gerry O'Sullivan. *Satanism in America.*
Carr, Joseph J. *The Twisted Cross.*
Carus, Paul. *History of the Devil.*
Cavandish, Richard. *The Black Arts.*
————. *Encyclopedia of the Unexplained.*
————. *A History of Magic.*
————. *The Powers of Evil.*
Clavex, Adrian. *Satanicon, Book of Evil.*
Cohen, Daniel. *The Encyclopedia of Ghosts.*
Colin, Wilson. *The Occult: A History.*
Conway, D. J. *Celtic Magic.*
Cooper, John C. *The Black Mask: Satanism in America Today.*
Copper, Basil. *Vampire in Legend and Fact.*
Cox, H. G. *Seduction of the Spirit: The Use and Misuse of People's Religion.*
Crowley, Aleister. *The A. A.*
————. *Aceldama.*

———. *The Book of the Law.*
———. *The Book of Lies.*
———. *The Book of Thoth.*
———. *City of God.*
———. *Confessions of Aleister Crowley.*
———. *Equinox (Journal),* 10 vols.
———. *Essay upon Number.*
———. *Fish.*
———. *Gems from the Equinox.*
———. *Heart of the Master.*
———. *The Holy Books of Thelema.*
———. *The Last Ritual.*
———. *The Law Is for All.*
———. *Magick in Theory and Practice.*
———. *Magick without Tears.*
———. *Moonchild.*
———. *Rites of Eleusis.*
———. *Satanic Extracts.*
———. *Scented Garden of Abdullah.*
———. *777 and Other Qabalistic Writings.*
———. *Tarot Divination.*
———. *Thelema.*
Crowley, Aleister, Leon M. Duquette, and Christopher S. Hyatt, Ph.D. *The Enochian World of Aleister Crowley: Enochian Sex Magick.*
Cunningham, Scott. *Earth Magic.*
———. *Living Wicca.*
———. *Magical Herbalism.*
———. *The Truth about Witchcraft Today.*
———. *Wicca: A Guide for the Solitary Practitioner.*
Daraul, Arkon. *A History of Secret Societies.*
de Givry, Emile Grillot. *Illustrated Anthology of Sorcery, Magic, and Alchemy.*
DeHaan, Richard W. *Satan, Satanism, and Witchcraft.*
Denning, Melita, and Osborne Phillips. *The Magick of the Tarot.*
Dickason, C. Fred. *Angels Elect and Evil.*
Drury, Neville, and Tillett G. Drury. *The Occult Sourcebook.*
Dunwich, Gerina. *Candlelight Spells.*
Farrer, Janet, and Stewart Farrer. *A Witch's Compleat.*
Fatunmbi, Awo. *Awo, Ifa, and Theology Divination.* (Santeria)
———. *Obatala, Ifa, and the Chief Spirit(s).* (Santeria)
Flowers, Stephen. *Fire and Ice.*
Fuller, J. F. C. *Bibliotheca Crowleyana.*
Gardener, Gerald. *The Meaning of Witchcraft.*
Gonzalez and Woppler. *Santeria Powers of the Orishas.*
Grant, Kenneth. *Aleister Crowley and the Hidden God.*
———. *The Magical Revival.*
———. *Remembering Aleister Crowley.*
Gray, William. *Tree of Evil, How to Use the Tree of Life.*

Green, Marian. *A Witch Alone.*

Guiley, Rosemary Ellen. *The Encyclopedia of Witches and Witchcraft.*

Hay, George. *The Necronomicon.*

Hicks, Robert D. *In Pursuit of Satan: The Police and the Occult.*

Hughs, Goeff, and Alan Richardson. *Ancient Magicks for a New Age.*

Hunt, Stoker. *Ouija: The Most Dangerous Game.*

Johnston, Jerry. *The Edge of Evil.*

Jung, Carl. *Psychology and the Occult.*

K., Amber. *True Magick.*

King, L. *Babylonian Magic and Sorcery.*

Koch, Kurt. *Christian Counselling and Occultism.*

Koltov, Barbara. *The Book of Lilith.*

Larson, Bob. *Satanism: The Seduction of America's Youth.*

LaVey, Anton. *The Satanic Bible.*

———. *The Satanic Rituals.*

———. *The Satanic Witch.*

Lenormant, F. *Science Occult; La Magie chez les Chaldeo-Assyriennes.*

Lovecraft, H. P. *At the Mountains of Madness.*

———. *The Dunwich Horror.*

———. *The Lurker at the Threshold.*

———. *Tales of the Cthulhu Mythos.*

Lindsey, Hal. *Satan Is Alive and Well on Planet Earth.*

Martin, Malachai. *Hostage to the Devil: The Possession and Exorcism of Five Living Americans.*

McDowell, Josh, and Don Stewart. *The Occult.*

Medici, Marina. *Love Magic.*

Moore, Raymond S. *The Abbaddon Conspiracy.*

Morgan, Keith. *How to Use a Ouija Board.*

Morrison, Sarah L. *The Modern Witches Book of Home Remedies.*

Nahmad, Claire. *Earth Magic.*

Neimark, Philip John. *The Way of Orisha.* (Santeria)

Oribello, William B. *King Solomon's Magick.*

Parker, Derek, and Julia Parker. *The Power of Magic.*

Paulsen, Kathryn. *Magic and Witchcraft.*

Pentecost, Dwight. *Your Adversary the Devil.*

Pratney, Wilkie. *Devil Take the Youngest: The War on Childhood.*

Rapacki, Lyle J. *Satan: The Not So New Problem.*

Ravenwolf, Silver. *To Ride a Silver Broomstick: New Generation of Witchcraft.*

Reed, Ellen C. *The Goddess and the Tree.*

Regardie, Israel. *Eye in the Triangle, Aleister Crowley.*

———. *The Golden Dawn.*

———. *Legend of Aleister Crowley.*

Richards, Steve. *Invisibility: Mastering the Art of Vanishing.*

Richardson, James T., Joel Best, and David Bromley, eds. *The Satanism Scare.*

Riva, Anna. *Voodoo Handbook of Cult Secrets.*

Robertson, Sandy. *The Aleister Crowley Scrapbook.*

Rose, Donna. *Unhexing Jinx/Removing Spells.*

Rose, Elliot. *A Razor for a Goat.*
Russell, Jeffrey B. *The Devil: Perceptions of Evil from Antiquity to Primitive Christianity.*
———. *Lucifer—The Devil in the Middle Ages.*
———. *Mephistopheles: The Devil in the Modern World.*
———. *Satan: The Early Christian Tradition.*
———. *The Prince of Darkness: Radical Evil and the Power of Good in History.*
Scholem, Gershom. *Kabbalah.*
Schuler, Gerald, and Betty Schuler. *Enochian Magic.*
Schuster, Gerald. *Crowley's Apprentice.*
Sebald, Hans. *Witchcraft: The Heritage of a Heresy.*
Seligmann, Kurt. *The History of Magic and the Occult.*
———. *Magic, Supernaturalism, and the Occult.*
Shah, Sirdar Ikbal Ali. *Occultism: Its Theory and Practice.*
———. *Oriental Magic.*
———. *The Secret Lore of Magic.*
———. *The Sufis.*
Simon. *The Necronomicon.*
Smith, Frederick W. *Cattle Mutilation: The Unthinkable Truth.*
Spence, Lewis. *The Encyclopedia of the Occult.*
Stratford, Lauren. *Satan's Underground.*
Summers, Montague. *History of Witchcraft and Demonology.*
Suster, Gerald. *Crowley's Apprentice.*
———. *Legacy of the Beast: Aleister Crowley.*
Terry, Maury. *The Ultimate Evil.*
Thompson, C. J. S. *The Mysteries and Secrets of Magic.*
Thompson, Janet. *Of Witches.*
Thorsson, Edred. *A Handbook of Rune Magic.*
Unger, Merril F. *Demons in the World Today.*
Waite, Arthur. *The Holy Kaballah.*
Wall, J. Charles. *Devils.*
Webb, James. *The Occult Establishment.*
———. *The Occult Underground.*
Warnke, Mike. *The Satan Seller.*
———. *The Schemes of Satan.*
Wedge, Thomas. *The Satan Hunter.*
Wendell, Leilah. *Necromantic Ritual Book.*
———. *Our Name Is Melancholy: Complete Books of Azrael.*
Wentz, W. Y., ed. *The Tibetan Book of the Dead.*
White, Thomas. *The Believer's Guide to Spiritual Warfare.*
Wilson, Colin. *The Occult of History.*
Wurmbrand, Richard. *Was Karl Marx a Satanist?*

## General End-Time Christian Books

Bass, Clarence G. *Background to Dispensation.*
Bates, Leon. *Projection for Survival.* Dallas: Bible Believers Evangelistic Association.

Blackstone, James. *Israel's Sure Tomorrow: A Prophetic Odyssey.*
Bloomfield, Arthur E. *Before the Last Battle—Armageddon.*
Breese, Dave. *Europe and the Prince Who Shall Come.*
———. *The Mid-East Wars—Who Will Win?*
Burkett, Larry. *The Coming Economic Earthquake.* (1994 revised edition).
———. *Whatever Happened to the American Dream?*
Campbell, Roger, and David Campbell. *Prosperity in the End Time.*
Cantelon, Willard. *The Day the Dollar Dies.*
———. *New Money or None?*
Clark, Doug. *Shockwaves of Armageddon.*
Crowley, Dale. *The Soon Coming of Our Lord.*
Darby, John N. *The Hopes of the Church of God in Connexion with the Destiny of Jews and the Nations as Revealed in Prophecy.*
DeHaan, Richard W. *Israel and the Nations in Prophecy.*
Dyer, Charles. *The Rise of Babylon.*
Erickson, Millard J. *Contemporary Options in Eschatology: A Study of the Millennium.*
Evans, Mike. *Israel: America's Key to Survival.*
———. *The Return.*
Faid, Robert W. *Gorbachev! Has the Real Antichrist Come?*
Goetz, William R. *Apocalypse Next and the New World Order.*
Graham, Billy. *Approaching Hoofbeats: The Four Horsemen of the Apocalypse.*
———. *Reentry.*
Hocking, David. *The Coming World Leader: Understanding the Book of Revelation.*
Hoyt, Herman A. *The End Times.*
Hubbard, David Allan. *The Second Coming: What Will Happen When Jesus Returns.*
Hunt, David. *Beyond Seduction: A Return to Biblical Christianity.*
———. *Global Peace and the Rise of Antichrist.*
———. *How Close Are We?*
———. *Peace, Prosperity, and the Coming Holocaust.*
Hunt, David, and T. A. McMahon. *The Seduction of Christianity.*
Ice, Thomas, and Randall Price. *Ready to Rebuild.*
Jeffrey, Grant R. *Armageddon: Appointment with Destiny.*
Kirban, Salem. *Guide to Survival.*
———. *I Predict.*
———. *Kissinger: Man of Peace?*
———. *Satan's Angel's Exposed.*
———. *666.*
Kolfield, Ellis H. *Sozo: Survival Guide for a Remnant Church.*
Lalonde, Peter, and Paul Lalonde. *Blueprint for Building a One-World Order.*
———. *Left Behind.*
———. *One World under Antichrist.*
———. *Racing toward the Mark of the Beast.*
———. *Why We Believe We're Living in the Last Days.*
Levitt, Zola. *The Cairo Connection: Egypt in Prophecy.*

————. *The Coming Invasion of Israel.*

————. *Israel My Beloved.*

————. *Satan and the Sanctuary.*

Lewis, David A. *Magog 1982 Cancelled.*

————. *Prophecy 2000.*

Lindsell, Harold. *The Armageddon Spectre.*

Lindsey, Hal. *The Final Battle.*

————. *The Late Great Planet Earth.*

————. *The 1980's: Countdown to Armageddon.*

————. *Planet Earth 2000 A.D.*

————. *The Rapture.*

————. *Road to the Holocaust.*

————. *There's a New World Coming.*

Lindsey, Hal, and C. C. Carlson. *The Terminal Generation.*

Locklear, Herbert. *Cameos of Prophecy: Are These the Last Days?*

Marrs, Texe. *Dark Majesty: The Secret Brotherhood and the Magic of "A Thousand Points of Light."*

————. *Mega Forces.*

————. *Ravaged by the New Age.*

————. *Texe Marrs' Book of New Age Cults and Religions.*

McClain, Alva. *Daniel's Prophecy of the Seventy Weeks.*

McConkey, James H. *The End of the Age.*

McKeever, Jim. *Christians Will Go through the Tribulation and How to Prepare for It.*

————. *Close Encounters of the Highest Kind.*

————. *The Rapture Book: Victory in the End Times.*

McPherson, Dave. *The Incredible Coverup.*

Overbey, Scot. *Vladimir Zhirinovsky: The Man Who Would Be Gog.*

Poland. Peter. *How to Prepare for the Coming Persecution.*

Reese, Alexander. *The Approaching Advent of Christ: An Examination of the Teaching of J. N. Darby.*

Relfe, Mary S. *The New Money System.*

————. *When Your Money Fails.*

Roberts, Oral. *The Drama of the End Time.*

Robertson, Pat. *The New Millennium: Ten Trends Which Will Impact Your Family by the Year 2000.*

————. *The New World Order.*

Rosen, Moishe. *Overture to Armageddon.*

Rushdoony, Rousas J. *Thy Kingdom Come: Studies in Daniel and Revelation.*

Ryrie, Charles C. *The Final Countdown.*

Sharrosh, Anis A. *Jesus, Prophecy, and the Middle East.*

Smith, Chuck. *What the World Is Coming To.*

Smith, Sherman S. *Exploding the Money Myths.*

Smith, Timothy. *Revivalism and Social Reform: American Protestantism on the Eve of the Civil War.*

Smith, Wilber. *The Arab/Israeli Conflict.*

Sutton, Hilton. *World War III: God's Conquest of Russia.*

Taylor, Charles. *The Destiny of America.*
———. *Those Who Remain.*
Unger, Merrill F. *Beyond the Crystal Ball.*
Van Impe, Jack. *11:59 . . . And Counting!*
———. *Everything You Always Wanted to Know About Prophecy.*
———. *Israel's Final Holocaust.*
———. *Revelation Revealed Verse by Verse.*
———. *Sabotaging the World Church.*
———. *Your Future: An A–Z Index to Prophecy.*
Viguerie, Richard. *The New Right: We're Ready to Lead.*
Wager, W. Warren. *Terminal Visions: The Literature of Last Things.*
Walvoord, John F. *Armageddon, Oil and the Middle East Crisis.*
———. *Israel in Prophecy.*
———. *The Rapture Question.*
Webber, David, and Noah Hutchings. *Is This the Last Century?*
Weber, Timothy. *The Future Explored.*
———. *Living in the Shadow of the Second Coming: American Premillennialism, 1875–1925.*
Whitaker, Robert, ed. *The New Right Papers.*
Wiersbe, Warren W. *Be Ready.*
Wilkerson, David. *Purple Violet Squish.*
———. *Racing toward Judgement.*
———. *The Vision.*
Wilson, Clifford, and John Weldon. *1980's: Decade of Shock.*
Wilson, Dwight. *Armageddon Now!*
Wood, Leon. *The Bible and Future Events.*
Wuest, Kenneth. *Prophetic Light in This Present Darkness.*
Youssef, Michael. *America, Oil, and the Islamic Mind.*

**Audiotapes**

Alexander, Brooks. "The Occult Dynamics of Visualization." SCP (A–005).
Baker, Jeff. "AIDS—The Politics of Death." 2 tapes. The Baker Group.
Brooke, Tal. "The New World Order and Gaia." SCP (A–001).
Crane, Stuart. "Best of Stuart Crane, 1983." TP–183.
———. "Dr. Crane Lectures on Evolution." TP–111.
———. "Dr. Stuart Crane Speaks Out on Religion." TP–182.
———. "Lecture, May 1981." TP–181.
———. "Wheat Receipts." TP–109.
Fagan, Myron. "The Illuminati-CFR." TP–107.
———. "Red Stars over Hollywood." TP–106.
Kellogg, William. "Authority Cults." SCP (A–004).
Marrs, Texe. "America's Secret SS Establishment."
———. "Bankruptcy USA: How You Can Escape the Coming Financial Nightmare."
———. "Black Science."
———. "Blood and Dynasty."

———. "The Bloodstained Hands of Big Brother Government."

———. "The Coming Shroud of Death." Texe Marrs Ministries.

———. "Concentration Camps."

———. "Days of Hunger, Days of Chaos: The Coming Great Food Shortages in America."

———. "Death and Sickness at the Hands of Big Brother."

———. "En Route to Global Occupation—an Update" (on Gary Kah's book).

———. "The Illuminati Plan for South Africa."

———. "Is Bill Clinton a Servant of the Skull and Bones Society?"

———. "July 1995: Ten Signs of the End of the World."

———. "The Last Days of Pope John Paul II: The Illuminist Scheme to Take Over the Vatican." 2 tapes.

———. "Law Enforcement, the US Armed Forces, and the New World Order Threat."

———. "The Light That Was Dark—The New Age 'Illumination' of the Christian Church."

———. "March 1995: Illuminata: The Secret New Age Occultism of Bill and Hillary Clinton."

———. "More Revelation about the New Age Bible Versions and the Men behind Them."

———. "NASA's Space Program—Hoaxes and Deceptions."

———. "The New World Order and American Sovereignty."

———. "November 1994: All Fall Down: The Plot to Crown the Pope the Prince of Peace."

———. "October 1995: The Inner Circle of the Illuminati: Ten Men Who Rule the World."

———. "The Oklahoma City Bombing, the Waco Massacre, and Other Media Lies."

———. "Ordo Abo Chao: The Great Work of the Illuminati."

———. "Pigs in the Parlour." Texe Marrs Ministries.

———. "The Pink Swastika: Homosexuality in the Nazi Party."

———. "Project Abaddon: Bible Prophecy and the Astonishing Truth about UFO's and Alien Abductions."

———. "Project Abaddon II: Bible Prophecy and UFOs—the Demonic Dimension."

———. "Promise Keepers: The Seduction and Demonization of Christianity."

———. "Report from Iron Mountain." (Analysis of 1963 Report)

———. "The Ross Perot That Nobody Knows."

———. "Secrets of the Bilderbergers."

———. "Secrets, vol. 1–3."

———. "The Skull and Bones Society."

———. "Strange Glory: Satan's Plan for a One World Bible." Texe Marrs Ministries.

———. "The United Nations Conspiracy in Bible Prophecy."

Mueller, Marc. "The West's Crisis of Belief and the New World Order." SCP (A–007).

Prophecy Portfolio. Van Impe Ministries.

SCP Conference. "Challenges for the 1990's." SCP (A–008). 7 tapes.
Weldon, John. "Freemasonry's Concept of God." SCP (A–003).

## Videotapes

*Academy under Siege.* SJS Productions. John Birch Society.
*Africa and the New World Order.* John McManus. John Birch Society.
*The AIDS Coverup.* Van Impe Ministries.
*Aids: Last Days Plague.* Midnight Call.
*The Alchemical Processing of Humanity.* Texe Marrs Ministries.
*America in Prophecy: The Decline and Fall of the American Empire.* Van Impe
    Ministries.
*America under Siege.* Texe Marrs Ministries.
*Americans Abandoned.* American Defense Institute. John Birch Society
*Appointment with Destiny.* Peter Lalonde, et al.
*Armageddon Scenario.* Hal Lindsey Ministries.
*Bible Prophecy and the World Conspiracy.* Texe Marrs Ministries.
*Big Sister Is Rising: Hillary's Hellcats.* Texe Marrs Ministries.
*The Bloodstained Hands of Big Brother Government.* Texe Marrs Ministries.
*The Clinton Chronicles.* Texe Marrs Ministries.
*Concentration Camps in America.* Texe Marrs Ministries.
*Dollars and Sense.* John McManus. John Birch Society.
*Europe 1992: The Revived Roman Empire.* Peter Lalonde.
*Everything You Always Wanted to Know about Prophecy.* Van Impe Ministries.
*The Evolution Conspiracy.* Jeremiah Films.
*Exposing the New Age Lie.* Peter Lalonde.
*Fascist Terror Stalking America.* Texe Marrs Ministries.
*The Final Battle.* Hal Lindsey Ministries.
*The Final Warning.* Grant Jeffrey.
*500 Years after Columbus.* Midnight Call.
*The Fourth Reich.* Midnight Call.
*Front Row Seats.* Peter Lalonde.
*Gods of the New Age.* Jeremiah Films.
*The Gospel of Hollywood.* Peter Lalonde.
*The Great Escape.* Van Impe Ministries.
*The Hidden Agenda.* Norman Dodd. John Birch Society.
*The Holocaust: A Critical Review.* Emissary, VHS–36.
*Image of the Beast.* Van Impe Ministries.
*The Insiders,* I and II. John McManus. John Birch Society.
*International Wilderness Congress and the New World Bank.* Emissary, VHS–31.
*Israel: How Close to War?* Midnight Call.
*Jesus: Psychic or Prophet?* Van Impe Ministries.
*The John Birch Society Speaks.* Armor, Griffin, and McManus. John Birch
    Society.
*Katanga: The Untold Story.* American Media. John Birch Society.
*The Late Great Planet Earth.* Hal Lindsey Ministries.
*Liberty in the Balance: America, the Fed and the IRS.* Emissary Publications.

*Mark of the Beast.* Peter Lalonde.
*Mark of the Beast II.* Peter Lalonde.
*Mark of the New World Order.* Van Impe Ministries.
*Massacre at Ruby Ridge.* Emissary Publications, VHS–37.
*Mideast Masquerade.* John McManus. John Birch Society.
*Mideast Peace.* Midnight Call.
*The Millennium and the Last Judgement.* Hal Lindsey Ministries.
*The Millennium: Greatest Deception in History.* Van Impe Ministries.
*Mysterious Monuments to the Beast.* Texe Marrs Ministries.
*New Age Spirits from the Underworld.* Van Impe Ministries.
*The New Age World Religion Is Here, Now!* Texe Marrs Ministries.
*The New Russia, World War III, and Armageddon.* Van Impe Ministries.
*New World Order 1993.* Peter Lalonde.
*No I.D. Found: The Mark of the Beast System Revealed.* Texe Marrs Ministries.
*The Occult World.* Van Impe Ministries.
*The Other Israel: The Whole Story of the Zionist Conspiracy.* Emissary, VHS–33.
*The Pagan Invasion.* vol. 2. Jeremiah Films.
*The Pagan Invasion.* 13 vols. (tapes). Peter Lalonde.
*The Peace That Destroys Israel.* Hal Lindsey Ministries.
*Pope John Paul II: Startling Revelations.* Van Impe Ministries.
*The Pope over Jerusalem.* Texe Marrs Ministries.
*The Prodigal Planet.* Van Impe Ministries.
*Prophecy Talk!* 3 vols. (tapes). Peter and Paul Lalonde, et al.
*The Rapture Factor.* Hal Lindsey Ministries.
*The Real Janet Reno.* Jack Thompson. Emissary Publications.
*Revelation Revealed.* 5 vols. (tapes). Van Impe Ministries.
*The Rise of the Antichrist.* Midnight Call.
*Russia's Last War.* Midnight Call.
*Russia, World War III . . . and Armageddon.* Van Impe Ministries.
*Satan's Fingerprints in the New Bible Versions.* Texe Marrs Ministries.
*Satan 2000: The Unity of World Religion.* Texe Marrs Ministries.
*The Search for Truth in History.* David Irving. Emissary Publications.
*666: The United States of Europe and the New World Order.* Van Impe Ministries.
*Superpower in Europe.* Midnight Call.
*Ten Signs of the End of the World.* Texe Marrs Ministries.
*Texe Marrs Exposes the New Age Plan for a One World Order.* Texe Marrs Ministries.
*This Generation Shall Not Pass.* Peter Lalonde.
*The Treaty from Hell.* Texe Marrs Ministries.
*20 Questions on Prophecy.* Midnight Call.
*2001: Countdown to Eternity.* Van Impe Ministries.
*UFO's . . . The Mystery Resolved.* By Hugh Ross, Reasons to Believe series.
*Unholy Bible Versions of the New Age.* Texe Marrs Ministries.
*The War to End All Wars.* Hal Lindsey Ministries.
*The Whore of Babylon.* Midnight Call.
*Why I Believe in the King James Bible.* Texe Marrs Ministries.
*The World's Affair with the Antichrist.* Hal Lindsey Ministries.
*World Unity and the Church.* Midnight Call.

## Comic Books Dealing with Conspiracy (Chick Publications)

Chick, Jack. *Alberto.*
———. *Angel of Light.*
———. *The Ark.*
———. *The Broken Cross.*
———. *Chaos.*
———. *The Crusaders: Operation Budapest.*
———. *Double-Cross.*
———. *The Exorcists.*
———. *The Force.*
———. *Four Horsemen.*
———. *The Gift.*
———. *The Godfathers.*
———. *Primal Man?*
———. *The Prophet.*
———. *Sabotage?*
———. *Scarface.*
———. *Spellbound?*

# Sources of Conspiracy Advocate Materials

**Selected Addresses of Leading Conspiracy Advocate Publishing Houses and/or Distributors and Ministries**

A-albionic Research
P.0. Box 20273
Fernsdale, MI 48220-0273

Adventures Unlimited
303 Main Street
P.O. Box 74
Kempton, IL 60946

Brother Stair
P.O. Box 691
Wallenboro, SC 29488

Emissary Publications
9205 S.E. Clackamas Road, #1776
Clackamas, OR 97015

Flatland
Department K 10
P.O. Box 2420
Fort Bragg, CA 95437-2420

Gary Kah
P.O. Box 509283
Indianapolis, IN 46250-9283

Illuminet Press
P.O. Box 2808
Lilburn, GA 30221

Institution for Creation Research
2716 Madison Avenue
San Diego, CA 92116

Jane's Book Service
P.O. Box 3622
Reno, NV 89505

Jeffrey Baker, President
Group I—The Baker Group, Inc.
4275—34th Street South #150
St. Petersburg, FL 33711

John Birch Society
P.O. Box 8040
Appleton, WI 54913

Loompanics Unlimited
P.O. Box 1197
Port Townsend, WA 98121

National Center for Constitutional
Studies
P.O. Box 31776
Salt Lake City, UT 84131

New American View
P.O. Box 999
Herndon, VA 22070

Noontide Press
1822 1/2 Newport Blvd.
Suite 183
Costa Mesa, CA 92627

Operation Right to Know (ORTK)
(UFO/ET Group)
P.O. Box 3173
Gaithersburg, MD 20885

Paragon Research Publications
2269 Chesnut Street, Suite 301
San Francisco, CA 94123

The Pleiades Project (UFO/ET
  group)
P.O. Box 386
Atwood, CA 92601

The Space Between
211 Town House Road
Hamden, CT 06514

Spotlight
Liberty Lobby
300 Independence Avenue S.E.
Washington, DC 20003

Summit Ministries
P.O. Box 207
Manitou Springs, CO 80829

Texe Marrs
Living Truth Ministries
1708 Patterson Road
Austin, TX 78733

UNWNNPM Research Institute
Box 66
Lutherville, MD 21094

## Newsletters Advocating a Conspiratorial Viewpoint

ADI News
1055 North Fairfax Street
Suite 200
Alexandria, VA 22314

Aid and Abet Police Newsletter
1001 North 43rd Avenue E-84
Phoenix, AZ 85009

Aura-Z
P.O. Box 224
Moscow, 117463, Russia

The Baker Report
Jeff Baker
4275 34th Street South, #150
St. Petersburg, FL 33711

Chalcedon Report
R. J. Rushdoony
P.O. Box 158
Vallecito, CA 95251

The Christian World Report
Omega—Letter, Inc.
P.O. Box 1440
Niagara Falls, NY 14302

The Eco-Profiteer
Larry Abraham
1350 Center Drive, #100
Dunwoody, GA 30338

Family Research Center
Dr. Paul Cameron
P.O. Box 2091
Washington, DC 20013

Flashpoint
Texe Marrs
1708 Patterson Road
Austin, TX 78733-6507

Foundations of Liberty
900 46th Avenue
East Moline, IL 61244

The Goodloe Report
P.O. Box 25736
Seattle, WA 98125-1236

The Insider Report
Larry Abraham
P.O. Box 467939
Atlanta, GA 30346-7939

The Leading Edge Research Group
P.O. Box 481-MU58
Yelm, WA 98597

The McAlvany Intelligence Report
Don S. McAlvany
P.O. Box 84904
Phoenix, AZ 85071

Dr. Stanley Monteith
P.O. Box 1835
Soquel, CA 95073

Gary North's Remnant Review
Gary North, Ph.D.
P.O. Box 84906
Phoenix, AZ 85071

The Ron Paul Survival Report
18333 Egret Bay Blvd.
P.O. Box 84906
Phoenix, AZ 85071

The Howard Phillips Issues and
    Strategies Bulletin
Policy Analysis, Inc.
9520 Bent Creek Lane
Vienna, VA 22182

The Weaver Report
Mark Weaver
U.S. Taxpayers Party
450 Maple Avenue East
Vienna, CA 22180

World News Digest
Larry Abraham
1350 Center Drive, #100
Dunwoody, GA 30338

## Council on Foreign Relations and Trilateral Commission

No list would be complete without providing the mailing addresses of conspiracy theory's major foes since the early 1920s (the CFR); and since the early 1970s, the Trilateral Commission:

Council on Foreign Relations
Harold Pratt House
58 E. 68th Street
New York, NY 10021
Telephone: 212-734-0400
FAX: 212-861-1789

Council on Foreign Relations
Washington Office
2400 N Street N.W.
Washington, DC 20037
Telephone: 202-862-7786

Trilateral Commission
345 E. 46th Street
New York, NY 10017
Telephone: 212-661-1180

## Christian Journals and Newsletters

Prophecy and/or conspiracy-related information do not necessarily appear in every issue of the Christian publications.

Apologia: Newsletter of Christian
   Research Associates
Bible Prophecy News
Charisma
Christian Beacon
Christian Century
Christian Research Journal
Christian Research Newsletter
Christianity Today
Cornerstone
Endtime News Digest
Eternity
Fundamentalist Journal
King's Business
Midnight Call
Moody Monthly
News from Israel
New Wine
Omega Letter
Pat Robertson's Perspective
Perhaps Today
Rapture Alert News Report
Spiritual Counterfeits Project (SCP)
   Journal
Spiritual Counterfeits Project (SCP)
   Newsletter
Sunday School Times
This Week in Bible Prophecy

## Selected New Age Journals or Journals with New Age and/or Occult Themes

(Not all of the magazines and journals
given are exclusively New Age or occultic in content. Many will, however,
carry stories from time to time about
such topics.)

Acupuncture News
Ahimsa Monthly
Astrologer's Magazine (Modern
   Astrology)
The Black Flame
Body, Mind, and Spirit
Breitenbush Newsletter

Broughton's Monthly Planet Reader
   and Astrological Journal
Church of Light Quarterly
Circle Guide of Wicca and Pagan
   Resources
The Cloven Hoof
Common Boundary
Conscious Choice
Conscious Connection
Cryptozoology
Cycles
East/West Journal
Ecology Center Newsletter
Evolving Time
Fate
Fireheart
Flying Saucer Review
Folklore
Fortean Times
Fully Alive
Gnosis
International Review of Mental
   Imagery
International UFO Reporter
ISC Newsletter
Journal of German Acupuncture
Journal of Religion and Psychical
   Research
The Journal of Traditional
   Acupuncture
Life Times
Llewellyn Publications (topical and
   book orders available)
Meditation
Mother Jones
MUFON UFO Journal
Mystic Trader
New Age
New Age Chicago (updated yearly)
New Age Community Guidebook
   (updated yearly)
New Dimensions
New Directions
New Frontier
New Realities
New Scientist
The New Sun

New York Folklore Quarterly
Notes and Queries
OMNI
Pathways
PhenomeNews (New Age directory
    for Michigan)
Psychic Guide
Psychology Today
Pursuit
The "Q" Directory (United Kingdom
    New Age directory)
The Quest
Reflections
Renewal
Saga
Saucer News
Skeptic
Skeptical Inquirer
Stigmata
Strange Magazine
Trajectories
UFO

UFO Quarterly
UFO Reporter
The Unexplained
Vegetarian Times
Western Folklore
Whole Life Monthly
Whole Life Times
Yoga Journal

## Other Sources Dealing with the World of Conspiracy

Klanwatch
Intelligence Report
400 Washington Avenue
Montgomery, AL 36104

Steamshovel Press
c/o Kenn Thomas, editor
P.O. Box 23715
Saint Louis, MO 63121

## Radio

Sadly, one of the chief sources of conspiracy theory information these days is spewed forth from a Christian source: the World-Wide Christian Radio (WWCR) shortwave broadcast out of Nashville. While not alone, it is one of the primary mouthpieces of bigotry disguised as gospel and broadcasts weekly programs such as Texe Marrs's *Voice of Prophecy* program. Other radio shows, although not necessarily on the Nashville station, include Radio Free America (sponsored by Liberty Lobby, a rabidly anti-Semitic organization); Intelligence Report with Mark Koernke; and For the People with Tom Harder. These are just a very few of the programs that can be found on shortwave radio these days. Those interested in keeping up with the latest conspiracy theory would do well to monitor the shortwave broadcasts; they contain some of the most blatant conspiracy theories out there today.

## Information Superhighway

The Internet has a large and growing number of resources available on the occult and material established by adherents of the lifestyle. Moreover, the Internet provides the interested with a host of sources on conspiracy theory, the Illuminati, and so forth. The "Information Superhighway" is a fountain of information and resources on these and other topics. I highly recommend surfing the Net for topics of interest. Given below are just a very few sites containing information (mostly pro) on the occult and conspiracy.

**Yahoo Directory:**

http://www.yahoo.com/Entertainment/Paranormal_Phenomena/Occult/
Items such as "Dark Side of the Net," vampires, gothic, Wiccan, Pagan, occult,
Satanism, Order of the Golden Dawn, O.T.O., Aleister Crowley.

**Yahoo Directory:**

Look under the Yahoo section on "Politics," click in, then hit "Conspiracies."

**Illuminati Home Page:**

http://www.mit.edu/~boogles/Illuminati

### *Conspiracy Central!:*

http://www.paranoia.com/~fraterk/conspire.html
A collection of strange conspiracy theory ideas about a host of topics: inter-
planetary conspiracy, privacy, UFOs, Black Magick, foreign agents, secret
societies.

### *Enchanter's Conspiracy Emporium:*

http://www.gate.net/~asia/
A good collection of interesting items on various conspiracy theory items
ranging from a brief history of the Illuminati to Carroll Quigley reviews. A
good starting point, well written and reasoned. Regardless of whether the
Net surfer agrees with Enchanter's view of conspiracy, it is most definitely
worth a stop and thorough reading.

### *Oklahoma Bombing . . . Conspiracy?*

http://www.gate.net/~asia/okie.html

### *A-albionic Consulting & Research Information Bulletin:*

http://a-albionic.com/a-albionic/info
Paradigms, Archives, and Research

### *John Birch Society:*

http://www.primenet.com/~tevans/jbs.html
One of America's better-known conspiracy supporters, the John Birch Society is apparently alive and well.

### *Patriots against the New World Order Totalitarian Index:*

http://www.10pht.com/~oblivion/patriot.html
The title pretty much tells you what you can expect here: in-your-face "there
is a conspiracy out there bent on getting us" sort of stuff.

### Foreign Affairs Magazine:

http://www.psi.com/chapterone/foreignaffairs/index.html
*Foreign Affairs* magazine is the mouthpiece of the Council on Foreign Relations, one of the boogeymen for conspiracy buffs. I do not doubt that if such conspiracy-minded persons tried, they could find the number "666" in the http address above!

### Very Occult Page:

http://www.uib.no/zoo/wolf/bjorn/occult.html
Items such as Astrology, Magick, Wicca, Mage's Guide to the Internet.

### Anders Magick Page:

http://www.nada.kth.se/~nv91-asa/magick.html.
Highly recommended site for a host of occult-related material. The researcher should be aware that like most all occult sites on the Web, items are presented from a distinctly non-Christian point of view.

### Christian Research Institute Homepage:

http://www.iclnet.org/pub/resources/text/cri/cri-home.html.
This site will provide the "surfer" with a host of valuable apologetic material. Articles from *Christian Research Journal* are available here, among other interesting documentation. A must.

### Christian Apologetics:

http://www.gate.net.net/~copeland/ca.html
Despite the Net address, this site is not run by Kenneth Copeland Ministries—at least insofar as I know.

### Apologia:

http://diakonos.hum.utah.edu/philosophy/religion/apologia
Another worthwhile site on the Net for a look at church history and other interesting topics for the intellectually inclined surfer.

There is also now available a database for the conspiracy theorist, or those just curious. Called NameBase, it was the work of a corporation of the same name under Daniel Brandt. It cross-references thousands of articles, books, newspapers, and any other source of conspiracy-related topics. It contains some 173,000 citations and is, without a doubt, a monumental work of significance for researchers of the conspiracy theory topic. The disks are formatted for either Macintosh or DOS-compatible computers.

Likewise, Christian Research Institute offers a database (FYI, version 2.5) for a host of publications found in its own journal and newsletter, as well as that of the Berkeley-based Spiritual Counterfeits Project.

Finally, there is even a board game dealing with conspiracy theory in history. Appropriately called "The Illuminati," the game's objective is to take over as much of the world as possible through hook or crook. The game and its copyright are owned by Steve Jackson Games, Inc., an organization that also has its own sites on the Internet. The game has achieved something of a quasi-cult status.

# The Conspiracy That Never Ends

*George Johnson*

The following rule of thumb concerning conspiracy theories was written by George Johnson, author of an award-winning book on the topic entitled *Architects of Fear.* Appearing in the *New York Times* April 30, 1995, Sunday Late Edition, section 4, page 5, column 2, Week in Review Desk column, it carried the appropriate title "The Conspiracy That Never Ends." The piece was written in the aftermath of the Oklahoma City tragedy and prompted the following response from Mr. Johnson. It is reproduced here with the kind permission of the author and the *New York Times.*

While most of the world waited for news of the official investigation into the Oklahoma bombing, callers and talk show hosts on World Wide Christian Radio, the Nashville shortwave station that has become the shrill voice of the far right, had it all figured out: the Federal Building was destroyed as part of a plot by the United States Government, acting on behalf of a secret international cabal, the New World Order, whose symbol, the cold staring eye in the pyramid, mocks Americans from the back of every dollar bill.

Within days, the bombing had been tightly woven into the sprawling conspiracy theories that have obsessed some Americans since the beginning of the Republic. The historian Richard

Hofstadter coined the phrase "the paranoid style in American politics" to describe this pathological world view in which history is a Manichean struggle between the forces of light and darkness. The conspiratorial fantasies are not simply an expression of inchoate fear. There is a shape, an architecture, to the paranoia.

Rule No. 1: The conspirators are internationalists in their sympathies. In this century the main targets of conspiracy theories have been Jews, depicted as people whose loyalty to fellow Jews makes them endemically antipatriotic, and international Communism. The United Nations is suspect, as is the Trilateral Commission, the Council on Foreign Relations, Interpol and even the Red Cross because they supposedly place international agendas above patriotic concerns. In the 19th century, the chief conspirators were said to be the Vatican and the Freemasons. In the mind of today's paranoiacs, which include some militia members, followers of the Liberty Lobby (the Holocaust-is-a-myth crowd) and the Ku Klux Klan, all these groups are mushed together into the New World Order, or One World Government.

The first rule is of more than academic historical interest because of Rule No. 2: In conspiracy theory, nothing is ever discarded. Right-wing mail order bookstores still sell the "Protocols of the Elders of Zion," the anti-Semitic fantasy hatched in Russia a century ago. Another big seller is "Proofs of a Conspiracy," a 1797 book reprinted by the John Birch Society, which fueled speculation that a Freemasonic group called the Order of the Illuminati plotted with the Jeffersonians to turn the fledgling United States to followers of French Enlightenment philosophy—the 18th century equivalent of secular humanism.

This brings us to Rule No. 3: Seeming enemies are actually secret friends. As evil as the Communists, in the right wing mind, are the Rockefellers and international bankers (often a synonym for Jews). Through the lens of conspiracy theorists, capitalists and Communists work hand in hand.

To what end? That's Rule No. 4: The takeover by the international godless government will be ignited by the collapse of the economic system. In an elaborate decades-long check-kiting scheme since the dollar was removed from the gold standard, the Federal Reserve has been creating money out of thin air. Once the conspirators give the word, the bankers will yank the rug from this house of cards and your money will be worthless.

As a sign that the conspirators have taken over the currency, they had printed on the back a Freemasonic symbol: the all-seeing eye of the enlightened ones perched atop the pyramid. And there, under the emblem, is their name: Novus Ordo Seclorum.

Finally, Rule No. 5: It's all spelled out in the Bible. For those with a fundamentalist bent, the New World Order or One World Government is none other than the international kingdom of the Antichrist, described in the Book of Revelation. Revelation also speaks of the "mark of the beast," a symbol of the satanic leader that will be imprinted on everyone's forehead and right hand. Fundamentalist preachers like Hal Lindsey have popularized the notion that the mark of the beast is the zebra-striped Universal Product Code, which will be tattooed on everyone by laser to increase the acuity of the panoptic big eye.

We may never know what went through the real conspirators' minds when, as investigators say, they rented a truck, packed it full of fertilizer and fuel oil, and ignited it where it would do the most harm. But if they hung out at militia meetings, or even just occasionally tuned to WWCR, they would have been exposed to this kind of thinking, over and over and over again.[1]

# Notes

## Introduction

1. Christian writers of this genre are numerous and will be detailed in later chapters. However, a prime example is Texe Marrs of Austin, Texas, whose entire ministry is seemingly based on the drive to "expose" the schemes of the New Age, Illuminati, International Bankers, and so forth.

Indeed, Marrs goes so far as to accuse President and Mrs. Clinton of being Satan worshipers. See (or hear) Marrs's audiotape, *Illuminata*, in which he "proves" his point with such laughable examples as Clinton supposedly giving a Satanic hand signal to those around him.

2. Not his real name.

3. Myron Fagan, *The Illuminati-Council on Foreign Relations*, taped copies of the original vinyl LP released in 1967, TP–107 (Clackamas, Ore.: Emissary Publications, n.d.).

4. Fagan also recorded an exposé titled *Red Star over Hollywood*, TP–106 available through Emissary Publications. This LP dealt with the "Red Scare" in Hollywood during the 1940s and 1950s, as well as television in the 1960s.

5. Victor E. Marsden, ed., *Protocols of the Learned Elders of Zion* (reprint, Clackamas, Ore.: Emissary Publications, n.d.); Henry Ford Sr., *The International Jew: The World's Foremost Problem* (reprint, Clackamas, Ore.: Emissary Publications, n.d.). Other hate literature dealing with Judaism and Jewish culture is, unfortunately, myriad. Besides those listed above, a few other such works include Martin Luther, *The Jews and Their Lies;* Kenneth Goff, *The Jewish Power* and *Still 'Tis Our Ancient Foe;* Paul Fisher, *Their God Is the Devil;* Wesley Swift, *Jesus Christ Was Not a Jew;* and Gerald Winrod, *The Jewish Assault on Christianity.*

One of my concerns is the growing movement within the evangelical and Charismatic movements to shrug off Judaism and its place in traditional prophetic dogmas with what has become known as "Dominion" or "Kingdom Now" theology. Some of its proponents offer little more than old-fashioned anti-Semitism while couching it in pious-sounding Christian terminology. The "Church as Israel" idea in particular is an erroneous and potentially dangerous interpretation of Jewish history. It has been used to justify persecutions and pogroms against those of Jewish faith across the spectrum of church history. At best, this Church as Israel idea will fade as the false doctrine it is; at worst, it could encourage renewed anti-Semitism. See Hal Lindsey, *The Road to Holocaust* (New York: Bantam, 1990), for an evangelical warning against Dominion or Kingdom theology. A lamentably anti-Semitic treatise in response to Lindsey's book is Gordon L. Ginn, *The Late Great Road to Holocaust* (Fortunea, Calif.: Smyrna, 1991).

## Chapter 1 *The Illuminati*

1. George Johnson, *Architects of Fear* (Los Angeles: Jeremy Tarcher, 1983), 25–27. Although books by contemporary conspiracy theory believers are legion, I will list only a few here: Gary Allen, *None Dare Call It Conspiracy* (Rossmoor, Calif.: Concord, 1971), 78–97; Gary H. Kah, *En Route to Global Occupation* (Lafayette, La.: Huntington House, 1992), 51–65; Des Griffin, *Fourth Reich of the Rich* (reprint, Clackamas, Ore.: Emissary Publications, 1993), 141–62. See also Jeffrey A. Baker, *Cheque Mate: The Game of Princes* (St. Petersburg, Fla.: The Jeffrey Baker Group, 1993); James Perloff, *The Shadows of Power: The Council on Foreign Relations and the American Decline* (Appleton, Wis.: Western Islands, 1988); and Holly Sklar, *Trilateralism: The Trilateral Commission and Elite Planning for World Management* (Boston: South End, 1980), for examples of "next generation" conspiracy theorists. Some of these are evangelical Christians, too. For a more comprehensive listing, please refer to appendix A.

2. Robert Middlekauf, *The Mathers: Three Generations of Puritan Intellectuals, 1596–1728* (New York: Oxford University Press, 1971), 330–42; Paul Boyer, *When Time Shall Be No More* (Cambridge: Belknap Harvard, 1992), 68–70; Robert Fuller, *Naming the Antichrist: The History of an American Obsession* (New York: Oxford University Press, 1995), 61–68.

3. Boyer, *When Time Shall Be No More*, 71; Fuller, *Naming the Antichrist*, 65–68.

4. Johnson, *Architects of Fear*, 45–47; Nesta H. Webster, *Secret Societies and Subversive Movements* (reprint, Los Angeles: Christian Book Club of America, n.d.), 255–57. It has been alleged that Webster was active in the British Fascist movement during the 1920s. See also John Robison, *Proofs of a Conspiracy* (1798; reprint, Appleton, Wis.: Western Islands, 1968). Gerald Winrod, *Adam Weishaupt: A Human Devil* (reprint, Clackamas, Ore.: Emissary Publications, n.d.), provides an interesting look at a 1930s resurrection of the Illuminati legend. Winrod, after a visit to Nazi Germany during the 1930s, returned to the United States as an ardent supporter of Hitler. In the

text of his book, Winrod praises Mussolini for restricting Masonry in Italy. His chief targets were Jews, the Illuminati, and Catholics. See Seymour Martin Lipset and Earl Raab, *The Politics of Unreason* (New York: Harper and Row, 1970), 159–62.

For other fine overviews of Radical Right conspiracy theory, see David B. Davis, *The Fear of Conspiracy: Images of Un-American Subversion from the Revolution to the Present* (Ithaca: Cornell University Press, 1971); Daniel Bell, *The Radical Right* (Garden City, N.Y.: Doubleday, 1963); Richard Curry and Timothy Brown, eds., *Conspiracy: The Fear of Subversion in American History* (New York: Holt, Rinehart, and Winston, 1972); and Phillip Finch, *God, Guts, and Guns—A Close Look at the Radical Right* (New York: Seaview/ Putnam, 1983).

5. James Billington, *Fire in the Minds of Men* (New York: Basic Books, 1980), 94–98; Tal Brooke, *When the World Will Be as One* (Eugene, Ore.: Harvest House, 1989), 249–51. See also Fritz Springmeier, *The Top 13 Illuminati Bloodlines* (Portland, Ore.: self-published, 1995).

6. Webster, *Secret Societies*, 196–99. See also Seth Payson, *Proofs of the Real Existence and Dangerous Tendency of Illuminism* (Charleston, S.C., 1802); Arkin Daraul, *A History of Secret Societies*, 2nd ed. (New York: Citadel Press, 1990), 225–32.

7. Robison, *Proofs of a Conspiracy*, 64.

8. Ibid., 64–65.

9. Ibid., passim; Davis, *The Fear of Conspiracy*, 37–39.

10. Pat Robertson, *The New World Order* (Dallas: Word, 1991), 180; Webster, *Secret Societies*, 199–200.

11. Robison, *Proofs of a Conspiracy*, passim; Billington, *Fire in the Minds of Men*, 95; Michael Howard, *The Occult Conspiracy: Secret Societies, Their Influence and Power in World History* (Rochester, Vt.: Destiny, 1989), 61–64.

12. J. P. L. de la Roche, Marquis de la Luchet, *Essai sur la sect des illumines*, 2nd ed. (Paris, 1789), 73–76, quoted in Billington, *Fire in the Minds of Men*, 98–99.

13. Webster, *Secret Societies*, 196–209; Robison, *Proofs of a Conspiracy*, 60–62; Lady Queensborough (Edith Starr Miller), *Occult Theocracy*, vol. 1 (1933; reprint, Los Angeles: Christian Book Club of America, n.d.), 370–75. See also Neil Wilgus, *The Illuminoids* (New York: Pocket Books, 1979), for an overview of the Illuminati legend.

14. William Still, *New World Order: Ancient Plans of Secret Societies* (Lafayette, La.: Huntington House, 1991), 80–81; Kah, *En Route to Global Occupation*, 25–26. For more level-headed approaches in the Christian community, I suggest Bill Alnor, *Soothsayers of the Second Advent* (Grand Rapids: Revell, 1989).

15. Billington, *Fire in the Minds of Men*, 95–96.

16. Webster, *Secret Societies*, 99–124.

Alcibiades was an Athenian general during the Second Peloponnesian War (431–404 B.C.) who was noted for political intrigue. Cardinal Richelieu was the power behind the throne during the reign of French King Louis XIII. Both names have become bywords for underhanded political dealing.

17. Nesta H. Webster, *World Revolution* (reprint, Devon, United Kingdom: Britons Publishing Company, 1971), 31.

18. Webster, *Secret Societies*, 203–9; Brooke, *When the World Will Be as One*, 250–51. Some conspiracy researchers even claim that the Illuminati transferred its operations to the United States in the wake of its exposure in Bavaria. See Rev. Clarence Kelly, *Conspiracy against God and Man* (Appleton, Wis.: Western Islands, 1974), 55–57.

19. See Count Mirabeau, *The Prussian Monarchy under Frederick the Great* (Paris, 1788); Billington, *Fire in the Minds of Men*, 19–20, 96. Mirabeau was a French ambassador in Berlin during the 1790s.

20. Billington, *Fire in the Minds of Men*, 96–97.

21. Henry Cabot Lodge, ed., *History of Nations: The French Revolution*, 4th ed., vol. 10 (New York: P. F. Collier and Son, 1916), 84–85. See Max Savelle, *The Origins of American Diplomacy: The International History of Anglo-America, 1492–1763* (New York, 1967); Douglas Edward Leach, *Arms for Empire* (New York: MacMillan, 1973); and Lawrence Gipson, *The British Empire before the American Revolution*, 14 vols. (New York, 1935–67), for comprehensive overviews of French losses in the contest for empire.

For a look at French domestic issues, see Gaetano Salvemini, *The French Revolution, 1788–1792* (New York: Norton Library, 1962), offers a dated but still good overview of Revolutionary-era issues. See also R. R. Palmer, *The Age of Democratic Revolution*, 2 vols. (Princeton, N.J.: Princeton University Press, 1956); R. R. Palmer, *Twelve Who Ruled: The Committee of Safety during the Reign of Terror* (Princeton, N.J.: Princeton University Press, 1941); and Billington, *Fire in the Minds of Men*, 98–99. See also a review quoted in Billington, book 1, chapter 4, footnote 85, stating, "If it is ridiculous to explain the [French] Revolution by an Illuminist plot, it is no less ridiculous to suppose that the friends and ideas of the Illuminists played no role in it."

22. Stanley Elkins and Eric McKintrick, *The Age of Federalism: The Early American Republic, 1788–1800* (London: Oxford University Press, 1993), 590–93, 694–95, 700–701; John Miller, *Crisis in Freedom: The Alien and Sedition Acts* (Boston: Houghton Mifflin, 1951), 83.

For a superb overview of the Alien and Sedition Acts and their impact, see James M. Smith, *Freedom's Fetters: The Alien and Sedition Acts and American Civil Liberties* (Ithaca, N.Y.: Cornell University Press, 1956).

For a short overview of the political parties and politics, see Morton Bordon, *Parties and Politics in the Early Republic, 1789–1815* (New York: Thomas Crowell, 1967); and Henry Cabot Lodge, *Alexander Hamilton* (reprint, New York: Chelsea House, 1980).

23. Davis, *The Fear of Conspiracy*, 37–42; Abbe Barruel, *Memoires pour servir à l'histoire du Jacobinisme*, vol. 1 (Hamburg, 1803), ix–x; Richard Hofstadter, *The Paranoid Style in American Politics* (New York: Knopf, 1965), 10–16; Lipset and Raab, *The Politics of Unreason*, 35–36; Johnson, *Architects of Fear*, 51–57. Barruel was a Jesuit who had been expelled from France. During his exile he wrote a four-volume history of the Jacobin movement in which he includes the Illuminati and their influence. Barruel and Robison's works

were among the two best-selling books in the United States around the turn of the century.

24. Jedediah Morse, *A Sermon, Exhibiting the Present Dangers and Consequent Duties of the Citizens of the United States of America: Delivered at Charlestown, April 25, 1799* (Charlestown, Mass., 1799); David Tatten, *A Concourse Delivered in the Chapel of Harvard College, June 19, 1798* (Boston, 1798). See also Davis, *The Fear of Conspiracy;* and Hofstadter, *The Paranoid Style in American Politics.*

25. Dumas Malone, *Jefferson and the Ordeal of Liberty,* vol. 3 (New York: Little, Brown, and Company, 1962), 395–408.

26. Timothy Dwight, *The Duty of Americans in the Present Crisis* (New Haven, Conn., 1798), 20; Hofstadter, *The Paranoid Style in American Politics,* 13; Vernon Stauffer, *New England and the Bavarian Illuminati* (New York: Columbia University Press, 1918), 283; Lipset and Raab, *The Politics of Unreason,* 36–39; George Washington, *Writings of George Washington,* vol. 20 (Washington, D.C.: Government Printing Office, 1941), 518; Johnson, *Architects of Fear,* 57–58. See also Washington's Famous "Farewell Address," James D. Richardson, ed., *A Compilation of the Messages and Papers of the Presidents, 1789–1897,* vol. 1 (Washington, D.C.: Government Printing Office, 1896), 213–14.

27. See Abraham Bishop, *Proofs of a Conspiracy against Christianity and the Government of the United States; Exhibited in Several Views of the Union of Church and State in New England* (Hartford, Conn., 1802).

28. Bordon, *Parties and Politics in the Early Republic,* 57–58.

29. Ibid., 58–59; Lodge, *Alexander Hamilton,* 162–84.

30. Rosemary Ellen Guiley, *Harper's Encyclopedia of Mystical and Paranormal Experience* (Edison, N.J.: Castle, 1990), 280–81. See also Aleister Crowley, *Gems from the Equinox* (Scottsdale, Ariz.: Falcon Press, 1992), for selections from the ten-volume *Equinox* journal.

### Chapter 2 *Nineteenth-Century Conspiracy Theories*

1. Robert V. Remini, *Andrew Jackson and the Course of American Freedom, 1822–1832,* vol. 2 (New York: Harper and Row, 1981), 138–40. William Morgan, *Illustrations of Masonry* (1827; reprint, Palmdale, Calif.: Omni Publications), iii–iv.

2. Remini, *Andrew Jackson,* 139–40.

For a first-rate contemporary evangelical Christian evaluation of the teachings of Freemasonry, I highly recommend John Ankerberg and John Weldon, *The Secret Teachings of the Masonic Lodge* (Chicago: Moody Press, 1990).

For conspiracy-related works on Freemasonry, see the following: Queensborough, *Occult Theocracy;* Webster, *Secret Societies;* Martin L. Wagner, *Freemasonry* (Clackamas, Ore.: Emissary Publications, reprint ed., n.d.); Jim Shaw, *The Deadly Deception* (Shreveport, La.: Huntington House, 1988); William Schnoebelen, *Masonry beyond the Light* (Chino, Calif.: Chick Publications, 1991); Jose Maria Cardinal Caro, *The Mystery of Freemasonry* (reprint, Clackamas, Ore.: Emissary Publications, 1992); David Carrico, *The Masonic-*

*Egyptian-Satanic Connection* (Clackamas, Ore.: Emissary Publications, 1991); and also by Carrico, *Manley P. Hall: The Honored Masonic Author* (Clackamas, Ore.: Emissary Publications, 1992), and *Lucifer-Eliphas Levi-Albert Pike and the Masonic Lodge* (Clackamas, Ore.: Emissary Publications, 1991).

I also recommend Albert Pike's *Morals and Dogma of the Ancient and Accepted Rite of Freemasonry* (Charleston, S.C.: The Supreme Council of the 33rd Degree for the Southern Jurisdiction of the United States, 1906); John J. Robinson, *Born in Blood: The Lost Secrets of Freemasonry* (New York: M. Evans and Company, 1989); Stephen Knight, *The Brotherhood: The Secret World of the Freemasons* (New York: Dorset Press, 1984); Martin Short, *Inside the Brotherhood: Further Secrets of the Freemasons* (New York: Dorset Press, 1989).

Finally, for books of related interest see Stephen Howarth, *The Knights Templar* (New York: Dorset Press, 1982); Ernle Bradford, *The Knights of the Order* (New York: Dorset Press, 1972); Magnus Incognito, *The Secret Doctrine of the Rosicrucians* (New York: Barnes and Noble, 1993); and Arthur Edward Waite, *The Brotherhood of the Rosy Cross* (New York: Barnes and Noble, 1993).

3. Remini, *Andrew Jackson,* 139–40.

4. Ralph C. H. Catterall, *The Second Bank of the United States* (Chicago: University of Chicago Press, 1960), 1–2.

5. Arthur Schlesinger Jr., *The Age of Jackson* (Boston: Little, Brown, and Company, 1945), 74–87; Remini, *Andrew Jackson,* 331–44; Edward Pessen, *Jacksonian America: Society, Personality, and Politics* (revised ed., Homewood, Ill.: Dorsey Press, 1978), 122–48; "Jackson's Veto Message, July 10, 1832," *House Miscellaneous Documents,* 53rd Congress, 2nd Session, reprinted in *Problems in American Civilization* series, "Jackson vs. Biddle: The Struggle over the Second Bank of the United States" (Boston: D. C. Heath Company, 1949), 7–22.

Some historians and bankers have gone so far as to accuse the House of Rothschild of seeking to saddle the United States with yet another chartered national bank, only to be thwarted by President Jackson. The Rothschild response to this rebuff, according to at least one author, was to cause the panic of 1837. See Henry Clews, *Twenty-eight Years in Wall Street* (New York: Irving Company, 1908), 106.

6. Leland H. Jenks, *The Migration of British Capital to 1875* (New York: Knopf, 1927), 106.

7. Whitney R. Cross, *The Burned-over District: The Social and Intellectual History of Enthusiastic Religion in Western New York* (New York: Harper Torchbooks, 1950), 3–13. See also Charles Finney, *The Heart of Truth* (reprint, Minneapolis: Bethany, 1976); Charles Finney, *Autobiography* (Minneapolis: Bethany, 1977); Charles Finney, *Systematic Theology* (Minneapolis: Bethany, 1976); and Lewis Drummond, *The Life and Ministry of Charles G. Finney* (Minneapolis: Bethany, 1985). For a critical look at the revivals of the day, see Paul E. Johnson, *A Shopkeeper's Millennium: Society and Revivals in Rochester, New York, 1815–1837* (New York: Hill and Wang, 1978).

8. *Signs of the Times,* January 25, 1843. See also Sylvester Bliss, *Memoirs of William Miller* (Boston, 1853); and Leon Festinger, Henry W. Riecken, and

Stanley Schachter, *When Prophecy Fails* (Minneapolis: University of Minnesota Press, 1956).

9. Festinger, *When Prophecy Fails,* 12–23; Walter Martin, *Kingdom of the Cults,* 3rd ed. (Minneapolis: Bethany, 1985), 411–13; Boyer, *When Time Shall Be No More,* 81–83. See C. E. Sears, *Days of Delusion: A Strange Bit of History* (Boston: Houghton Mifflin, 1924); and Francis D. Nichols, *The Midnight Cry* (Washington, D.C.: Review and Herald, 1944), for anti and pro accounts respectively of the Millerite movement.

10. Boyer, *When Time Shall Be No More,* 81–83.

11. Ibid. See also Henry Pickering, *Chief Men among the Brethren* (London: Pickering and Inglis, 1961; reprint, 1981); John Darby, *The Hopes of the Church of God in Connection with the Destiny of the Jews and the Nations as Revealed in Prophecy,* translated from French (London, 1842); Alexander Reese, *The Approaching Advent of Christ: An Examination of the Teaching of J. N. Darby* (London: Marshall, Morgan, and Scott, 1937).

12. Boyer, *When Time Shall Be No More,* 86–90.

13. Eric Foner, *Reconstruction: America's Unfinished Revolution, 1863–1877* (New York: Harper and Row, 1988), 565–66; Avery Craven, *Reconstruction: The Ending of the Civil War* (New York: Holt, Rinehart, and Winston, 1969), 267–68, 274–76, 279–83, 288–96. See also C. Van Woodward, *Reunion and Reaction: The Compromise of 1877 and the End of Reconstruction* (Boston: Little, Brown, and Company, 1951); William S. McFeely, *Grant: A Biography* (New York, 1981); William B. Hesseltine, *Ulysses S. Grant, Politician* (New York, 1935); and John Hope Franklin, *Reconstruction: After the Civil War* (Chicago: University of Chicago Press, 1961).

14. Norman J. Ware, *The Labor Movement in the United States, 1860–1895* (New York: Vintage, 1929), 1–21; Allan Nevins, *The Emergence of Modern America, 1865–1878* (Chicago: Triangle Books, 1955), 178–203.

15. Thomas C. Cochran and William Miller, *The Age of Enterprise: A Social History of Industrial America* (New York: Harper and Row, 1961), 129–53, 154–80; Matthew Josephson, *The Robber Barons* (New York: Harcourt, Brace, and Company, 1934), 68–69, 141–48.

16. Josephson, *The Robber Barons,* 50–74; Cochran and Miller, *The Age of Enterprise,* 145–46. See also Burton J. Hendrick, *The Life of Andrew Carnegie,* 2 vols. (New York: Doubleday, 1932); Andrew Carnegie, *Autobiography* (Boston: Houghton Mifflin, 1920); Andrew Carnegie, *The Empire of Business* (New York: Doubleday, 1912); Raymond B. Fosdick, *John D. Rockefeller* (New York: Harper and Brothers, 1955); and Peter Collier and David Horowitz, *The Rockefellers: An American Dynasty* (New York: Holt, Rinehart, and Winston, 1976).

17. Richard Hofstadter, *The Age of Political Reform* (reprint, New York: Vintage, 1955), passim.

18. See Gilbert Fite, *The Farmer's Frontier* (reprint, Albuquerque: University of New Mexico Press, 1974).

19. See John Hicks, *The Populist Revolt* (Lincoln: University of Nebraska Press, 1968); and Lawrence Goodwyn, *The Populist Moment* (Oxford: Oxford

University Press, 1978), for excellent overviews of the Populist movement, its leaders, and its goals.

20. Ignatius Donnelly, *Caesar's Column* (Chicago, 1891). See also Hofstadter, *Age of Reform*, 77–79.

21. See Mary Lease, *The Problem of Civilization Solved* (Chicago, 1895); Hofstadter, *Age of Reform*, 82–85.

22. Hofstadter, *Age of Reform*, 73.

23. Ibid.

24. James Corcoran, *Bitter Harvest* (New York: Penguin, 1990), 43–69. See also Capstan Turner, *There Was a Man: The Saga of Gordan Kahl* (Nashville: Sozo, 1985), for a sympathetic, conspiratorial presentation of the Posse and its most famous member.

25. Quoted in Hofstadter, *Age of Reform*, 74.

26. Ibid., 75. Hofstadter includes period books such as Mrs. S. E. V. Emery, *Seven Financial Conspiracies Which Have Enslaved the American People*, and Gordon Clark, *Shylock: As Banker, Bondholder, Corruptionist, Conspirator*, as examples of fear of big banker money manipulation. Some of the arguments found therein are identical to writings contending manipulation today.

27. William H. Harvey, *Coin's Financial School* (Chicago: Coin Publishing Company, 1894), 96–99; Hicks, *The Populist Revolt*, 310–20; Goodwyn, *The Populist Moment*, 230–63; Frederick Merk, *History of the Westward Movement* (New York: Knopf, 1978), 479; Ray Allen Billington, *Westward Expansion*, 4th ed. (New York: Macmillan, 1974), 645–48; C. Van Woodward, *The Burden of Southern History* (Baton Rouge: LSU Press, 1960), 141–61. See also Theodore Salutos, *Farmer Movements in the South, 1865–1933* (Berkeley, Calif.: University of California Press, 1933).

28. M. R. Werner, *William Jennings Bryan* (New York: Chelsea House, 1983), 50, 53–55. See also William Jennings Bryan and Mary Baird Bryan, *Memoirs* (reprint, New York: Haskell House, 1971); and William Jennings Bryan, *The First Battle* (1896), for a description of William Jennings Bryan's views on the issues surrounding the election.

29. Werner, *William Jennings Bryan*, 50.

30. Hofstadter, *The Paranoid Style in American Politics*, 246–49; Harvey, *Coin's Financial School*, 165–72.

31. Harvey, *Coin's Financial School*, 249.

32. William H. Harvey, *Coin on Money, Trusts, and Imperialism* (Chicago: Coin Publishing Company, 1900).

33. Hofstadter, *The Paranoid Style in American Politics*, 312–15.

34. Boyer, *When Time Shall Be No More*, 86–90.

35. Ibid., 96–98; see also Cyrus Scofield, *What Do the Prophets Say?* (Philadelphia: Philadelphia School of the Bible, 1918); and Moody, et al., *The Second Coming of Christ* (Chicago: Moody Press, n.d.).

**Chapter 3** *Money Trusts and the Federal Reserve*

1. William O. Weyforth, *The Federal Reserve Board: A Study of Federal Reserve Structure and Credit Control* (Baltimore: Johns Hopkins Press, 1933),

6–7; 35 *Stat.L.* 552, May 30, 1908; see Paul M. Warburg, *The Federal Reserve System: Its Origin and Growth*, vol. 1 (New York: Macmillan, 1930).

2. Charles A. Lindbergh, *Banking and Currency and the Money Trust* (Clackamas, Ore.: Emissary Publications, n.d.), 185.

3. Ibid., 94–97.

Conspiracy theorists have further ideas about what was to happen with a central bank; see G. Edward Griffin, *The Creature from Jekyll Island* (Westlake Village, Calif.: American Media, n.d.), 437–43.

4. G. L. Bach, *Federal Reserve Policy-Making* (New York: Knopf, 1950), 3–5; George W. Edwards, *The Evolution of Finance Capitalism* (New York: Longmans, Green, 1938), 194–95.

5. Carroll Quigley, *Tragedy and Hope* (New York: Macmillan, 1966), 529–30; Pat Robertson, *The New World Order*, 123–25. See also Edwards, *The Evolution of Finance Capitalism*.

6. Quigley, *Tragedy and Hope*, 530.

7. Cochran and Miller, *The Age of Enterprise*, 182, 196–97. See also Lewis Corey, *The House of Morgan* (New York: G. H. Watt, 1930). As one might expect, Morgan denied that anything like a "money trust" existed. Herbert L. Satterlee, *J. Pierpont Morgan* (New York: Macmillan, 1939), 556–58. See also Frederick Lewis Allen, *The Great Pierpont Morgan* (New York: Harper and Brothers, 1949), and Frederick L. Allen, "Morgan the Magnificent," *Life* (April 25, 1949); John Winkler, *Morgan the Magnificent* (New York: Vanguard Press, 1930); and Louis Brandeis, *Other People's Money* (New York: Frederick Stokes, 1914).

Brandeis served as Jacob Schiff's attorney until Woodrow Wilson appointed him to a vacant seat on the U.S. Supreme Court. See also *The Congressional Record*, v. 51, December 22, 1913, p. 1446 for Charles Lindbergh Sr.'s explanation of the 1907 panic; and Perloff, *Shadows of Power*, 2.

8. Quigley, *Tragedy and Hope*, 72.

9. Greider, *Secrets of the Temple: How the Federal Reserve Runs the Country* (New York: Simon and Schuster, 1987), 275–76; Eustace Mullins, *The Secrets of the Federal Reserve* (reprint, Stanton, Va.: Bankers Research Institute, 1993), 1–3; Warburg, *The Federal Reserve System*, 1:58. Of course all of those who attended the meeting were sworn to secrecy, pledging not to discuss what transpired at the meetings. Warburg himself, two decades later, would not offer much in the way of information about the discussions at Jekyll Island.

10. Ron Chernow, *The Warburgs* (New York: Random House, 1993), 133–34. See also T. W. Lamont, *Henry P. Davison* (New York: Harper, Row and Company, 1933).

11. Weyforth, *The Federal Reserve Board*, 1933, 10–11; *Report of the National Monetary Commission* (Washington, D.C.: Government Printing Office, 1913), 11.

12. Nathaniel W. Stephenson, *Nelson Aldrich: A Leader in American Politics* (New York: Charles Scribner's Sons, 1930), 485; Mullins, *Secrets of the Federal Reserve*, 6.

13. *Saturday Evening Post* (February 9, 1935). See Roy Hoops, "Follow Me to Jekyll Island," *Washington Post* (March 27, 1983), quoted in Mullins, *Secrets of the Federal Reserve,* 8; Greider, *Secrets of the Temple,* 276.

14. Warburg, *The Federal Reserve System,* 1:58–69; Mullins, *Secrets of the Federal Reserve,* 7.

15. See Andrew Carnegie, *Triumphant Democracy* (London, 1886); E. C. Knuth, *The Empire of "The City"* (Milwaukee, 1946), 60; David Graham Phillips, "Aldrich, the Head of It All," *Cosmopolitan Magazine* (April 1906).

16. Mullins, *Secrets of the Federal Reserve,* 16–17.

17. "House Committee Hearings on the Money Trust," *House Report No. 1593,* III (Washington, D.C.: Government Printing Office, 1913). See Emanuel Josephson, *The "Federal" Reserve Conspiracy and the Rockefellers* (New York: Chedney Press, 1968), for an incredibly convoluted mishmash of conspiratorial rantings. This book serves as a good example of how conspiracy theorists have, from time to time, pointed the finger at each other as being part of the "Plan."

For a good overview and listing of some of the era's more important writings and documents, see Richard Hofstadter, ed., *The Progressive Movement, 1900–1915* (reprint, Englewood Cliffs, N.J.: Prentice-Hall, 1963).

18. George E. Mowry, *Theodore Roosevelt and the Progressive Movement* (reprint, New York: Hill and Wang, 1960), 284–305; William Henry Harbaugh, *The Life and Times of Theodore Roosevelt* (reprint, New York: Collier, 1963), 410–23.

19. Quoted in Mullins, *Secrets of the Federal Reserve,* 21.

20. See Elisha E. Garrison, *Roosevelt, Wilson, and the Federal Reserve Law* (Boston: Christopher Publications, 1931); Mullins, *Secrets of the Federal Reserve,* 16.

21. Edward Mandell House, *Phillip Dru: Administrator* (New York: B. W. Huebsch, 1912). See also Charles Seymour, *The Intimate Papers of Colonel House,* 4 vols. (Boston: Houghton Mifflin, 1928), passim, for the subject's views of the Federal Reserve System; and Ray Stannard Baker, *Woodrow Wilson: Life and Letters, Governor, 1910–1913,* vol. 3 (London: William Heinemann, 1932), 294–309.

22. Woodrow Wilson, *Messages and Papers,* vol. 1 (New York: The Review of Reviews Corporation, 1924), 10–14; Seymour, *Intimate Papers of Colonel House,* 1:157.

23. Mullins, *Secrets of the Federal Reserve,* 26–27. See also George S. Viereck, *The Strangest Friendship in History: Woodrow Wilson and Colonel Edward Mandell House* (New York: Liverlight, 1932); Greider, *Secrets of the Temple,* 280–81.

24. Mullins, *Secrets of the Federal Reserve,* 33–35.

25. See Robertson, *The New World Order;* Still, *New World Order.*

## Chapter 4 *The Council on Foreign Relations*

1. Quigley, *Tragedy and Hope,* 130–31.

2. Ibid., 131; Carroll Quigley, *The Anglo-American Establishment* (reprint, New York: Books in Focus, 1981), 84–100; 117–39.

3. Ibid., 132–33.

4. Ibid., 582–83.

5. Arthur Schlesinger Jr., *A Thousand Days* (Boston: Houghton Mifflin, 1965), 128; Quigley, *Tragedy and Hope*, 951. See also David Halberstam, *The Best and Brightest* (New York: Random House, 1972); and Perloff, *Shadows of Power.*

It is interesting to note that early leaders of the Council on Foreign Relations included John Davis as president and Paul Cravath as vice president, as well as a council of thirteen—all of whom were associates of the Morgan bank.

6. Ibid., 36–37; *Foreign Affairs* was and is the chief public voice for the Council on Foreign Relations. Although sometimes readers complain of the dullness and arcane nature of the topics, it is nonetheless an extremely valuable source for understanding the positions of the Council itself. It has rightly been said that today's article in *Foreign Affairs* is tomorrow's United States' foreign policy.

7. Quigley, *Tragedy and Hope*, 952.

8. Ibid., 953.

9. Ibid., 954.

10. Ibid., 950.

11. Boyer, *When Time Shall Be No More*, 100–102. See also Scofield, *What Do the Prophets Say?* among other prophecy-based writings of the day.

12. See Anthony Sutton, *Wall Street and the Bolshevik Revolution* (New Rochelle, N.Y.: Arlington House, 1974), for a conspiracy-laced presentation of the author's interpretation of how the Russian Revolution succeeded.

13. Allen, *None Dare Call It Conspiracy*, 58–59.

14. Brooke, *When the World Will Be as One*, 254–55.

15. John M. Thompson, *Revolutionary Russia* (New York: Macmillan, 1989), 37–39.

Also valuable in understanding the background and Russian Revolution itself are Michael Kort, *The Soviet Colossus: A History of the USSR* (New York: Charles Scribner's Sons, 1985); Leonard Shapiro, *The Government and Politics of the Soviet Union* (reprint, New York: Vintage, 1967), 15–79; and V. I. Lenin, *The State and Revolution* (reprint, Moscow: Progress Publishers, 1969).

16. Sutton, *Wall Street and the Bolshevik Revolution*, 25. See Perloff, *Shadows of Power*, 39.

17. There are numerous such articles in the first few volumes of *Foreign Affairs*, of which Phillip Kerr, "From Empire to Commonwealth," 1, no. 2 (December 1922), could well serve as an example. I would also suggest that the researcher look at the CFR's publication: Robert J. Palmer, comp., *Foreign Affairs: A Fifty Year Index*, vols. 1–50 (New York: R. R. Bowler Company, 1973), for specific topics found in *Foreign Affairs*.

18. See W. E. Leuchtenberg, *The Perils of Prosperity: 1914–1932* (Chicago: University of Chicago Press, 1958); Daniel M. Smith, *The Testing of America, 1914–1945* (St. Louis: Forum Press, 1979); Robert K. Murray, *Red Scare* (reprint, New York: McGraw Hill, 1964); and George Soule, *Prosperity Decade* (New York: Rinehart, 1947).

19. John Kenneth Galbraith, *The Great Crash* (Boston: Houghton Mifflin, 1955), 8–28; Lionel Robbins, *The Great Crash* (New York: Macmillan, 1934), 53. See also Herbert Hoover, *Memoirs of Herbert Hoover: The Great Depression, 1929–1941* (New York: Macmillan, 1952); Seymour Harris, *Twenty Years of Federal Reserve Policy* (Cambridge, Mass.: Harvard University Press, 1933); Carter Glass, *An Adventure in Creative Finance* (New York, 1927); Carter Glass, *The Facts about the Fiscal Policy of Our Government* (Washington, D.C.: Government Printing Office, 1933); and Earl Sparling, *Mystery Men of Wall Street* (New York: Greenberg, 1930).

For a highly conspiratorial story relating to the presence of Winston Churchill at the stock exchange, see Pat Riott, *The Greatest Story Never Told: Winston Churchill and the Crash of 1929* (Oak Brook, Ill.: Nanoman Press, 1994).

20. Irving Fisher, *The Stock Market Crash and After* (New York: Macmillan, 1930), 1–20, 31–55; Galbraith, *The Great Crash*, 28–47; Bernard Baruch, *Baruch: The Public Years* (New York: Holt, Rinehart, and Winston, 1960), 217–35; Margaret L. Coit, *Mr. Baruch* (Boston: Houghton Mifflin, 1957), 376–411.

21. Anthony Sutton, *Wall Street and FDR* (New Rochelle, N.Y.: Arlington House, 1975), 18; Perloff, *Shadows of Power*, 53–54.

22. Ibid., 55. See also Curtis Dall, *FDR: My Exploited Father-in-Law* (Washington, D.C.: Action Associates, 1970), for the author's contention that the president was merely a mouthpiece for the Council on Foreign Relations.

23. Johnson, *Architects of Fear*, 99–100; Alfred McClung Lee and Elizabeth Briant Lee, eds., *The Fine Art of Propaganda: A Study of Father Coughlin's Speeches* (New York: Harcourt, Brace and Company, 1939), 8–13, 26–46; David H. Bennett, *The Party of Fear* (Chapel Hill: University of North Carolina Press, 1992), 253–66.

24. Fuller, *Naming the Antichrist*, 137–43; Winrod, *Adam Weishaupt*, 41–51; Gerald Winrod, *The Jewish Assault on Christianity* (Wichita: Defender Publications, 1935).

25. Boyer, *When Time Shall Be No More*, 104–12. See also Arthur Maxwell, *History's Crowded Climax* (Mountain View, Calif.: Pacific Press, 1940); and James Spink, *Will Hitler Gain World Domination?* (New York: Loizeaux Bros., 1942).

26. Books and articles are quite numerous for this period, but a few noteworthy ones include Roland N. Stromberg, "American Business and the Approach of War, 1935–1941," *Journal of Economic History* 13 (Winter 1953): 58–78; Winston Churchill, *The Gathering Storm*, vol. 1 (reprint, Boston: Houghton Mifflin, 1967); Robert Ferrell, "Pearl Harbor and the Revisionists," *The Historians* 17 (Spring 1955): 215–33; Herbert Feis, "War Came at Pearl Harbor: Suspicions Considered," *Yale Review* 45 (March 1956): 378–90; Arthur M. Schlesinger Jr., "Roosevelt and His Detractors," *Harpers* 200 (June 1950); Donald Drummond, *The Passing of American Neutrality, 1937–1941* (Ann Arbor, Mich.: University of Michigan Press, 1955).

27. Arthur Schlesinger Jr., *The Age of Roosevelt* (Boston: Houghton Mifflin, 1958), 389–91.

28. Samuel Elliot Morison, comp. and ed., *The United States Navy in World War II* (New York: Ballantine, 1967), 3–107; A. J. Barker, *Pearl Harbor* (New

York: Ballantine, 1969), 21–64; Tracy B. Kitteridge, "The Muddle before Pearl Harbor," *U.S. News and World Report* 27 (December 3, 1954): 52–63. See also Samuel Elliot Morison, *The Rising Sun in the Pacific, 1931–1942* (Boston, 1948). Also of great assistance, although requiring a great deal of sometimes tedious reading, is the collected report of the U.S. Naval Institute on the Pearl Harbor attack.

29. Adolf Hitler, *Mein Kampf* (reprint, Boston: Houghton Mifflin, 1971), 3–18; William L. Shirer, *The Rise and Fall of the Third Reich* (New York: Fawcett, 1960), 17–52; Joachim Fest, *The Face of the Third Reich* (New York: Pantheon, 1970), 3–26; Dusty Sklar, *The Nazis and the Occult* (reprint, New York: Dorset Press, 1988), 17.

30. Hitler, *Mein Kampf*, 141–43; Fest, *Face of the Third Reich*, 13–14; Alan Wykes, *Hitler* (New York: Ballantine, 1970), 20–31.

31. Perloff, *Shadows of Power*, 65; Winston Churchill, *The Grand Alliance* (Boston: Houghton Mifflin, 1950), 23; William Stephenson, *A Man Called Intrepid* (New York: Harcourt, Brace, and Jovanovich, 1976), 157.

32. See B. H. Liddell Hart, *History of the Second World War*, 2 vols. (reprint, New York: G. P. Putnam's Sons, 1970); Carl Berger, *B–29: The Superfortress* (New York: Ballantine, 1970), 148–59; Brian J. Ford, *Allied Secret Weapons: The War of Science* (New York: Ballantine, 1971), 27–46. See also John Strawson, *The Battle for North Africa* (New York: Charles Scribner's Sons, 1969); Harry Butcher, *My Three Years with Eisenhower* (New York: Simon and Schuster, 1946); and Albert Speer, *Inside the Third Reich* (reprint, New York: Avon, 1971).

33. K. J. Macksey, *Afrika Korps* (New York: Ballantine, 1968), 122–27; Charles Whiting, *Patton* (New York: Ballantine, 1970), 20–21; Martin Blumenson, *Kasserine Pass* (New York: Tower, 1967), 179–253; Ladislas Farago, *Patton: Ordeal and Triumph* (reprint, New York: Dell, 1970), 228–55. See also Paul Carell, *Hitler Moves East, 1941–1943* (reprint, New York: Ballantine, 1970); and Paul Carell, *Scorched Earth* (reprint, New York: Ballantine, 1971).

34. Martin Gilbert, *The Holocaust: A History of the Jews of Europe during the Second World War* (New York: Holt, Rinehart, and Winston, 1985), 784–810, 811–28; David S. Wyman, *The Abandonment of the Jews: America and the Holocaust, 1941–1945* (New York: Pantheon, 1984), 311–40; Howard M. Sacher, *The Course of Modern Jewish History* (reprint, New York: Vintage, 1990), 504–56; Paul Johnson, *A History of the Jews* (New York: Harper and Row, 1987), 423–517. See also Walter Laqueur, *A History of Zionism* (reprint, New York: Schocken, 1989), 505–62.

## Chapter 5 *The Cold War: 1945–1963*

1. Walter LaFeber, *America, Russia, and the Cold War, 1945–1975*, 3rd ed. (New York: John Wiley and Sons, 1976), 30–49; Martin J. Sherwin, "The Atomic Bomb and the Origins of the Cold War," *American Historical Review* 78 (October 1973): 945–68; John Spanier, *American Foreign Policy Since World War II*, 2nd ed. (New York: Frederick Praeger, 1965), 18–37; Stephen Ambrose, *Rise to Globalism: American Foreign Policy 1938–1970*, 4th ed. (New York: Penguin, 1985), 55–78. See also Zbigniew Brzezinski, *The Grand Failure: The*

*Birth and Death of Communism in the Twentieth Century* (reprint, New York: Collier, 1990).

2. Perloff, *Shadows of Power*, 70–71.

3. Lawrence Shoup and William Minter, *Imperial Brain Trust: The Council on Foreign Relations and United States Foreign Policy* (New York: Monthly Review Press, 1977), 16; Thomas Bailey, *A Diplomatic History of the American People*, 6th ed. (New York: Appleton Century Crofts, 1955), 802–3; Brooke, *When the World Will Be as One*, 265–66; Robertson, *The New World Order*, 52. See also Anthony Sutton, *National Suicide: Military Aid to the Soviet Union* (New York: Arlington House, 1974), for a conspiratorial interpretation of this era.

4. Collier and Horowitz, *The Rockefellers*, 246–47; Perloff, *Shadows of Power*, 71–72; Whittaker Chambers, *Witness* (New York: Random House, 1952), 331.

5. Bailey, *A Diplomatic History of the American People*, 796–804; Ambrose, *Rise to Globalism*, 102–35. See also William Appleman Williams, *The Tragedy of American Diplomacy* (reprint, New York: Dell, 1978).

6. See Wilbur M. Smith, "World Crisis and the Prophetic Scriptures," *Moody Monthly* (June 1950); Wilbur Smith, *Before I Forget* (Chicago: Moody, 1971); Wilbur Smith, *The Atomic Age and the Word of God* (Boston: W. A. Wilde, 1948); and Boyer, *When Time Shall Be No More*, 118–19.

7. Boyer, *When Time Shall Be No More*, 115–19.

8. Ibid., 296.

9. Bailey, *Diplomatic History of the American People*, 796–97; *Congressional Record*, 8th Congress, 1st Session (March 12, 1947), 1981. See also George Kennan, *Realities of American Foreign Policy* (Princeton, N.J.: Princeton University Press, 1954); and Harry Truman, *Memoirs of Harry S. Truman*, 2 vols. (New York: New American Library, 1956).

10. Ambrose, *Rise to Globalism*, 192–216; Spanier, *American Foreign Policy since World War II*, 86–96. See also John Spanier, *The Truman-MacArthur Controversy and the Korean War* (Cambridge, Mass.: Harvard University Press, 1959); and Norman Graebner, ed., "The Cold War: Ideological Conflict or Power Struggle," *Problems in European Civilization* (Boston: D. C. Heath, 1966).

11. Earl Latham, ed., "The Meaning of McCarthyism," *Problems in American Civilization* (Boston: D. C. Heath, 1965), iv.

12. See Reinhard H. Luthin, *American Demagogues* (New York: Beacon Press, 1954); and Richard M. Fried, *Nightmare in Red* (New York: Oxford University Press, 1990).

13. Quigley, *Tragedy and Hope*, 946–50; Stephen Ambrose, *Eisenhower*, vol. 2 (New York: Simon and Schuster, 1983), 5.

14. Ambrose, *Eisenhower*, 5; Earl Latham, *The Communist Controversy in Washington* (Cambridge, Mass.: Harvard University Press, 1966), 296–316; René Wormser, *Foundations: Their Power and Influence* (reprint, Sevierville, Tenn.: Covenant House, 1993), 32–40, 67–75, 125–29.

15. Quigley, *Tragedy and Hope*, 950.

16. Fagan, *Red Star over Hollywood*, tape number TP–106 (Clackamas, Ore.: Emissary Publications). Fagan and others were part of an organization seeking to expose what they saw as a massive Communist infiltration of the

entertainment, especially movie, industry. Fagan worked in this capacity into the 1960s, periodically putting out tracts containing the names of alleged Hollywood Communists or Communist sympathizers. See also Neil Gaebler, *An Empire of Their Own* (New York: Doubleday, 1989).

17. Perloff, *Shadows of Power,* 106–8.

18. Ambrose, *Eisenhower,* 2:57.

19. LaFeber, *America, Russia, and the Cold War,* 175–76.

20. Today the event is celebrated in Israel and the Diaspora as Yom Haatzmaut, Israel Independence Day.

21. Chaim Herzog, *The Arab-Israeli Wars: War and Peace in the Middle East* (reprint, New York: Vintage, 1984), 111–40; Ambrose, *Rise to Globalism,* 161–62, 164–65; Bailey, *A Diplomatic History of the American People,* 840–47; Spanier, *American Foreign Policy Since World War II,* 120–22; Johnson, *A History of the Jews,* 533–34. See also Moshe Dayan, *Diary of the Sinai Campaign* (London: Weidenfeld and Nicolson, 1966); Col. T. N. Dupuy, *Elusive Victory: The Arab-Israeli Wars, 1947–1974* (New York: Harper and Row, 1978); R. Henriques, *A Hundred Hours to Suez: An Account to Israel's Campaign in the Sinai Peninsula* (reprint, New York: Viking Press, 1957); and Isaac Alteras, *Eisenhower and Israel: U.S./Israel Relations, 1953–1960* (Tallahassee: University of Florida Press, 1993).

22. A single kiloton is equivalent to one thousand tons of TNT. The blast that leveled Hiroshima was estimated to be equal to twenty thousand tons of TNT. Thus when the United States detonated a fifteen-megaton bomb, its explosive power was equal to fifteen million tons of TNT.

23. LaFeber, *America, Russia, and the Cold War,* 199–207; Russell F. Weigley, *The American Way of War: A History of United States Military Strategy and Policy* (reprint, Bloomington: University of Indiana Press, 1977), 399–440. See also George Kennan, *Russia, the Atom, and the West* (reprint, New York: Greenwood Press, 1974); and George Kennan and Anna Nelson, eds., *The State Department Policy Staff Papers,* 3 vols. (New York: Garland, 1983).

24. Ambrose, *Rise to Globalism,* 173–75.

25. Ibid., 176–79; Spanier, *American Foreign Policy since World War II,* 222–34. See also Theodore Draper, *Castro's Revolution* (New York: Frederick A. Praeger, 1962); and Robert F. Smith, *What Happened to Cuba?* (New York, 1963).

26. See Ellie Abel, *The Missile Crisis* (New York: Lippincott, 1966).

27. Ibid., 19–23, 23–27, 83–99. See also *The Public Papers of the Presidents, John F. Kennedy* (Washington, D.C.: Government Printing Office, 1962).

28. Robert McNamara, *Blundering into Disaster* (New York: Pantheon, 1986), 8–16; Ambrose, *Rise to Globalism,* 189–200.

29. Conspiracy books on this period are legion, and I refer the reader to the select bibliography in appendix A. Some of the classics are William Guy Carr, *Pawns in the Game* (Clackamas, Ore.: Emissary Publications, n.d.); and William Guy Carr, *Red Fog over America* (reprint, Clackamas, Ore.: Emissary Publications, 1968).

30. For a conspiratorial view of this period, see Perloff, *Shadows of Power;* Carr, *Red Fog over America;* and Des Griffin, *Martin Luther King: The Man Behind the Myth* (reprint, Clackamas, Ore.: Emissary Publications, 1987).

### Chapter 6 *The Cold War: 1964–1989*

1. Gary Allen, *Say NO! to the New World Order* (Rossmoor, Calif.: Concord Press, 1987), 177–78.

2. John A. Stormer, *None Dare Call It Treason* (Florissant, Mo.: Liberty Bell Press, 1964), 7–14, 93–98, 99–123, 124–35; Allen, *None Dare Call It Conspiracy,* 9–16.

3. M. R. DeHaan, *Coming Events in Prophecy* (Grand Rapids: Zondervan, 1962); James Reid, *God, the Atom, and the Universe* (Grand Rapids: Zondervan, 1968); and Charles Taylor, *The Destiny of America* (reprint, Van Nuys, Calif.: Time-Life, 1972). For representative works of the period, see Boyer, *When Time Shall Be No More,* 122–30, 190.

4. Hugh Sydney, *A Very Personal Presidency: Lyndon Johnson in the White House* (New York: Athenaeum, 1968), 3–25. See also Doris Kearnes, *Lyndon Johnson and the American Dream* (New York: New American Library, 1976); Bertram Gross, ed., *The Great Society* (Rossmoor, Calif.: Concord Press, 1971), 9–16; and Bernard J. Firestone and Robert Voight, *Lyndon Baines Johnson and the Uses of Power* (New York: Greenwood Press, 1988), 1–6 and passim.

5. Spanier, *American Foreign Policy since World War II,* 146–71.

6. Ambrose, *Rise to Globalism,* 201–30.

7. Herbert S. Parmet, *Richard Nixon and His America* (Boston: Little, Brown, and Company, 1990), 506–7; Richard M. Nixon, *Memoirs* (New York: Grosset and Dunlap, 1978), 449–53, passim; Stephen Ambrose, *Nixon: Triumph of a Politician,* vol. 2 (New York: Simon and Schuster, 1989), 277–78, passim. See also Rowland Evans Jr. and Robert Novak, *Nixon and the White House* (New York: Random House, 1971).

8. Ambrose, *Nixon,* 341–45, 347–48; Nixon, *Memoirs,* 394, 547–48; Ambrose, *Rise to Globalism,* 253–58; Richard McMannus on C-SPAN, March 28, 1994.

9. See also Gary Allen, *The Man behind the Mask* (Appleton, Wis.: Western Islands, 1971).

10. Peggy Mann, *Golda: The Life of Israel's Prime Minister* (New York: Coward, McCann, and Georghegan, 1971), 211–24, 230–47; Yehoshafat Harkabi, *Arab Strategies and Israel's Response* (London: Collier Macmillan, 1977), 94–96; Herzog, *The Arab-Israeli Wars,* 143–91; Ann Mosely Lesch and Mark Tessler, *Israel, Egypt, and the Palestinians: From Camp David to Intifada* (Bloomington: University of Indiana Press, 1989), 3–22, 140–73.

11. Mann, *Golda,* 222; Herzog, *The Arab-Israeli Wars,* 180–82. See also David Dolan, *Holy War for the Promised Land* (Nashville: Thomas Nelson, 1991).

It should be noted that "Zionism" and "Jew" have often been used interchangeably during the twentieth century. Conspiracy theorists who are enemies of Israel or those of an anti-Semitic bent will sometimes claim to hate Zionism, not Jews. The record often speaks otherwise, however; such arguments some-times tend to be little more than thinly veiled hatred of Jews in general.

12. Julian Becker, *The PLO: The Rise and Fall of the Palestine Liberation Organization* (New York: St. Martin's Press, 1984), 55–56; Neil C. Livingston and David Halvery, *Inside the PLO* (New York: Quill/William Morrow, 1990), 79–85; Mann, *Golda*, 225–26. See also Hoag Levins, *Arab Reach* (New York: Doubleday, 1983); Alan Hart, *Arafat: A Political Biography* (reprint, Bloom-ington: University of Indiana Press, 1984); and Randolph Churchill, *The Six Day War* (reprint, Boston: Houghton Mifflin, 1967), 123–46.

13. Thomas Ice and Randall Price, *Ready to Rebuild* (Eugene, Ore.: Har-vest House, 1992); Hal Lindsey, *The Late Great Planet Earth* (Grand Rapids: Zondervan, 1970), 52–58.

14. Herzog, *The Arab-Israeli War*, 195–221.

15. See James Ennes, *The Assault on the* Liberty: *The True Story of the Israeli Attack on an American Intelligence Ship* (New York: Random House, 1979); and Alfred M. Lilienthal, *The Zionist Connection II* (reprint, New Brunswick, N.J.: North American, 1982), 561–76.

16. Herzog, *The Arab-Israeli Wars*, 227–323.

17. William B. Branst, *Camp David: Peacemaking and Politics* (Washing-ton, D.C.: The Brookings Institute, 1986), 320–39, 397–406; Burton I. Kauf-man, *James Earl Carter* (Lawrence: University of Kansas Press, 1993), 117–23, 144–45; Jimmy Carter, *Keeping the Faith: Memoirs of a President* (New York: Bantam, 1982), 273–318; Eitan Haber, *Menachem Begin* (New York: Dela-corte Press, 1978), 309–10; Yehoshafat Harkabi, *Israel's Fateful Hour* (New York: Harper and Row, 1986), 87–92.

18. Wim Malgo, *Begin with Sadat: A Stunning Revelation of the Latest Mideast Development* (Columbia, S.C.: Midnight Call, 1978), 85–87.

19. Mary Stewart Relfe, *The New Money System* (Montgomery, Ala.: Min-istries, 1982), 218.

20. Mary Stewart Relfe, *When Your Money Fails* (Montgomery, Ala.: Min-istries, 1981), 140–43.

21. Boyer, *When Time Shall Be No More*, 304–5.

22. Ibid., 306.

23. See Shlomo Nakdimon, *First Strike: The Exclusive Story of How Israel Foiled Iraq's Attempt to Get the Bomb* (New York: Simon and Schuster, 1987); and Dan McKinnon, *Bullseye Iraq* (reprint, New York: Berkeley, 1988).

24. Lesch and Tessler, *Israel, Egypt, and the Palestinians*, 255–84. See also Aryeh Shalev, *The West Bank: Line of Defense* (New York: Praeger, 1985); and Mark Heller, *A Palestinian State: Implications for Israel* (Cambridge, Mass.: Harvard University Press, 1983).

25. Anti-Semitic literature among conspiracy theorists is unfortunately plentiful. Please refer to the bibliography for a sampling of these unsavory publications.

26. See The Trilateral Commission, *The Trilateral Commission: Questions and Answers* (New York: North American Office, 1986); Zbigniew Brzezin-ski, *Between Two Ages: America's Role in the Technotronic Age* (New York: Pen-guin, 1970); and Kah, *En Route to Global Occupation*, 44–49.

27. See Larry Berman, ed., *Looking Back at the Reagan Presidency* (Baltimore: Johns Hopkins University Press, 1990); and William Muir Jr., *The Bully Pulpit: The Presidential Leadership of Ronald Reagan* (San Francisco: ICS Press, 1992).

28. See Lou Cannon, *President Reagan: The Role of a Lifetime* (Sacramento: Cal Journal, 1991); Coral Bell, *The Reagan Paradox* (New Brunswick, N.J.: Rutgers University Press, 1989), 152–72; and Jeff McMahan, *Reagan and the World: Imperial Policy in the New Cold War* (New York: Monthly Review Press, 1985), 10–25.

29. Michael Coffman, *Saviors of the Earth?* (Chicago: Northfield, 1994), 195–213, 217–20; Kah, *En Route to Global Occupation*, 54–55; Perloff, *Shadows of Power*, 167–75.

For a controversial document from the mid-1960s supposedly detailing secret conspiratorial planning, see Leonard C. Lewin, ed., *Report from Iron Mountain on the Possibility and Desirability of Peace* (New York: Dial Press, 1967).

30. See *Spotlight on the Bilderbergers: Irresponsible Power* (reprint, Washington, D.C.: Liberty Lobby, 1991); Kah, *En Route to Global Occupation*, 38–40; Ralph Epperson, *The Unseen Hand* (Tucson: Publius Press, 1985), 206. See also Jim Lucier, "Bilderbergers," *American Opinion* (November 1964). *American Opinion* is a journal of the John Birch Society.

31. Harry E. Figgie Jr. and Gerald J. Swanson, *Bankruptcy 1995* (Boston: Little, Brown, and Company, 1992), 34–43, based on the Grace Commission projections; James Dale Davidson and Lord William Rees-Mogg, *The Great Reckoning: How the World Will Change in the Depression of the 1990s* (New York: Summit, 1991), 12–14, 91–111. See also Larry Burkett, *The Coming Economic Earthquake* (rev. ed., Chicago: Moody Press, 1994).

32. The Iran-Contra hearings made for some highly rated television, but despite the hearings and an immensely expensive Walsh investigation, virtually nothing came of it. See Thomas L. Friedman, *From Beirut to Jerusalem* (New York: Farrar, Straus, Giroux, 1989), 506–7; and Samuel Segev, *The Iranian Triangle: The Untold Story of Israel's Role in the Iran-Contra Affair* (New York: Free Press, 1988).

33. Nicholas King, *George Bush: A Biography* (New York: Dodd, Mead, and Company, 1980), 61–70.

34. Ibid., 113–46.

35. *Conduct of the Gulf War*, United States Department of Defense (Washington, D.C.: Government Printing Office, 1992), 2–3, 18–19, 30–46; Time-Life Editors, *Desert Storm: The War in the Persian Gulf* (Boston: Little, Brown, and Company, 1991). See also David Fromkin, *A Peace to End All Peace: The Fall of the Ottoman Empire and the Creation of the Modern Middle East* (reprint, New York: Avon, 1989), for an overview of how the modern Middle East was divided up.

36. Time-Life Editors, *Desert Storm*, 155–66.

37. Ibid., 187–225.

38. *Conduct of the Gulf War*, 88–181.

## Chapter 7 *Conspiracy and the Age of Aquarius*

1. See Marilyn Ferguson, *The Aquarian Conspiracy: Personal and Social Transformation in the 1980s* (reprint, Los Angeles: Jeremy Tarcher, 1980), for a New Age advocate's view of this cultural transformation in the United States. For a more balanced historical account, I highly recommend James R. Lewis and J. Gordon Melton, eds., *Perspectives on the New Age* (Ithaca: State University of New York Press, 1994).

2. Reincarnation, of course, is a staple belief in Hinduism and the New Age movement. Some sources dealing with the topic range from the classic to Americanized versions. See A. C. Bhaktivedanta Swami Prabhupada, *Bhagavad-Gita: As It Is* (Los Angeles: Bhaktivedanta Book Trust, ISKC, 1968), as well as traditional Hindu scriptures such as the Upanishads and Srimad-Bhagavatam. For Americanized versions or interpretations of reincarnation, although much less intellectual in content, see a few of the selected following works: Elizabeth Claire Prophet, *The Lost Teachings of Jesus*, vol. 1 (reprint, Livingston, Mont.: Summit University Press, 1988); and Carlos Castaneda, *The Teachings of Don Juan* (Berkeley: University of California Press, 1969).

3. See Genesis 10:8–10. It has been suggested that the reference to Nimrod was part of a larger epic from the Middle East dealing with Tukulti-Ninurta I, who ruled Assyria around 1244–1208 B.C. This ruler once controlled both Babylon and Assyria.

The Genesis account also makes mention of the land of Shinar, an area now considered to be ancient Sumer. See also *The Torah: A Modern Commentary* (New York: Union of American Hebrew Congregations, 1981).

The story of Semiramis is also a key part of conspiracy theory. According to the story, Semiramis and Nimrod provided the core beliefs for both Masonry and Roman Catholicism. It is a sort of pick-and-choose affair here for whichever conspiracy belief you want to accept.

4. Brooke, *When the World Will Be as One*, 242–44. See also Alexander Hislop, *The Two Babylons*, 2nd American ed. (Neptune, N.J.: Loizeaux Bros., 1959), for a well-researched but lamentably anti-Catholic monograph.

5. Brooke, *When the World Will Be as One*, 242–44.

6. Ibid., 245. See also Tal Brooke, *Riders of the Cosmic Circuit* (Batavia, Ill.: Lion, 1986).

For good accounts of the *Kaballah*, see Gershom Scholem, *Kabbalah* (New York: Dorset Press, 1974), 187–89; and *The Zohar*, 5 vols. (New York: Jonathan David, n.d.), for an extensive guide through the world of medieval Jewish mysticism as related to the *Kaballah*.

7. Ferguson, *Aquarian Conspiracy*, 23–43.

8. Cult expert and evangelical Christian Dave Hunt has suggested that the event that would catapult the world into a one-world economic and political system would be the literal bodily removal of Christians from the earth during a long-anticipated event historically known as the rapture or "blessed hope." Such an event, I imagine, would go far in solidifying acceptance of this new global faith; still, a global faith of the sort Hunt anticipates does not yet exist.

See Dave Hunt, *Peace, Prosperity, and the Coming Holocaust* (Eugene, Ore.: Harvest House, 1983); and Boyer, *When Time Shall Be No More*, 254–57, 279–80.

9. Guiley, *Harper's Encyclopedia of Mystical and Paranormal Experience*, 64. See also Madame Helene Blavatsky, *The Secret Doctrine*, 2 vols. (reprint, Pasadena: Theosophical University Press, 1988); Madame Helene P. Blavatsky, *Isis Unveiled* (reprint, Pasadena: Theosophical University Press, 1988); and Peter Washington, *Madame Blavatsky's Baboon* (New York: Schocken, 1995), 26–40.

Theosophy means "divine wisdom."

10. Martin, *Kingdom of the Cults*, 246–60; Irving Cooper, *Theosophy Simplified* (reprint, Wheaton, Ill.: Theosophical Press, 1964), 22–23. See also L. W. Rogers, *Elementary Theosophy* (Wheaton, Ill.: Theosophical Press, 1956); and Baseden G. Butt, *Madame Blavatsky* (London: Marchard Brothers, 1926).

11. I highly recommend Robert Muller, *New Genesis: Shaping of Global Spirituality* (New York: Doubleday, 1984), for a New Ager's perspective on global political ramifications.

12. John Ankerberg and John Weldon, *The Facts on the New Age* (Eugene, Ore.: Harvest House, 1988), 29–30. I recommend the entire "Facts on" series of Ankerberg-Weldon booklets for those seeking short overviews on a variety of cult-related topics.

13. See Darylann Whitemarsh and Bill Reisman, *Subtle Serpent* (Lafayette, La.: Huntington House, 1993), for a look at the intrusion of Aquarian philosophy into American public education.

Occultist Aleister Crowley popularized the phrase "Do what thou wilt" in his 1904 work, *The Book of the Law* (reprint, New York: Magickal Childe Publishing, O.T.O., 1990), and embodied it like few before or since. Sometimes misunderstood as a grand statement of "do whatever you want," the credo instead speaks more to "doing what you must." Crowley died in 1947 but has become the patron saint to self-styled occultists ever since. A popular contemporary example is Jimmy Page, the immensely talented former lead guitarist of supergroup Led Zeppelin. Page bought Crowley's home (Boleskine House) on Loch Ness in Scotland; has a collection of Crowley memorabilia, including original manuscripts and ritual robes; and is himself reportedly a devotee of the "Great Beast's" version of occultism. The guitarist even once owned an occult bookstore named Equinox after Crowley's published journal of the same name. On early issues of Zeppelin's third album, the phrase "Do what thou wilt" can be found etched in the vinyl near the label. Although both Page and Led Zeppelin vocalist Robert Plant have little good to say about the following books, they at least provide a place to start—flawed as they may be: Stephen Davis, *The Hammer of the Gods: The Led Zeppelin Saga* (reprint, New York: Bantam, 1990), 95, 106–8, 154, 211, 272–74; Richard Cole, *Stairway to Heaven: Led Zeppelin* (New York: HarperCollins, 1992), 11–12, 184–85, 256, 300–301, 366–67, 390. See also Sandy Robertson, *The Aleister Crowley Scrapbook* (York Beach, Maine: 1988), 117–21, for statements concerning Page's interest in Crowley and his collection of related artifacts.

Although rock stars have lionized Crowley over the past thirty years, his true importance and influence was and still is in a host of occult organizations. Ranging from the Golden Dawn and Stella Matutina to the Ordo Templi Orientis (O.T.O.), Crowley's imprint and influence can be seen. To say he is a heavyweight in the world of the occult would be a grand understatement.

There are many books by and about Crowley, some terribly difficult to find. A few of the more common include Aleister Crowley, Parts I–IV, *Magick in Theory and Practice* (reprint, New York: Castle Books); Aleister Crowley, *The Confessions of Aleister Crowley* (reprint, New York: Bantam, 1969); Israel Regardie and P. R. Stephensen, *The Legend of Aleister Crowley* (reprint, Las Vegas: New Falcon, 1990). Any serious student of the occult or of Aleister Crowley must become familiar with *Equinox,* the "Beast 666's" journal. Volume 1 (in ten tomes) and the famous "Blue" *Equinox* (portions of vol. 3). Both are available through Samuel Weiser Publishers.

14. I encourage those interested in a Westerner's comparative view of spiritual life in India to read Tal Brooke, *Lord of the Air* (Eugene, Ore.: Harvest House, 1990); and Brooke, *Riders of the Cosmic Circuit.*

15. Mike Warnke, *The Satan Seller* (Plainfield, N.J.: Logos, 1972). See also Mike Warnke, *Schemes of Satan* (Tulsa, Okla.: Victory House, 1991). I also highly recommend Mike Hertenstein and Jon Trott, *Selling Satan: The Tragic History of Mike Warnke* (Chicago: Cornerstone Ministries, 1993). This book is a first-rate work of investigative journalism. Sadly, the authors have been victims of a "kill the messenger" mentality among some Christian groups; the idea seems to be that so-called unity of the brethren is more important than truth.

16. See Jeffrey S. Victor, *Satanic Panic: The Creation of a Contemporary Legend* (Chicago: Open Court, 1993), for a fine sociological look at the phenomenon. The author does a first-rate job in pointing out the evangelical and fundamentalist Christian tendency to overreact to the fear of the occult in general and Satanism in particular. See also Bob and Gretchen Passantino, "The Hard Facts about Satanic Abuse," *Christian Research Journal* (Winter 1992), 20, for a fine account of many of the Satanic hysterias afflicting American Christendom today.

17. See George Hay, ed., *The Necronomicon* (reprint, London: Skoob, 1992); Simon, *The Necronomicon* (New York: Avon, 1977); Leilah Wendell, *The Necromantic Ritual Book* (New Orleans: Westgate Press, 1994); Jeffrey Burton Russell, *The Prince of Darkness* (Ithaca, N.Y.: Cornell University Press, 1988).

18. Leviticus 19:31; 20:6, 27; Deuteronomy 18:10–11; 1 Samuel 28:3, 7–9.

19. See Hertenstein and Trott, *Selling Satan;* and Rebecca Brown, *He Came to Set the Captives Free* (Springdale, Pa.: Whitaker House, 1992), 6–82, (the entire book is filled with stories all too common in the "Satanic Panic" genre). Lauren Stratford, *Satan's Underground* (Eugene, Ore.: Harvest House, 1988), takes the reader on a white-knuckle ride through alleged Satanic abuse—a story since proven false. Although not as bad, Texe Marrs's *Ravaged by the New Age* dedicates a chapter to the rise of Satanism among teens titled "Teens Trip Out on Satan: The Rise of Hard-core Devil Worship and Witchcraft among Our Youth" (Austin: Living Truth Publishers, 1989), 230–49.

I highly recommend Bob and Gretchen Passantino's article in *Cornerstone* 19, no. 92, titled "Satan's Sideshow" pertaining to the Stratford story. Like Trott and Hertenstein's work, it is first-class investigative journalism.

20. See Walter Martin, *The Maze of Mormonism* (reprint, Ventura, Calif.: Regal, 1978).

21. Ankerberg and Weldon, *Facts on the New Age*, 1–2. Also highly recommended are Douglas R. Groothuis, *Unmasking the New Age* (Downers Grove, Ill.: InterVarsity, 1986); and Douglas R. Groothuis, *Revealing the New Age Jesus* (Downers Grove, Ill.: InterVarsity, 1990).

22. See Bob Larson, *Straight Answers on the New Age* (Nashville: Thomas Nelson, 1989), for the controversial, bombastic author and broadcaster's dealing with a host of Aquarian issues.

23. See Shirley MacLaine, *Out on a Limb* (New York: Bantam, 1983).

24. For but one example, see the introduction to Levi, *Aquarian Gospel of Jesus the Christ* (reprint, Marina del Ray, Calif.: DeVorss and Co., 1964). This classic of Aquarian literature is said to be based on the Akashic Records, mystical imprints forever recorded everywhere in the metaphysical universe. This less than objective "source" is not atypical of New Age writings today based on mystical experience.

25. *Los Angeles Times*, April 25, 1982.

26. The rise of Mother Meera is nothing short of phenomenal. From approximately the age of thirteen, she was recognized as possessing highly advanced spiritual awareness; by the time she reached her twenties and moved to Germany, thousands sought her out as an avatar. See Andrew Harvey, *Hidden Journey* (New York: Arkana/Penguin, 1991); Mother Meera, *Answers* (Ithaca, N.Y.: Meeramma Publications, 1991); Mark Matousek, "The Feminine Face of God," *Common Boundary* (May/June 1992), 32–37; and "Mother Meera: Burning with Divine Light," *Yoga Journal* (July/August 1933). For a seminal work on the Hindu concept of the Divine Mother, see Sri Aurobindo, *The Mother* (Pondicherry, India: Sri Aurobindo Ashram, 1972).

27. Ferguson, *Aquarian Conspiracy*, 216–17; Russell Chandler, *Understanding the New Age* (Grand Rapids: Zondervan, 1993), 96–97.

28. Hunt, *Peace, Prosperity, and the Coming Holocaust*, 9–19, 47–60, 61–73; Chandler, *Understanding the New Age*, 210–16; Teilhard de Chardin, *Building the Earth* (New York: Avon, 1969), 49–59. Chandler's book gives a good critique of Constance Cumby's grossly conspiratorial *Hidden Dangers of the Rainbow* (Lafayette, La.: Huntington House, 1983). See also Dave Hunt, *The Seduction of Christianity* (Eugene, Ore.: Harvest House, 1985); and Dave Hunt, *Beyond Seduction* (Eugene, Ore.: Harvest House, 1987), for accounts of how Aquarian philosophy has infiltrated the church. Two highly recommended comparative studies of non-Christian (many of them New Age) teachings increasingly permeating the church, primarily through the health and wealth, "name it and claim it" doctrines of Kenneth Hagin, Kenneth Copeland, and Frederick Price are D. R. McConnell, *A Different Gospel* (Peabody, Mass.: Hendrickson Publishers, 1988); and Hank Hanegraaff, *Christianity in Crisis* (Eugene, Ore.: Harvest House, 1992).

29. For examples of Marrs's use of secular conspiracy theory writers, some of whom come from Fascist Party backgrounds, see the endnotes to his *Dark Majesty* (Austin, Tex.: Living Truth Publishers, 1992), chapters 8–15.

See also Texe Marrs, *America Shattered* (Austin, Tex.: Living Truth Publishers, 1991), for a short but sensationalized account of the alleged New Age plan for a "One World Government." It is a short and sadly typical example of Marrs's publications, tapes, and video publications.

30. See Kah, *En Route to Global Occupation*, 214–24, for a listing of sources used.

31. See Lady Queensborough, *Occult Theocracy*, 721–41, for her "labeling" of Jews, Masons, or Martinists.

## Chapter 8 *The New World Order*

1. See Quigley, *Tragedy and Hope*. Quigley taught at Georgetown University's Foreign Service School, names himself as one of the "insiders" in favor of world government, and even had access to the records of these secretive organizations. The book, along with his *Anglo-American Establishment* monograph, traces the history of Round Table discussion groups from England, the British Commonwealth, and the United States to encourage a form of globalism. Many of those he names formed or helped to form the Council on Foreign Relations.

One of Quigley's students in the 1960s was a young man from Arkansas named Bill Clinton. Conspiracy theorists have made much of this fact, pointing out the mentor-student relationship the two apparently enjoyed. Indeed, Clinton went so far as to give credit to Quigley during a speech at the 1988 Democratic Presidential Convention. When Clinton was elected in 1992, one can imagine that many in conspiracy theory circles gave a knowing smirk, as though it were all planned.

2. Harry Figgie Jr. and Gerald Swanson, *Bankruptcy 1995* (Boston: Little, Brown, and Company, 1992), 26–34; Burkett, *The Coming Economic Earthquake*, 113–25. For an excellent counterpoint, I highly recommend Sherman Smith's *Exploding the Doomsday Myths* (Nashville: Thomas Nelson, 1994).

Government records from the Office of Management and Budget, Budget of the United States Government for the Fiscal Year 1993 (Washington, D.C.: Government Printing Office, 1993), provide the basis for many of the projections in the works cited above.

3. Figgie and Swanson, *Bankruptcy 1995*, 34–37; Davidson and Rees-Mogg, *The Great Reckoning*, 91–111, 331–47.

4. See OMB's Fiscal Budget for 1993.

5. Figgie and Swanson, *Bankruptcy 1995*, 63–73.

6. Burkett, *The Coming Economic Earthquake*, 164–70; Larry Burkett, *Whatever Happened to the American Dream?* (Chicago: Moody Press, 1993). Burkett has also appeared in two separate segments on the highly respected *John Ankerberg Show* concerning an impending economic collapse.

7. Larry Burkett, *Investing for the Future* (Wheaton, Ill.: Victor, 1992), 20. See also Smith, *Exploding the Doomsday Money Myths*, 14.

8. See John McManus, *Financial Terrorism: Hijacking America under the Threat of Bankruptcy* (Appleton: Wis.: The John Birch Society, 1993); and Larry Burkett, *The Illuminati* (Nashville: Thomas Nelson, 1991).

9. See Still, *New World Order*, 45–46. Still also appeared on the *Lowell Lundstrom Live* radio program in which he again held forth what could be called Christian conspiracy theories. He and co-guest Larry Bates were unfortunately unable to address the Fascist Party origins of many of their sources, as well as those coming from the John Birch Society. I was lucky enough to be one of the call-in guests with either a question or comment on this particular program. Instead of addressing my questions on their sources, Bates chose to insult me for having a Ph.D. in history ("Piled higher and deeper" was the comment). Such a response is sadly typical of what is given to someone who questions or challenges a strongly held conspiratorial view of history and government. See Lowell Lundstrom, "The Coming World Order Government," February 14, 1995, broadcast; and Robertson, *The New World Order*, chapters 5–8 in particular.

10. Texe Marrs, *Report from Iron Mountain* audiotape, Texe Marrs Ministries, 1995. See also *The Report from Iron Mountain* (New York: Dial Press, 1967)—reportedly authored by John Kenneth Galbraith but since admitted to be authored by Leonard C. Lewin, the book's editor—for the original edition of the document railed on by Texe Marrs. See also Texe Marrs, *Circle of Intrigue* (Austin, Tex.: Living Truth Publishers, 1995), for Marrs's most comprehensive treatment to date on the world conspiracy in which he so fervently believes.

Again, I do not doubt for a moment the sincerity of the Austin-based author; I merely believe he is quite wrong and lacking in historical understanding.

11. Marrs, *Circle of Intrigue*, ix–xiii; 49–75; *Flashpoint* 96, no. 1 (January 1996), 1.

12. Texe Marrs, *AIDS/The Secret Power of Foundations* tape, available through Texe Marrs Ministries. On this tape, Marrs continues to insult those not holding his conspiratorial view as "stupid" or "in the Stone Age" and so on. Marrs also considers the King James Bible as the only authorized, spiritually reliable version. The other Bible translations are tagged "New Age" and perhaps part of the global conspiracy. See G. A. Ripplinger, *New Age Versions* (Munroe Falls, Ohio: AV Publications, 1994), for a heavily Marrs endorsed book on the topic.

Marrs has even gone so far as to call C. S. Lewis, author of books such as *Mere Christianity* and the *Chronicles of Narnia* a New Ager! See Texe Marrs, *The Light That Was Dark: New Age Illumination of the Christian Church*, audiotape.

13. Apparently Marrs might just believe that Billy Graham is in on some sort of plot, or at least is a sellout to Christianity. See Marrs's *Flashpoint: A Newsletter Ministry of Texe Marrs*, August 1995, for an unmerciful attack on Billy Graham and his ministry.

14. Texe Marrs, "New World Order and American Sovereignty," *World of Prophecy*, Texe Marrs Ministries, Austin, Texas, 1995.

15. Texe Marrs, "NASA's Space Program—Hoaxes and Deceptions," *World of Prophecy*, Living Truth Ministries, 1995.

16. Grant R. Jeffrey, *Prince of Darkness: Antichrist and the New World Order* (Toronto: Frontier Research Publications, 1994), 59–90. See also Jeffrey, *Apocalypse: The Coming Judgment of the Nations* (reprint, Toronto: Frontier Research Publications, 1993).

17. David Allen Lewis, *Prophecy 2000*, 6th ed. (Green Forest, Ariz.: New Leaf Press, 1990), 43–46. See also Don S. McAlvany, "America and the New World Order," in William T. James, ed., *Earth's Final Days* (Green Forest, Ariz.: New Leaf Press, 1995), 179–216, in which the same themes of international conspiracy so familiar in secular circles are set forth as spiritual fact.

18. Coffman, *Saviors of the Earth?* 193–213; Cumby, *Hidden Dangers of the Rainbow*.

19. Constance Cumby, "Special Report on Pat Robertson," *New Age Monitor* (August–December, 1987), quoted in Alnor, *Soothsayers of the Second Advent*, 23.

Cumby was a guest on *Lowell Lundstrom Live* on February 20, 1995, during which she suggested to a caller that Spiritual Counterfeits Project directors (Tal Brooke and Brooks Alexander, both highly respected experts in the field of cult and occult research) were New Agers, and that Dr. Walter Martin or CRI, too, had questionable motives. See *Lowell Lundstrom Live*, February 20, 1995.

20. Perloff, *Shadows of Power*, 199–208. See Griffin, *Fourth Reich of the Rich*, for an extensive conspiracy theory interpretation of where the world is headed. Likewise, Griffin's *Descent into Slavery?* (reprint, Clackamas, Ore.: Emissary Publications, 1991) should be read by all serious students of conspiracy theory. Other books dealing with this subject include the late Allen, *Say NO! to the New World Order*. Allen, who wrote the best-selling *None Dare Call It Conspiracy* in the 1970s probably did more than any single author to bring conspiracy theory to the attention of the American people.

See also the July 1, 1995, Texe Marrs radio program, *World of Prophecy*, in which Marrs and a guest proclaimed the United Nations to be the system through which the Beast of Revelation will emerge and govern. This, of course, is a considerable departure from other prophecy teachings in recent decades, which had the Antichrist arising out of some sort of reborn Roman Empire, presumably the European Common Market.

21. Interview with Barbara Walters, *20/20* ABC News program, March 25, 1994.

22. Zbigniew Brzezinski, *Out of Control* (New York: Charles Scribner's Sons, 1993), ix–xv, 203–31; Richard Nixon, *1999: Victory without War* (New York: Simon and Schuster, 1988), 308–21.

23. The rapture theory follows closely with the view of millennialism. For instance, some Christians believe in a pretribulation view of the event, others in a midtribulation position, others in a posttribulation position. I have personally witnessed some very heated arguments concerning this matter. See Dennis Engleman, *Ultimate Things: An Orthodox Christian Perspective on*

*the End Times* (Ben Lomond, Calif.: Conciliar Press, 1996); and Boyer, *When Time Shall Be No More*, for views of this rather silly argument.

24. See Jack Van Impe's videos *2001: Countdown to Eternity* (Troy, Mich.: Jack Van Impe Ministries, 1995) and *Millennium: Greatest Deception in History!* (Troy, Mich.: Jack Van Impe Ministries, 1995) for a couple of classic examples of the literalist view of the second coming so common in today's prophecy ministries.

25. Ibid. See also virtually any of Jack Van Impe's weekly programs dedicated to the subject over the past two years or more.

26. Lindsey, *The Late Great Planet Earth*.

Regardless of one's agreement or disagreement with Mr. Lindsey's prophecy interpretation, it is difficult to overstate his contribution to the genre in the last quarter of the twentieth century. Lindsey has written many prophecy books, of course, but recently published a summarization titled *Planet Earth—2000 A.D.* (Palos Verde, Calif.: Western Front, 1994) in which he restates old themes and fine-tunes others.

27. Lindsey, *Planet Earth—2000 A.D.*, 57. See also Lindsey's videos, including *The World's Affair with Antichrist*.

28. Salem Kirban, *666* (Huntington Valley, Pa.: Salem Kirban, Inc., 1970). See also the following booklets by Kirban: "Kissinger: Man of Peace?" (1974) and "What in the World Will Happen Next?" (1974).

See Edgar C. Whisenant, *88 Reasons Why the Rapture Will Be in 1988* (Nashville: World Bible Society, 1988); Merrill Unger, *Beyond the Crystal Ball* (Chicago: Moody Press, 1973); Jack Van Impe, *Signs of the Times* (Royal Oak, Mich.: Jack Van Impe Ministries, 1979); and William R. Goetz, *Apocalypse Next and the New World Order* (Camp Hill, Pa.: Horizon House, 1991).

29. See Peter Lemesurier, *Nostradamus: The Next Fifty Years* (New York: Berkeley, 1993), and Charles A. Ward, *Oracles of Nostradamus* (New York: Barnes and Noble, 1993); Russell Chandler, *Doomsday* (Ann Arbor, Mich.: Servant, 1993), 57–68, 275–85.

30. Jack Van Impe weekly television program aired June 18, 1995. See also Alnor, *Soothsayers of the Second Coming*, 108–20; Elliot Miller and Craig Hawkins, "Nostradamus," *Christian Research Newsletter* 1, no. 3 (1988); and from Dr. Gene Scott's Dolores Press, at least fifty audio tapes on the Great Pyramid as a tool of prophecy and at least four VHS tapes on the topic. Dolores Press also offers the following books on the topic of pyramidology: E. Raymond, *The Great Pyramid Decoded, The Glory of the Stars,* and *Jacob's Pillar.*

31. See the Jack Van Impe television programs aired May 7, 1995, and June 25, 1995, on the topic of conspiracy theories as he does in his 1995 video, *666.* I again recommend William Alnor's *Soothsayers of the Second Advent* for an effective refutation of the conspiracy issue. See also Hertenstein and Trott, *Selling Satan,* for another effective refutation of the Illuminati issue and its ties to end-time prophecy.

32. See John Hagee, *Beginning of the End* (Nashville: Thomas Nelson, 1996), for a predictable premillennial end-time rollercoaster ride in which

the author seeks to incorporate contemporary events with ancient documents. He certainly is not the first (nor will he be the last) to do so.

33. Peter and Patti Lalonde, *Left Behind* (Eugene, Ore.: Harvest House, 1995), Trinity Broadcasting Network spot ads during the month of February 1996. See also Peter and Paul Lalonde's *One World under Antichrist* (Eugene, Ore.: Harvest House, 1991), 103–9; and *Racing toward the Mark of the Beast* (Eugene, Ore.: Harvest House, 1994).

34. Reference to the Illuminati tie to Catholicism is found in Jack Chick, *Alberto: Part One* (Chino, Calif.: Chick Publications, 1979), 27–29. Additional Chick publications with anti-Catholic themes include the following: *Double-Cross: Alberto, Part II* (1981); *The Godfathers: Alberto, Part III* (1982); *The Force: Alberto, Part IV* (1983); *Four Horsemen: Alberto, Part V* (1985); and *The Big Betrayal* (1981).

See also *Christian Research Journal*, no. 2 (Fall 1981) for a fine article entitled "Alberto Rivera: The Truth about His Story" and Johnson, *Architects of Fear*, 85–102. Johnson's book, although now dated, is an excellent overview of conspiracy theory in America.

### Appendix C *The Conspiracy That Never Ends*

1. Copyright © 1995 by the New York Times Company. Reprinted by permission.

# Recommended Reading

Alnor, William. *Soothsayers of the Second Advent*. Grand Rapids: Revell, 1989.
Bennett, David H. *The Party of Fear*. Rev. ed. New York: Vintage, 1995.
Billington, James. *Fire in the Minds of Men*. New York: Basic Books, 1980.
Boyer, Paul. *When Time Shall Be No More*. Cambridge, Mass.: Belknap Harvard, 1992.
Brooke, Tal. *When the World Will Be as One*. Eugene, Ore.: Harvest House, 1989.
Chandler, Russell. *Doomsday*. Ann Arbor, Mich.: Servant, 1993.
———. *Understanding the New Age*. Grand Rapids: Zondervan, 1993.
Davis, David Brion. *The Fear of Conspiracy: Images of an Un-American Subversion from the Revolution to the Present*. Ithaca, N.Y.: Cornell University Press, 1971.
Fuller, Robert. *Naming the Antichrist: The History of an American Obsession*. New York: Oxford University Press, 1995.
Hertenstein, Mike, and Jon Trott. *Selling Satan*. Chicago: Cornerstone Ministries, 1993.
Hofstadter, Richard. *The Paranoid Style in American Politics*. New York: Knopf, 1965.
Johnson, George. *Architects of Fear: Conspiracy Theories and Paranoia in American Politics*. Los Angeles: Jeremy Tarcher, 1983.
Oropeza, B. J. *99 Reasons Why No One Knows When Christ Will Return*. Downers Grove, Ill.: InterVarsity Press, 1994.
Rhodes, Ron. *The Culting of America*. Eugene, Ore.: Harvest House, 1994.
Shaw, Eva. *Eve of Destruction*. Los Angeles: Lowell House, 1995.
Smith, Sherman. *Exploding the Doomsday Money Myths*. Nashville: Thomas Nelson, 1994.
Wilgus, Neil. *The Illuminoids*. New York: Pocket Books, 1979.

# Bibliography

## Books

Abel, Ellie. *The Missile Crisis.* New York: Lippincott, 1966.

Abel, George O., and Barry Singer. *Science and the Paranormal.* New York: Charles Scribner's Sons, 1981.

Adler, Margot. *Drawing Down the Moon.* Rev. ed. Boston: Beacon Press, 1986.

Albrecht, Mark. *Reincarnation: A Christian Appeal.* Downers Grove, Ill.: InterVarsity, 1982.

———. *Reincarnation: A Christian Critique of a New Age Doctrine.* Downers Grove, Ill.: InterVarsity, 1987.

Allen, Frederick Lewis. *The Great Pierpont Morgan.* New York: Harper and Brothers, 1949.

Allen, Gary. *None Dare Call It Conspiracy.* Rossmoor, Calif.: Concord Press, 1971.

———. *The Rockefeller File.* Seal Beach, Calif.: '76 Press, 1976.

———. *Say NO! to the New World Order.* Rossmoor, Calif.: Concord Press, 1987.

Alnor, Bill. *Soothsayers of the Second Advent.* Grand Rapids: Revell, 1989.

Ambrose, Stephen E. *Eisenhower.* 2 vols. New York: Simon and Schuster, 1983.

———. *Nixon: Triumph of a Politician.* 2 vols. New York: Simon and Schuster, 1989.

———. *Rise to Globalism: American Foreign Policy 1938–1970.* 4th ed. Baltimore: Penguin, 1985.

Ankerberg, John, and John Weldon. *The Coming Darkness.* Eugene, Ore.: Harvest House, 1993.

———. *The Facts on the New Age Movement.* Eugene, Ore.: Harvest House, 1988.

———. *The Secret Teachings of the Masonic Lodge*. Chicago: Moody Press, 1990.

Appel, Willa. *Cults in America*. New York: Henry Holt, 1983.

Armstrong, George. *Rothschild Money Trust*. Clackamas, Ore.: Emissary Publications, n.d.

Athern, Robert G. *Union Pacific Country*. Reprint, Lincoln: University of Nebraska Press, 1976.

Aurobindo, Sri. *Mother*. Pondicherry, India: Sri Aurobindo Ashram, 1972.

Bach, G. L. *Federal Reserve Policy-Making*. New York: Knopf, 1950.

Baer, Randall N. *Inside the New Age Nightmare*. Shreveport, La.: Huntington House, 1989.

Bailey, Alice A. *Death: The Great Adventure*. Reprint, New York: Lucis, 1985.

———. *Education and the New Age*. New York: Lucis, 1954.

———. *The Reappearance of the Christ*. New York: Lucis, 1948.

Bailey, Thomas A. *A Diplomatic History of the American People*. 6th ed. New York: Appleton Century Crofts, 1955.

Baker, Jeffrey A. *Cheque Mate: The Game of Princes*. St. Petersburg, Fla.: The Jeffrey Baker Group, 1993.

Baker, Ray Stannard. *Woodrow Wilson: Life and Letters, Governor, 1910–1913*. 4 vols. London: William Heinemann, 1932.

Baldwin, Samuel D. *Armageddon, or the Overthrow of Romanism and Monarch: The Existence of the United States Foretold in the Bible, Its Future Greatness, Invasion by Allied Powers; Annihilation of the Monarch; Expansion into the Millennial Republic, and Its Dominion over the Whole World*. Cincinnati: Applegate and Company, 1884.

Barker, A. J. *Pearl Harbor*. New York: Ballantine, 1969.

Barruel, Abbe. *Memoires pour servir à l'histoire du Jacobinisme*. 2 vols. Hamburg, Germany, 1803.

Bartley, W. W. *Werner Erhardt: The Transformation of a Man: The Founding of EST*. New York: Clarkson N. Potter, 1978.

Baruch, Bernard. *Baruch: The Public Years*. New York: Holt, Rinehart, and Winston, 1960.

Bates, Larry. *The New Economic Disorder*. Orlando, Fla.: Creation House, 1994.

Becker, Julian. *The PLO: The Rise and Fall of the Palestine Liberation Organization*. New York: St. Martin's Press, 1984.

Bell, Coral. *The Reagan Paradox*. New Brunswick, N.J.: Rutgers University Press, 1989.

Bell, Daniel. *The Radical Right*. Garden City, N.Y.: Doubleday, 1963.

Ben-Gurion, David. *Israel: Years of Challenge*. New York: Holt, Rinehart, and Winston, 1963.

———. *Rebirth and Destiny of Israel*. New York: Philosophical Library, 1954.

Benson, Ivor. *The Zionist Factor*. Torrance, Calif.: Noontide Press, 1992.

Berger, Carl. *B–29: The Superfortress*. New York: Ballantine, 1970.

Berman, Larry, ed. *Looking Back on the Reagan Presidency*. Baltimore: Johns Hopkins University Press, 1990.

Bhaktivedanta, A. C., Swami Prabhupada. *Bhagavad-Gita: As It Is.* Los Angeles: Bhaktivedanta Book Trust, ISKC, 1968.

Billington, James. *Fire in the Minds of Men.* New York: Basic Books, 1980.

Billington, Ray Allen. *Westward Expansion.* 4th ed. New York: Macmillan, 1974.

Bishop, Abraham. *Proofs of a Conspiracy against Christianity and the Government of the United States; Exhibited in Several Views of the Union of Church and State in New England.* Hartford, Conn., 1802.

Black, Ian, and Beny Morris. *Israel's Secret Wars: A History of Israel's Intelligence Services.* New York: Grove Weidenfeld, 1991.

Blavatsky, Helene P. *Isis Unveiled.* 2 vols. Reprint, Wheaton, Ill.: Theosophy Publishing House, 1971.

———. *The Secret Doctrine.* 2 vols. Reprint, Pasadena: Theosophical University Press, 1988.

Blitzer, Wolf. *Territory of Lies: The Exclusive Story of Jonathan Jay Pollard.* New York: Harper and Row, 1989.

Blum, John Morton. *Woodrow Wilson and the Politics of Morality.* Reprint, Boston: Little, Brown, and Company, 1956.

Blumenson, Martin. *Kasserine Pass.* New York: Tower, 1967.

———. *The Patton Papers.* 2 vols. Boston: Houghton Mifflin, 1972.

Bordon, Morton. *Parties and Politics in the Early Republic, 1789–1815.* New York: Thomas Crowell, 1967.

Boyer, Paul. *When Time Shall Be No More.* Cambridge, Mass.: Belknap Harvard, 1992.

Bradford, Ernle. *The Knights of the Order.* Reprint, New York: Dorset Press, 1991.

Brandeis, Louis. *Other People's Money.* New York: Frederick Stokes, 1914.

Breese, Dave. *Know the Marks of Cults.* Wheaton, Ill.: Victor, 1986.

Brooke, Tal. *Lord of the Air: Tales of a Modern Antichrist.* Eugene, Ore.: Harvest House, 1990.

———. *Riders of the Cosmic Circuit.* Bavaria, Ill.: Lion, 1986.

———. *When the World Will Be as One.* Eugene, Ore.: Harvest House, 1989.

Brookes, James H. *Maranatha.* Reprint, New York: Revell, 1989.

Brown, Morton. *Parties and Politics in the Early Republic, 1789–1815.* New York: Thomas Crowell, 1967.

Brown, Rebecca. *He Came to Set the Captives Free.* Springdale, Pa.: Whitaker House, 1992.

Bryan, William Jennings. *The First Battle.* Chicago, 1896.

Bryan, William Jennings, and Mary Baird Bryan. *Memoirs.* Reprint, New York: Haskell House, 1971.

Brzezinski, Zbigniew. *Between Two Ages: America's Role in the Technotronic Age.* New York: Penguin, 1970.

———. *The Grand Failure: The Birth and Death of Communism in the Twentieth Century.* Reprint, New York: Collier, 1990.

Burkett, Larry. *The Coming Economic Earthquake.* Rev. ed. Chicago: Moody Press, 1991, 1994.

———. *The Illuminati.* Nashville: Thomas Nelson, 1991.

——. *Investing for the Future.* Wheaton, Ill.: Victor, 1992.

——. *Whatever Happened to the American Dream?* Chicago: Moody Press, 1993.

Burns, Evelyn M. *Toward Social Security: An Explanation of the Social Security Act and a Survey of the Larger Issues.* New York, 1936.

Butcher, Harry C. *My Three Years with Eisenhower.* New York: Simon and Schuster, 1946.

Butt, Baseden G. *Madame Blavatsky.* London: Marchard Brothers, 1926.

Cannon, Lou. *President Reagan: The Role of a Lifetime.* Sacramento: Cal Journal, 1991.

Carell, Paul. *Hitler Moves East, 1941–1943.* Reprint, New York: Ballantine, 1970.

——. *Scorched Earth.* Reprint, New York: Ballantine, 1971.

Carnegie, Andrew. *Autobiography.* Boston: Houghton Mifflin, 1920.

——. *The Empire of Business.* New York: Doubleday, 1912.

——. *Triumphant Democracy.* London, 1886.

Carr, William Guy. *Pawns in the Game.* Clackamas, Ore.: Emissary Publications, n.d.

——. *Red Fog over America.* Reprint, Clackamas, Ore.: Emissary Publications, 1968.

Carrico, David, and Rick Doninger. *Lucifer-Eliphas Levi-Albert Pike and the Masonic Lodge.* Clackamas, Ore.: Emissary Publications, 1991.

——. *Manley P. Hall: The Honored Masonic Author.* Clackamas, Ore.: Emissary Publications, 1992.

——. *The Masonic-Egyptian-Satanic Connection.* Clackamas, Ore: Emissary Publications, 1991.

Carter, Jimmy. *Keeping the Faith: Memoirs of a President.* New York: Bantam, 1982.

Catterall, Ralph C. H. *The Second Bank of the United States.* Chicago: University of Chicago Press, 1960.

Chandler, Russell. *Doomsday.* Ann Arbor, Mich.: Servant, 1993.

——. *Understanding the New Age.* Grand Rapids: Zondervan, 1993.

Chernow, Ron. *The Warburgs.* New York: Random House, 1993.

Churchill, Randolph. *The Six Day War.* Reprint, Boston: Houghton Mifflin, 1967.

Churchill, Winston. *The Gathering Storm.* 5 vols. Reprint, Boston: Houghton Mifflin, 1967.

——. *The Grand Alliance.* Boston: Houghton Mifflin, 1950.

Clark, Gordon. *Shylock: As Banker, Bondholder, Corruptionist, Conspirator.* Chicago, n.d.

Clews, Henry. *Twenty-eight Years in Wall Street.* New York: Irving Company, 1908.

Cochran, Thomas C., and William Miller. *The Age of Enterprise: A Social History of Industrial America.* New York: Harper and Row, 1961.

Coffman, Michael S. *Saviors of the Earth?* Chicago: Northfield, 1994.

Coit, Margaret L. *Mr. Baruch.* Boston: Houghton Mifflin, 1957.

Cole, Richard. *Stairway to Heaven: Led Zeppelin.* New York: HarperCollins, 1992.

Collier, Peter, and David Horowitz. *The Rockefellers: An American Dynasty.* New York: Holt, Rinehart, and Winston, 1976.

Cooper, Irving. *Theosophy Simplified.* Reprint, Wheaton, Ill.: Theosophical Press, 1964.

Corcoran, James. *Bitter Harvest.* New York: Penguin, 1990.

Corey, Lewis. *The House of Morgan.* New York: G. H. Watt, 1930.

Council on Foreign Relations, *The United States in World Affairs, 1931–1945.* New York: CFR, 1946.

Craven, Avery. *Reconstruction: The Ending of the Civil War.* New York: Holt, Rinehart, and Winston, 1969.

Creme, Benjamin. *The Reappearance of the Christ and the Masters of Wisdom.* London: Tara Press, 1980.

Cross, Whitney R. *The Burned-Over District: The Social and Intellectual History of Enthusiastic Religion in Western New York.* New York: Harper Torchbooks, 1950.

Crowley, Aleister. *The Book of the Law* (LIBER AL vel LEGIS sub figura CCXX). New York: Magickal Childe, in association with Ordo Templi Orientis, 1990.

———. *The Confessions of Aleister Crowley.* Reprint, New York: Bantam, 1969.

———. *Equinox,* vols. 1–10. York Beach, Maine: Samuel Weiser, 1992.

———. *Gems from the Equinox.* 5th ed. Scottsdale, Ariz.: Falcon Press, 1992.

———. *Magick in Theory and Practice.* New York: Castle Books, n.d.

Curry, Richard, and Timothy Brown, eds. *Conspiracy: The Fear of Subversion in American History.* New York: Holt, Rinehart, and Winston, 1972.

Dall, Curtis. *FDR: My Exploited Father-in-Law.* New Rochelle, N.Y.: Arlington House, 1975.

Daraul, Arkin. *A History of Secret Societies.* 2nd ed. New York: Citadel Press, 1990.

Davidson, James Dale, and Lord William Rees-Mogg. *The Great Reckoning: How the World Will Change in the Depression of the 1990s.* New York: Summit, 1991.

Davis, David Brion. *The Fear of Conspiracy: Images of Un-American Subversion from the Revolution to the Present.* Ithaca, N.Y.: Cornell University Press, 1971.

Davis, Stephen. *The Hammer of the Gods: The Led Zeppelin Saga.* Reprint, New York: Bantam, 1990.

Dayan, Moshe. *Diary of the Sinai Campaign.* London: Weidenfeld and Nicolson, 1966.

de Chardin, Teilhard. *Building the Earth.* New York: Avon, 1969.

Decker, Ed, and Dave Hunt. *The God Makers.* Eugene, Ore.: Harvest House, 1984.

de Goulevitch, Arsene. *Czarism and the Revolution.* New York, n.d.

DeHaan, M. R. *Coming Events in Prophecy.* Grand Rapids: Zondervan, 1962.

de la Roche, J. P. L., Marquis de la Luchet. *Essai sur la secte des illumines.* 2nd ed. Paris, 1789.

Deyo, Stan. *The Cosmic Conspiracy.* Rev. ed. Kalamunda, Australia: West Australian Texas Trading, 1992.

Dolan, David. *Holy War for the Promised Land.* Nashville: Thomas Nelson, 1991.

Donnelly, Ignatius. *Caesar's Column.* Chicago, 1891.

Draper, Theodore. *Castro's Revolution.* New York: Frederick A. Praeger, 1962.

Drummond, Donald. *The Passing of American Neutrality, 1937–1941.* Ann Arbor, Mich.: University of Michigan Press, 1955.

Drummond, Lewis A. *The Life and Ministry of Charles G. Finney.* Minneapolis: Bethany House, 1985.

Dupuy, Colonel T. N. *Elusive Victory: The Arab-Israeli Wars, 1947–1974.* New York: Harper and Row, 1978.

Dwight, Timothy. *The Duty of Americans in the Present Crisis.* New Haven, Conn., 1798.

Edwards, George W. *The Evolution of Finance Capitalism.* New York: Longmans, Green, 1938.

Elkins, Stanley, and Erin McKintrick. *The Age of Federalism: The Early American Republic, 1788–1800.* London: Oxford University Press, 1993.

Emery, Mrs. S. E. V. *Seven Financial Conspiracies Which Have Enslaved the American People.* Chicago, n.d.

Ennes, James. *The Assault on the* Liberty: *The True Story of the Israeli Attack on an American Intelligence Ship.* New York: Random House, 1979.

Epperson, Ralph. *The Unseen Hand.* Tucson: Publius Press, 1985.

Evans, Rowland, Jr., and Robert Novak. *Nixon and the White House.* New York: Random House, 1971.

Farago, Ladislas. *Patton: Ordeal and Triumph.* Reprint, New York: Dell, 1970.

Ferguson, Marilyn. *The Aquarian Conspiracy: Personal and Social Transformation in the 1980s.* Reprint, Los Angeles: Jeremy Tarcher, 1980.

Fest, Joachim. *The Face of the Third Reich.* New York: Pantheon, 1970.

Festinger, Leon, Henry W. Riecken, and Stanley Schachter. *When Prophecy Fails.* Minneapolis: University of Minnesota Press, 1956.

Figgie, Harry E., Jr., and Gerald J. Swanson. *Bankruptcy 1995.* Boston: Little, Brown, and Company, 1992.

Finch, Phillip. *God, Guts, and Guns—A Close Look at the Radical Right.* New York: Seaview/Putnam, 1983.

Finney, Charles G. *Autobiography.* Reprint, Minneapolis: Bethany House, 1977.

———. *The Heart of Truth.* Reprint, Minneapolis: Bethany House, 1976.

———. *Systematic Theology.* Reprint, Minneapolis: Bethany House, 1976.

Firestone, Bernard J., and Robert C. Voight. *Lyndon Baines Johnson and the Uses of Power.* New York: Greenwood Press, 1988.

Fisher, Irving. *The Stock Market Crash and After.* New York: Macmillan, 1930.

Fite, Gilbert. *The Farmer's Frontier.* Reprint, Albuquerque: University of New Mexico Press, 1974.

Flexner, James Thomas. *Washington: The Indispensable Man.* 3rd ed. New York: Mentor, 1974.

Foner, Eric. *Reconstruction: America's Unfinished Revolution, 1863–1877.* New York: Harper and Row, 1988.

Ford, Brian J. *Allied Secret Weapons: The War of Science.* New York: Ballantine, 1971.

Ford, Henry, Sr. *The International Jew: The World's Foremost Problem.* Reprint, Clackamas, Ore.: Emissary Publications, n.d.

Fosdick, Raymond B. *John D. Rockefeller.* New York: Harper and Brothers, 1955.

Franklin, John Hope. *Reconstruction: After the Civil War.* Chicago: University of Chicago Press, 1961.

Freedman, Lawrence, and Efraim Karsh. *The Gulf Conflict, 1990–1991: Diplomacy and War in the New World Order.* Princeton, N.J.: Princeton University Press, 1993.

Freidal, Frank, ed. *The New Deal and the American People.* New York, 1964.

Fried, Richard M. *Nightmare in Red.* New York: Oxford University Press, 1990.

Friedman, Thomas L. *From Beirut to Jerusalem.* New York: Farrar, Straus, Giroux, 1989.

Fromkin, David. *A Peace to End All Peace: The Fall of the Ottoman Empire and the Creation of the Modern Middle East.* Reprint, New York: Avon, 1989.

Fulbright, J. William. *The Arrogance of Power.* Reprint, New York: Vintage, 1966.

———. *The Price of Empire.* New York: Pantheon, 1989.

Fuller, Robert. *Naming the Antichrist: The History of an American Obsession.* New York: Oxford University Press, 1995.

Gaebler, Neil. *An Empire of Their Own.* New York: Doubleday, 1989.

Galbraith, John Kenneth. *The Great Crash.* Boston: Houghton Mifflin, 1955.

Garrison, Elisha E. *Roosevelt, Wilson, and the Federal Reserve Law.* Boston: Christopher Publications, 1931.

Geisler, Norman. *The Reincarnation Sensation.* Wheaton, Ill.: Tyndale, 1986.

Gilbert, Martin. *The Holocaust: A History of the Jews of Europe during the Second World War.* New York: Holt, Rinehart, and Winston, 1985.

Ginn, Gordon L. *The Late Great Road to Holocaust.* Fortunea, Calif.: Smyrna, 1991.

Gipson, Lawrence. *The British Empire before the American Revolution.* 14 vols. New York: Knopf, 1935–67.

Glass, Carter. *An Adventure in Creative Finance.* New York, 1927.

———. *The Facts about the Fiscal Policy of Our Government.* Washington, D.C.: Government Printing Office, 1933.

Goetz, William R. *Apocalypse Next and the New World Order.* Camp Hill, Pa.: Horizon House, 1991.

Goodwyn, Lawrence. *The Populist Moment.* Oxford: Oxford University Press, 1978.

Graebner, Norman, ed. "The Cold War: Ideological Conflict or Power Struggle," in *Problems in European Civilization.* Boston: D. C. Heath, 1966.

Grebstein, Sheldon N., ed. *Monkey Trial.* Boston: Houghton Mifflin, 1960.

Greider, William. *Secrets of the Temple: How the Federal Reserve Runs the Country.* New York: Simon and Schuster, 1987.

Grenz, Stanley J. *The Millennial Maze: Sorting Out Evangelical Options*. Downers Grove, Ill.: InterVarsity, 1992.

Griffin, Des. *Anti-Semitism and the Babylonian Connection*. Reprint, Clackamas, Ore.: Emissary Publications, 1992.

———. *Descent into Slavery?* Reprint, Clackamas: Ore.: Emissary Publications, 1991.

———. *Fourth Reich of the Rich*. Reprint, Clackamas, Ore.: Emissary Publications, 1993.

———. *Martin Luther King: The Man behind the Myth*. Reprint, Clackamas, Ore.: Emissary Publications, 1987.

Griffin, Des, Pat Brooks, Dale Crowley, and Haviv Schieber. *Freedom or Slavery?* Fletcher, N.C.: New Puritan Press, 1990.

Griffin, G. Edward. *The Creature from Jekyll Island*. Westlake Village, Calif.: American Media, n.d.

Groothuis, Douglas R. *Revealing the New Age Jesus*. Downers Grove, Ill.: InterVarsity, 1990.

———. *Unmasking the New Age*. Downers Grove, Ill.: InterVarsity, 1986.

Gross, Bertram, ed. *The Great Society*. Rossmoor, Calif.: Concord Press, 1971.

Guiley, Rosemary Ellen. *Harper's Encyclopedia of Mystical and Paranormal Experience*. Edison, N.J.: Castle, 1990.

Gunther, John. *Roosevelt in Retrospective*. New York, 1950.

Haber, Eitan. *Menachem Begin*. New York: Delacorte Press, 1978.

Halberstam, David. *The Best and Brightest*. New York: Random House, 1972.

Hall, Manley. *An Encyclopedic Outline of Masonic Hermetic Qabbalistic and Rosicrucian Symbolical Philosophy*. Reprint, Los Angeles: The Philosophical Research Society, 1977.

Hanegraaff, Hank. *Christianity in Crisis*. Eugene, Ore.: Harvest House, 1992.

Harbaugh, William Henry. *The Life and Times of Theodore Roosevelt*. Reprint, New York: Collier, 1963.

Harkabi, Yehoshafat. *Arab Strategies and Israel's Response*. London: Collier Macmillan, 1977.

———. *Israel's Fateful Hour*. New York: Harper and Row, 1986.

Harris, Seymour. *Twenty Years of Federal Reserve Policy*. Cambridge, Mass.: Harvard University Press, 1933.

Hart, Alan. *Arafat: A Political Biography*. Reprint, Bloomington: University of Indiana Press, 1984.

Hart, B. H. Liddell. *History of the Second World War*. 2 vols. Reprint, New York: G. P. Putnam's Sons, 1970.

Harvey, Andrew. *Hidden Journey*. New York: Arkana/Penguin, 1991.

Harvey, William H. *Coin on Money, Trusts, and Imperialism*. Chicago: Coin Publishing Company, 1900.

———. *Coin's Financial School*. Chicago: Coin Publishing Company, 1894.

Hay, George, ed. *The Necronomicon*. Reprint, London: Skoob, 1992.

Heller, Mark. *A Palestinian State: Implications for Israel*. Cambridge, Mass.: Harvard University Press, 1983.

Hendrick, Burton J. *The Life of Andrew Carnegie*. 2 vols. New York: Doubleday, 1932.

Henriques, R. *A Hundred Hours to Suez: An Account of Israel's Campaign in the Sinai Peninsula.* Reprint, New York: Viking Press, 1957.

Hersch, Seymour M. *The Samson Option.* New York: Random House, 1991.

Hertenstein, Mike, and Jon Trott. *Selling Satan.* Chicago: Cornerstone Ministries, 1993.

Herzog, Chaim. *The Arab-Israeli Wars: War and Peace in the Middle East.* Reprint, New York: Vintage, 1984.

Hesseltine, William B. *Ulysses S. Grant, Politician.* New York, 1935.

Hicks, John D. *The Populist Revolt.* Reprint, Lincoln: University of Nebraska Press, 1974.

Hislop, Alexander. *The Two Babylons.* 2nd American ed. Neptune, N.J.: Loizeaux Bros., 1959.

Hitler, Adolf. *Mein Kampf.* Reprint, Boston: Houghton Mifflin, 1971.

Hofstadter, Richard. *The Age of Political Reform.* Reprint, New York: Vintage, 1955.

———. *The American Political Tradition.* New York: Random House, 1948.

———. *The Paranoid Style in American Politics.* New York: Knopf, 1965.

———, ed. *The Progressive Movement, 1910–1915.* Reprint, Englewood Cliffs, N.J.: Prentice-Hall, 1963.

Holzer, Hans. *The New Pagans.* Garden City, N.Y.: Doubleday, 1972.

Hoover, Herbert. *Memoirs of Herbert Hoover: The Great Depression, 1929–1941.* New York: Macmillan, 1952.

House, Edward Mandell. *Phillip Dru: Administrator.* New York: B. W. Huebsch, 1912.

Howard, Michael. *The Occult Conspiracy: Secret Societies, Their Influence and Power in World History.* Rochester, Vt.: Destiny, 1989.

Howarth, Stephen. *The Knights Templar.* Reprint, New York: Dorset Press, 1991.

Hunt, Dave. *Beyond Seduction.* Eugene, Ore.: Harvest House, 1987.

———. *The Cult Explosion.* Eugene, Ore.: Harvest House, 1978.

———. *Global Peace and the Rise of Antichrist.* Eugene, Ore.: Harvest House, 1990.

———. *Peace, Prosperity, and the Coming Holocaust.* Eugene, Ore.: Harvest House, 1983.

———. *The Seduction of Christianity.* Eugene, Ore.: Harvest House, 1985.

———. *Whatever Happened to Heaven?* Eugene, Ore.: Harvest House, 1988.

Ice, Thomas, and Randall Price. *Ready to Rebuild.* Eugene, Ore.: Harvest House, 1992.

Incognito, Magus. *The Secret Doctrine of the Rosicrucians.* Reprint, New York: Barnes and Noble, 1993.

James, William T., ed. *Earth's Final Days.* Green Forest, Ark.: New Leaf Press, 1995.

Jastrow, Robert. *God and the Astronomers.* New York: Norton, 1978.

Jeffrey, Grant R. *Prince of Darkness: Antichrist and the New World Order.* Toronto: Frontier Research Publications, 1994.

Jenks, Leland H. *The Migration of British Capital to 1875.* New York: Knopf, 1927.

Johnson, George. *Architects of Fear: Conspiracy Theories and Paranoia in American Politics.* Los Angeles: Jeremy Tarcher, 1983.

Johnson, Paul. *A History of the Jews.* New York: Harper and Row, 1987.

Johnson, Paul E. *A Shopkeeper's Millennium: Society and Revivals in Rochester, New York, 1815–1837.* New York: Hill and Wang, 1978.

Johnson, Walter. *The Battle against Isolation.* New York, 1944.

Josephson, Emanuel. *The "Federal" Reserve Conspiracy and the Rockefellers.* New York: Chedney Press, 1968.

Josephson, Matthew. *The Robber Barons.* New York: Harcourt, Brace, and Company, 1934.

Kah, Gary H. *En Route to Global Occupation.* Lafayette, La.: Huntington House, 1992.

Karsch, Efraim. *The Gulf Conflict, 1990–1991: Diplomacy and the War in the New World Order.* Princeton, N.J.: Princeton University Press, 1993.

Kaufman, Burton I. *James Earl Carter.* Lawrence: University of Kansas Press, 1993.

Kearnes, Doris. *Lyndon Johnson and the American Dream.* New York: New American Library, 1976.

Kelly, Rev. Clarence. *Conspiracy against God and Man.* Appleton, Wis.: Western Islands, 1974.

Kennan, George. *Realities in American Foreign Policy.* Princeton, N.J.: Princeton University Press, 1954.

———. *Russia, the Atom, and the West.* Reprint, New York: Greenwood Press, 1974.

Kennan, George, and Anna Nelson, eds. *The State Department Policy Staff Papers.* 3 vols. New York: Garland, 1983.

King, Nicholas. *George Bush: A Biography.* New York: Dodd, Mead, and Company, 1980.

Knight, J. *I Am Ramtha.* Portland, Ore.: Beyond Words Publishing, 1986.

Knuth, E. C. *The Empire of the "The City."* Milwaukee, 1946.

Kochan, Lionel. *Russia in Revolution.* New York, 1962.

Kole, Andrew, and Al Janssen. *Miracles or Magic?* Eugene, Ore.: Harvest House, 1984.

Korem, Dan. *Powers: Testing the Psychic and Supernatural.* Downers Grove, Ill.: InterVarsity, 1988.

Kort, Michael. *The Soviet Colossus: A History of the USSR.* New York: Charles Scribner's Sons, 1985.

LaFeber, Walter. *America, Russia, and the Cold War, 1945–1975.* 3rd ed. New York: John Wiley and Sons, 1976.

Lamont, T. W. *Henry P. Davidson.* New York: Harper, Row, and Company, 1933.

Laqueur, Walter. *A History of Zionism.* Reprint, New York: Schocken, 1989.

Larson, Bob. *Straight Answers on the New Age.* Nashville: Thomas Nelson, 1989.

Latham, Earl. *The Communist Controversy in Washington.* Cambridge, Mass.: Harvard University Press, 1966.

———, ed. "The Meaning of McCarthyism," in *Problems in American Civilization*. Boston: D. C. Heath, 1965.

Leach, Douglas Edward. *Arms for Empire*. New York: Macmillan, 1973.

Lease, Mary E. *The Problem of Civilization Solved*. Chicago, 1895.

Lemesurier, Peter. *Nostradamus: The Next Fifty Years*. New York: Berkeley, 1993.

Lenin, Vladimir I. *The State and Revolution*. Reprint, Moscow: Progress Publishers, 1969.

Lesch, Ann Mosely, and Mark Tessler. *Israel, Egypt, and the Palestinians: From Camp David to Intifada*. Bloomington: University of Indiana Press, 1989.

Leuchtenberg, W. E. *The Perils of Prosperity, 1914–1932*. Chicago: University of Chicago Press, 1958.

Levi. *The Aquarian Gospel of Jesus the Christ*. Reprint, Marina del Ray, Calif.: DeVorss and Company, 1964.

Levin, Murray B. *Political Hysteria in America: The Democratic Capacity for Repression*. New York: Basic Books, 1971.

Levins, Hoag. *Arab Reach*. New York: Doubleday, 1983.

Lewin, Leonard C. *Report from Iron Mountain on the Possibility and Desirability of Peace*. New York: Dial Press, 1967.

Lewis, James R., and J. Gordon Melton, eds. *Perspectives on the New Age*. Ithaca, N.Y.: State University of New York Press, 1994.

Lilienthal, Alfred M. *The Zionist Connection II*. Reprint, New Brunswick, N.J.: North American, 1982.

Lindburgh, Charles A., Sr. *Banking and Currency and the Money Trust*. Reprint, Clackamas, Ore.: Emissary Publications, n.d.

Lindsey, Hal. *The Late Great Planet Earth*. Reprint, Grand Rapids: Zondervan, 1970.

———. *The Road to Holocaust*. Reprint, New York: Bantam, 1990.

———. *There Is a New World Coming*. New York: Bantam, 1983.

Lipset, Seymour Martin, and Earl Raab. *The Politics of Unreason*. New York: Harper and Row, 1970.

Lipstadt, Deborah E. *Denying the Holocaust: The Growing Assault on Truth and Memory*. New York: Free Press, 1993.

Livingston, Neil C., and David Halvery. *Inside the PLO*. New York: Quil/William Morrow, 1990.

Lodge, Henry Cabot. *Alexander Hamilton*. Reprint, New York: Chelsea House, 1980.

———. *History of Nations: The French Revolution*. Vol. 10. 4th ed. New York: P. F. Collier and Son, 1916.

Luther, Martin. *The Jews and Their Lies*. Reprint, St. Louis: Christian Nationalist Crusade, 1948.

Luthin, Reinhard H. *American Demagogues*. New York: Beacon Press, 1954.

Mackenzie, Norman. *Secret Societies*. New York: Holt, Rinehart, and Winston, 1967.

Mackey, Albert. *The Symbolism of Freemasonry: Illustrating and Explaining Its Science and Philosophy, Its Legends, Myths, and Symbols*. Chicago: Charles T. Powner, 1975.

Macksey, K. J. *Afrika Korps.* New York: Ballantine, 1968.

MacLaine, Shirley. *Out on a Limb.* New York: Bantam, 1983.

Maharaj, Rabi. *Escape into the Light.* Eugene, Ore.: Harvest House, 1984.

Maharishi Mahesh Yogi. *Meditations of Maharishi Mahesh Yogi.* New York: Bantam, 1968.

Malgo, Wim. *Begin with Sadat.* Columbia, S.C.: Midnight Call, 1978.

Malone, Dumas. *Jefferson and the Ordeal of Liberty.* 6 vols. New York: Little, Brown, and Company, 1962.

Mann, Peggy. *Golda: The Life of Israel's Prime Minister.* New York: Coward, McCann, and Georghegan, 1971.

Marrs, Texe. *America Shattered.* Austin, Tex.: Living Truth Publishers, 1991.

———. *Circle of Intrigue.* Austin, Tex.: Living Truth Publishers, 1995.

———. *Dark Majesty.* Austin, Tex.: Living Truth Publishers, 1992.

———. *Millennium: Peace, Promises, and the Day They Take Our Money Away.* Austin, Tex.: Living Truth Publishers, 1990.

Marsden, George M. *Fundamentalism and American Culture: The Shaping of Twentieth Century Evangelicalism, 1870–1925.* New York: Oxford University Press, 1980.

Marsden, Victor, ed. *Protocols of the Learned Elders of Zion.* Reprint, Clackamas, Ore.: Emissary Publications, n.d.

Martin, Walter. *Kingdom of the Cults.* 3rd ed. Minneapolis: Bethany, 1985.

———. *The Maze of Mormonism.* Reprint, Ventura, Calif.: Regal, 1978.

———. *The New Age Cult.* Minneapolis: Bethany, 1989.

———. *The New Cults.* Ventura, Calif.: Regal, 1980.

Matrisciana, Caryl. *Gods of the New Age.* Eugene, Ore.: Harvest House, 1985.

Matzat, Don. *Inner Healing.* Eugene, Ore.: Harvest House, 1985.

Maxwell, Arthur. *History's Crowded Climax.* Mountain View, Calif.: Pacific Press, 1940.

McConnell, D. R. *A Different Gospel.* Peabody, Mass.: Hendrickson Publishers, 1988.

McKinnon, Dan. *Bullseye Iraq.* Reprint, New York: Berkeley, 1988.

McMahan, Jeff. *Reagan and the World: Imperial Policy in the New Cold War.* New York: Monthly Review Press, 1985.

McManus, John F. *Financial Terrorism: Hijacking America under the Threat of Bankruptcy.* Appleton, Wis.: The John Birch Society, 1993.

McNamara, Robert. *Blundering into Disaster.* New York: Pantheon, 1986.

Meera, Mother. *Answers.* Ithaca, N.Y.: Meeramma, 1991.

Merk, Frederick. *History of the Westward Movement.* New York: Knopf, 1978.

Miller, John. *Crisis in Freedom: The Alien and Sedition Acts.* Boston: Houghton Mifflin, 1951.

Mirabeau, Count. *The Prussian Monarchy under Frederick the Great.* Reprint, Paris: 1788.

Moody, Raymond. *Life after Life.* New York: Bantam, 1975.

Morgan, Capt. William. *Illustrations of Masonry.* 1827. Reprint, Clackamas, Ore.: Emissary Publications, n.d.

Morison, Samuel Elliot, comp. and ed. *The Rising Sun in the Pacific, 1931–1942.* Boston: Houghton Mifflin, 1948.

———. *The United States Navy in World War II*. New York: Ballantine, 1967.

Morlan, Robert L. *Political Prairie Fire: The Nonpartisan League, 1915–1922.* St. Paul: Borealis, 1985.

Morse, Jedediah. *A Sermon, Exhibiting the Present Dangers and Consequent Duties of the Citizens of the United States of America: Delivered at Charlestown, April 25, 1799.* Hartford: Hudson and Goodwin, 1799.

Mowry, George E. *Theodore Roosevelt and the Progressive Movement*. Reprint, New York: Hill and Wang, 1960.

Mowry, George E., ed. *The Twenties: Fords, Flappers, and Fanatics.* New York, 1963.

Muir, William K., Jr. *The Bully Pulpit: The Presidential Leadership of Ronald Reagan.* San Francisco: ICS Press, 1992.

Muller, Robert. *New Genesis: Shaping of Global Spirituality.* New York: Doubleday, 1984.

Mullins, Eustace. *The Secrets of the Federal Reserve.* Reprint, Stanton, Va.: Bankers Research Institute, 1993.

Murray, Robert K. *Red Scare.* Reprint, New York: McGraw Hill, 1964.

Nakdimon, Shlomo. *First Strike: The Exclusive Story of How Israel Foiled Iraq's Attempt to Get the Bomb.* New York: Simon and Schuster, 1987.

Nevins, Allan. *The Emergence of Modern America, 1865–1878.* Chicago: Triangle, 1955.

———. *Rockefeller.* 2 vols. New York: Charles Scribner's Sons, 1940.

Nichols, Francis D. *The Midnight Cry.* Washington, D.C.: Review and Herald, 1944.

Nixon, Richard M. *Memoirs.* New York: Grosset and Dunlap, 1978.

———. *1999: Victory without War.* New York: Simon and Schuster, 1988.

North, Gary. *Unholy Spirits: Occultism and New Age Humanism.* Tyler, Tex.: Dominion Press, 1986.

O'Driscoll, Robert, Des Griffin, Margarita Ivanoff Dubrowski. *The New World Order and the Throne of the Antichrist.* Clackamas, Ore.: Emissary Publications, 1993.

O'Neil, William L. *The Fundamentalist Controversy, 1918–1931.* New York, 1931.

Palmer, R. R. *The Age of Democratic Revolution.* 2 vols. Princeton, N.J.: Princeton University Press, 1956.

———. *Twelve Who Ruled: The Committee of Safety during the Reign of Terror.* Princeton, N.J.: Princeton University Press, 1941.

Parmet, Herbert S. *Richard Nixon and His America.* Boston: Little, Brown, and Company, 1990.

Payson, Seth. *Proofs of the Real Existence and Dangerous Tendency of Illuminism.* Charleston, S.C., 1802.

Perkins, Francis. *The Roosevelt I Knew.* New York, 1946.

Perloff, James. *The Shadows of Power: The Council on Foreign Relations and the American Decline.* Appleton, Wis.: Western Islands, 1988.

Permutter, Amos. *The Life and Times of Menachem Begin.* New York: Doubleday, 1987.

Pessen, Edward. *Jacksonian America: Society, Personality, and Politics.* Rev. ed. Homeweed, Ill.: Dorsey Press, 1978.

Pike, Albert. *Morals and Dogma of the Ancient and Accepted Scottish Rite of Freemasonry.* Charleston, S.C.: L. H. Jenkins, 1871.

Playfair, Guy L. *The Unknown Power.* New York: Pocket Books, 1975.

Prager, Dennis, and Joseph Telushkin. *Why the Jews?* Reprint, New York: Torchstone Books, 1985.

*Problems in American Civilization,* "Jackson vs. Biddle: The Struggle over the Second Bank of the United States," and "Evolution and Religion: The Conflict between Science and Theology in Modern America." Boston: D. C. Heath and Company, 1957.

Prophet, Elizabeth Claire. *The Lost Teachings of Jesus.* 3 vols. Reprint, Livingston, Mont.: Summit University Press, 1988.

Puharich, Andrijah. *Beyond Death's Door.* Nashville: Thomas Nelson, 1978.

Quandt, William B. *Camp David: Peacemaking and Politics.* Washington, D.C.: The Brookings Institute, 1986.

Queensborough, Lady (Edith Starr Miller). *Occult Theocracy.* 2 vols. 1933. Reprint, Los Angeles: Christian Book Club of America, n.d.

Quigley, Carroll. *The Anglo-American Establishment.* Reprint, New York: Books in Focus, 1981.

———. *Tragedy and Hope.* New York: Macmillan, 1966.

Raschke, Carl L. *The Interruption of Eternity: Modern Gnosticism and the Origins of the New Religious Consciousness.* Chicago: Nelson-Hall, 1980.

Raviv, Dan, and Yossi Meman. *Every Spy a Prince.* Boston: Houghton Mifflin, 1991.

Reed, Douglas. *The Controversy of Zion.* Torrance, Calif.: Noontide Press, 1985.

Regardie, Israel, and P. R. Stephensen. *The Legend of Aleister Crowley.* Reprint, Las Vegas: New Falcon, 1990.

Reid, James. *God, the Atom, and the Universe.* Grand Rapids: Zondervan, 1968.

Reisser, Paul C., Teri K. Reisser, and John Weldon. *The Holistic Healers.* Downers Grove, Ill.: InterVarsity, 1987.

———. *New Age Medicine.* Downers Grove, Ill.: InterVarsity, 1987.

Relfe, Mary Stewart. *The New Money System.* Montgomery, Ala.: Ministries, 1982.

———. *When Your Money Fails.* Montgomery, Ala.: Ministries, 1981.

Remini, Robert V. *Andrew Jackson and the Course of American Freedom,* Vol. 2. New York: Harper and Row, 1981.

Rhodes, Ron. *The Culting of America.* Eugene, Ore.: Harvest House, 1994.

Richardson, James D., ed. *A Compilation of the Messages and Papers of the Presidents, 1789–1897.* 10 vols. Washington, D.C.: Government Printing Office, 1896.

Riott, Pat. *The Greatest Story Never Told: Winston Churchill and the Crash of 1929.* Oak Brook, Ill.: Nanoman Press, 1994.

Robbins, Lionel. *The Great Crash.* New York: Macmillan, 1934.

Robertson, Pat. *The New World Order.* Dallas: Word, 1991.

―――. *The Turning Tide*. Dallas: Word, 1993.

Roberts, Jane. *The Seth Material*. Englewood Cliffs, N.J.: Prentice-Hall, 1970.

―――. *Seth Speaks*. Englewood Cliffs, N.J.: Prentice-Hall, 1972.

Robertson, Sandy. *The Aleister Crowley Scrapbook*. York Beach, Maine: Samuel Weiser, 1988.

Robinson, John J. *Born in Blood: The Lost Secrets of Freemasonry*. New York: M. Evans and Company, 1989.

Robison, John. *Proofs of a Conspiracy*. 1799. Reprint, Appleton, Wis.: Western Islands, 1968.

Rodriguez, José Maria Cardenal Caro. *The Mystery of Freemasonry Unveiled*. Reprint, Los Angeles: Christian Book Club of America, 1992.

Rogers, L. W. *Elementary Theosophy*. Wheaton, Ill.: Theosophical Press, 1956.

Roosevelt, Elliot, ed. *F. D. R.: His Personal Letters, 1905–1945*. 4 vols. New York, 1947–50.

Russell, Jeffrey Burton. *The Prince of Darkness*. Ithaca, N.Y.: Cornell University Press, 1988.

Russell, P. *The Global Brain*. Los Angeles: J. P. Tarcher, 1983.

Sacher, Howard M. *The Course of Modern Jewish History*. Reprint, New York: Vintage, 1990.

Salutos, Theodore. *Farmer Movements in the South, 1865–1933*. Berkeley: University of California Press, 1933.

Salvemini, Gaetano. *The French Revolution, 1788–1792*. New York: Norton Library, 1962.

Satterlee, Herbert L. *J. Pierpont Morgan*. New York: Macmillan, 1939.

Savelle, Max. *The Origins of American Diplomacy: The International History of Anglo-America, 1492–1763*. New York: Macmillan, 1967.

Schenck, Paul. *The Extermination of Christianity*. Lafayette, La.: Huntington House, 1993.

Schlesinger, Arthur, Jr. *The Age of Jackson*. Boston: Little, Brown, and Company, 1945.

―――. *The Age of Roosevelt*. Boston, 1958.

―――. *A Thousand Days*. Boston: Houghton Mifflin, 1965.

Schnoebelen, William. *Masonry beyond the Light*. Chino, Calif.: Chick Publications, 1991.

Scholem, Gershom. *Kabbalah*. New York: Dorset Press, 1974.

Scofield, Cyrus. *What Do the Prophets Say?* Philadelphia: Philadelphia School of the Bible, 1918.

Sears, C. E. *Days of Delusion: A Strange Bit of History*. Boston: Houghton Mifflin, 1924.

Segev, Samuel. *The Iranian Triangle: The Untold Story of Israel's Role in the Iran-Contra Affair*. New York: Free Press, 1988.

Seymour, Charles. *The Intimate Papers of Colonel House*. 4 vols. Boston: Houghton Mifflin, 1928.

Shalev, Aryeh. *The West Bank: Line of Defense*. New York: Praeger, 1985.

Shannon, Fred. *The Farmer's Last Frontier*. New York, 1945.

Shapiro, Leonard. *The Government and Politics of the Soviet Union*. Reprint, New York: Vintage, 1967.

Sharon, Ariel. *Warrior.* New York: Simon and Schuster, 1989.

Shaw, Jim, and Tom McKenney. *The Deadly Deception.* Lafayette, La.: Huntington House, 1988.

Shirer, William L. *The Rise and Fall of the Third Reich.* New York: Fawcett, 1960.

Short, Martin. *Inside the Brotherhood.* New York: Dorset Press, 1989.

Shoup, Lawrence, and William Minter. *Imperial Brain Trust: The Council on Foreign Relations and United States Foreign Policy.* New York: Monthly Review Press, 1977.

Simon. *The Necronomicon.* New York: Avon, 1977.

Simon, Merrill. *God, Allah, and the Great Land Grab.* New York: Jonathan David, 1989.

Sklar, Dusty. *The Nazis and the Occult.* Reprint, New York: Dorset Press, 1988.

Sklar, Holly. *Trilateralism: The Trilateral Commission and Elite Planning for World Management.* Boston: South End Press, 1980.

Skousen, W. Cleon. *The Naked Communist.* Reprint, Salt Lake City: Ensign, 1962.

Smith, Daniel M. *The Testing of America, 1914–1945.* St. Louis: Forum Press, 1979.

Smith, James M. *Freedom's Fetters: The Alien and Sedition Acts and American Civil Liberties.* Ithaca, N.Y.: Cornell University Press, 1956.

Smith, Robert F. *What Happened in Cuba?* New York, 1963.

Smith, Sherman. *Exploding the Doomsday Money Myths.* Nashville: Thomas Nelson, 1994.

Smith, Wilbur. *The Atomic Age and the Word of God.* Boston: W. A. Wilde, 1948.

———. *Before I Forget.* Chicago: Moody Press, 1971.

Sorenson, Theodore. *Kennedy.* New York, 1965.

Soule, George. *Prosperity Decade.* New York: Rinehart, 1947.

Spangler, David. *Reflections on the Christ.* Moray, Scotland: Findhorn, 1978.

Spanier, John. *American Foreign Policy since World War II.* 2nd ed. New York: Frederick Praeger, 1965.

———. *The Truman-MacArthur Controversy and the Korean War.* Cambridge, Mass.: Harvard University Press, 1959.

Sparling, Earl. *Mystery Men of Wall Street.* New York: Greenberg, 1930.

Speer, Albert. *Inside the Third Reich.* Reprint, New York: Avon, 1971.

Spink, James. *Will Hitler Gain World Domination?* New York: Loizeaux Bros., 1942.

*Spotlight on the Bilderbergers.* Reprint, Washington, D.C.: Liberty Lobby, 1991.

Springmeier, Fritz. *The Top 13 Illuminati Bloodlines.* Portland, Ore.: self-published, 1995.

St. John, Robert. *Ben-Gurion.* Garden City, N.Y.: Doubleday and Company, 1959.

Stauffer, Vernon. *New England and the Bavarian Illuminati.* New York: Columbia University Press, 1918.

Stephenson, William. *A Man Called Intrepid.* New York: Harcourt, Brace, and Jovanovich, 1976.

Stephenson, Nathaniel W. *Nelson Aldrich: A Leader in American Politics.* New York: Charles Scribner's Sons, 1930.

Still, William. *New World Order: Ancient Plans of Secret Societies.* Lafayette, La.: Huntington House, 1991.

Stimson, Henry, and McGeorge Bundy. *On Active Duty in Peace and War.* New York, 1948.

Stormer, John A. *None Dare Call It Treason.* Florissant, Mo.: Liberty Bell Press, 1964.

Stowe, Harriet Beecher. *The Second Coming of Christ.* Chicago: Moody Press, n.d.

Stratford, Lauren. *Satan's Underground.* Eugene, Ore.: Harvest House, 1988.

Strawson, John. *The Battle for North Africa.* New York: Charles Scribner's Sons, 1969.

Sutton, Anthony. *America's Secret Establishment: An Introduction to the Order of Skull and Bones.* Billings, Mont.: Liberty House, 1986.

———. *National Suicide: Military Aid to the Soviet Union.* New York: Arlington House, 1974.

———. *Wall Street and FDR.* New Rochelle, N.Y.: Arlington House, 1975.

———. *Wall Street and the Bolshevik Revolution.* New Rochelle, N.Y.: Arlington House, 1974.

Sydney, Hugh. *A Very Personal Presidency: Lyndon Johnson in the White House.* New York: Atheneum Books, 1968.

Taylor, Charles. *The Destiny of America.* Reprint, Van Nuys, Calif.: Time-Life, 1972.

Thompson, John M. *Revolutionary Russia.* New York: Macmillan, 1989.

Time-Life Editors. *Desert Storm: The War in the Persian Gulf.* Boston: Little, Brown, and Company, 1991.

Trilateral Commission, The. *The Trilateral Commission: Questions and Answers.* New York: North American Office, 1986.

Truman, Harry. *Memoirs of Harry S. Truman.* 2 vols. New York: New American Library, 1956.

Tugwell, Redford G. *The Democratic Roosevelt.* New York, 1957.

Unger, Merrill. *Beyond the Crystal Ball.* Chicago: Moody Press, 1973.

Van Buskirk, Michael. *Astrology: Revival in the Cosmic Garden.* Santa Ana, Calif.: Christian Apologetics, Research and Information Service.

Van Impe, Jack. *Signs of the Times.* Royal Oak, Mich.: Jack Van Impe Ministries, 1979.

Victor, Jeffrey S. *Satanic Panic: The Creation of a Contemporary Legend.* Chicago: Open Court, 1993.

Viereck, George S. *The Strangest Friendship in History: Woodrow Wilson and Colonel Edward Mandell House.* New York: Liverlight, 1932.

Wagner, Martin. *Freemasonry: An Interpretation.* Reprint, Clackamas, Ore.: Emissary Publications, n.d.

Waite, Arthur Edward. *The Brotherhood of the Rosy Cross.* Reprint, New York: Barnes and Noble, 1993.

Wall, Joseph Frazier. *Andrew Carnegie.* New York: Oxford University Press, 1970.

Wallace, D. M. *Russia on the Eve of the War and Revolution.* New York, 1962.

Warburg, Paul M. *The Federal Reserve System: Its Origin and Growth.* 2 vols. New York: Macmillan, 1930.

Ward, Charles A. *Oracles of Nostradamus.* New York: Barnes and Noble, 1993.

Ware, Norman J. *The Labor Movement in the United States, 1860–1895.* New York: Vintage, 1929.

Warnke, Mike. *The Satan Seller.* Plainfield, N.J.: Logos, 1972.

———. *Schemes of Satan.* Tulsa, Okla.: Victory House, 1991.

Washington, George. *Writings of George Washington.* Washington, D.C.: Government Printing Office, 1941.

Washington, Peter. *Madame Blavatsky's Baboon.* New York: Schlocken, 1993.

Webb, James. *The Occult Establishment.* La Salle, Ill.: Open Court, 1976.

———. *The Occult Underground.* La Salle, Ill.: Open Court, 1974.

Webster, Nesta H. *Secret Societies and Subversive Movements.* Reprint, Los Angeles: Christian Book Club of America, n.d.

———. *World Revolution.* Reprint, Devon, United Kingdom: Britons Publishing Company, 1971.

Weigley, Russell F. *The American Way of War: A History of United States Military Strategy and Policy.* Reprint, Bloomington: University of Indiana Press, 1977.

Weissman, Rudolph. *The New Federal Reserve System: The Board Assumes Control.* New York, 1936.

———. *The New Wall Street.* New York, 1939.

Wendell, Leilah. *The Necromantic Ritual Book.* New Orleans: Westgate Press, 1994.

Werner, M. R. *William Jennings Bryan.* New York: Chelsea House, 1983.

Weyforth, William O. *The Federal Reserve Board: A Study of Federal Reserve Structure and Credit Control.* Baltimore: Johns Hopkins Press, 1933.

Whisenant, Edgar C. *88 Reasons Why the Rapture Will Be in 1988.* Nashville: World Bible Society, 1988.

White, Thomas B. *The Believer's Guide to Spiritual Warfare.* Ann Arbor, Mich.: Vine Books, 1990.

Whitemarsh, Darylann and Bill Reisman. *Subtle Serpent.* Lafayette, La.: Huntington House, 1993.

Whiting, Charles. *Patton.* New York: Ballantine, 1970.

Wickersheim, Dwight N. *WWIV.* Littleton, Colo.: Aeternus Publishers, 1982.

Wilgus, Neil. *The Illuminoids.* New York: Pocket Books, 1979.

Williams, William Appleman. *The Tragedy of American Diplomacy.* Reprint, New York: Dell, 1978.

Wilson, Colin. *The Occult: A History.* New York: Random House, 1971.

Wilson, Woodrow. *Messages and Papers.* 2 vols. New York: The Review of Reviews Corporation, 1924.

Winkler, John. *Morgan the Magnificent.* New York: Vanguard Press, 1930.

Winrod, Gerald B. *Adam Weishaupt: A Human Devil.* Reprint, Clackamas, Ore.: Emissary Publications, n.d.

———. *The Jewish Assault on Christianity.* Wichita: Defender Publications, 1935.

Wise, David, and Thomas B. Ross. *The Invisible Government.* Reprint, New York: Random House, 1964.

Woodward, C. Vann. *The Burden of Southern History.* Baton Rouge: LSU Press, 1960.

———. *Reunion and Reaction: The Compromise of 1877 and the End of Reconstruction.* Boston: Little, Brown, and Company, 1951.

Wormser, René A. *Foundations: Their Power and Influence.* Reprint, Sevierville, Tenn.: Covenant House, 1993.

Wykes, Alan. *Hitler.* New York: Ballantine, 1970.

Wyman, David S. *The Abandonment of the Jews: America and the Holocaust, 1941–1945.* New York: Pantheon, 1984.

*Zolar's Encyclopedia of Ancient and Forbidden Knowledge.* Reprint, New York: Simon and Schuster, 1984.

**Journal Articles**

Allen, Frederick L. "Morgan the Magnificent." *Life Magazine* (April 25, 1949). *Saturday Evening Post* (February 9, 1935).

Kitteridge, Tracy B. "The Muddle before Pearl Harbor." *U.S. News and World Report* 27 (December 3, 1954).

Lucier, Jim. "Bilderbergers." *American Opinion* (November 1964).

Matousek, Mark. "The Feminine Face of God." *Common Boundary* (May/June 1992).

Miller, Elliot, and Craig Hawkins. "Nostradamus." *Christian Research Newsletter* 1, no. 3 (1988).

"Mother Meera: Burning with Divine Light." *Yoga Journal* (July/August 1993).

"New Age in America." *Time* (December 7, 1987).

Passantino, Bob, and Gretchen Passantino. "The Hard Facts about Satanic Ritual Abuse." *Christian Research Journal* (Winter 1992).

———. "Satan's Sideshow." *Cornerstone Magazine* 90, 1990.

Phillips, David G. "Aldrich, the Head of It All." *Cosmopolitan* (April 1906).

Sherwin, Martin J. "The Atomic Bomb and the Origins of the Cold War." *American Historical Review* 78 (October 1973).

Stromberg, Roland N. "American Business and the Approach of War, 1935–1941." *Journal of Economic History* 13 (Winter 1953).

**Statutes at Large**

35 *Stat.L.* 552, May 30, 1908.

**Government Records**

*Conduct of the Persian Gulf War.* United States Department of Defense. Washington, D.C.: Government Printing Office, 1992.

*Congressional Record* 51 (December 1913).

*Congressional Record* 80 (March 1947).

"House Committee Hearings on the Money Trust," *House Report No. 1593,* vol. III. Washington: D.C.: Government Printing Office, 1913.

*The Public Papers of the Presidents, John F. Kennedy.* Washington, D.C.: Government Printing Office, 1962.

*Report of the National Monetary Commission.* Washington, D.C.: Government Printing Office, 1913.

**Audiotapes**

Brooke, Tal. *The New World Order and Gaia.* Spiritual Counterfeits Project Conference, 1990.

Fagan, Myron. *The Illuminati/CFR.* 2 tapes. Cassette tape recording of an original long-playing vinyl LP, 1967. Available through Emissary Publications.

———. *Red Star over Hollywood.* 2 tapes. Cassette recording of an original long-playing vinyl LP, 1967. Available through Emissary Publications.

Marrs, Texe. *Illuminata.* Texe Marrs Ministries, Austin, Texas, 1995.

———. *NASA's Space Program—Hoaxes and Deceptions.* Texe Marrs Ministries, Austin, Texas, 1995.

———. *Report from Iron Mountain.* Texe Marrs Ministries, Austin, Texas, 1995.

———. *The Secret Power of Foundations/AIDS: The Unnecessary Epidemic.* Texe Marrs Ministries, Austin, Texas, 1995.

# Index

Gregory S. Camp is associate professor of history at Minot State University, in North Dakota. He holds an M.A. in American History (University of South Dakota) and a Ph.D. (University of New Mexico) that included advanced studies in U.S. history to 1860 and in the American West.